UNBROKEN

UNBROKEN

THE BRUSSELS TERROR
ATTACK SURVIVOR

NIDHI CHAPHEKAR

AMARYLLIS

AMARYLLIS

An imprint of Manjul Publishing House Pvt. Ltd.
•C-16, Sector 3, Noida, Uttar Pradesh 201301- India
Website: www.manjulindia.com
Registered Office:
•10, Nishat Colony, Bhopal 462 003 – India

This edition first published in 2020

ISBN 978-93-89647-01-3

Nidhi Chaphekar asserts the moral right to be identified
as the author of this work

Cover design by PealiDezine: peali.duttagupta@gmail.com

Front cover photo courtesy: Farhan Husain
Back cover photo courtesy: Ketevan Kardava

Printed and bound in India by Replika Press Pvt Ltd.

I dedicate this book to:

Mom and Dad for bringing me into this world.

God's blessings that ensured I tied the knot with Rupesh, who has weathered the storms my life brought along with a smile.

And God's love that bestowed upon us two precious boons — Vardaan and Vriddhi — my support system and my strongest sources of motivation.

INTRODUCTION

22 March 2016 — what should have been just another workday turned into the most horrific day of my life. Twin suicide bomb blasts shook Brussels airport in Zaventem, followed by another blast at Maalbeek metro station in Central Brussels, in one of the deadliest terror attacks Belgium had ever known. I was one among the three hundred people injured in those blasts. And a photo taken of me after the attack inadvertently made me the face of the blast across the globe.

The bomb blast nearly took my life. But after enduring much travails, like a phoenix rising from the ashes, I too was reborn. This book holds my story of the blast and my long journey of recovery with the help of my loving family and friends. Although I started writing my journal around three months after the incident, I have attempted to be as thorough as possible. I was in a medically induced coma immediately after the blast, so I had to rely on the accounts of my family members, the hospital staff, friends and colleagues who visited me to piece together what happened during those early months of my hospitalisation. I would initially jot down pointers on my calendar to remember what I was told. Then I started writing small paragraphs to note the events of the day. When I started writing, the skin grafts and wounds on my fingers made it difficult for me to hold the pen to write, causing a lot of pain. I still wanted to write my story, though. However, my chronicle does not follow the usual diary entry format. I wrote about a lot of things that happened in my life days or months later, as and when time and health would permit. Not just that, I was scared to write. I'm not a writer. What if I miswrote about an event or missed an important detail? On many days, I would sit holding the pen in my hand, not knowing how to start or what to write. But like how I have faced every other hurdle in life, I decided to tackle this too head on. I told myself not to be bogged down by negative thoughts of what may or may not happen. How would we know how things will turn out if we don't even give it a try?

Through the course of the book, you'll come to understand how important a role my positive state of mind played in my recovery. By no means was my journey an easy one. But what gave me courage was unwavering support and love from those around me. Their faith in me, and more importantly, my faith in my own abilities helped me emerge victorious. I learned many things along the way, the biggest lesson being the importance of positivity in our lives. You manifest what you feed your mind, so nurture only happiness and confidence. When you surround yourself with love and optimism, you can mould any situation in your favour. The path ahead of you may be long and dark, and the walk may be slow, but when you keep walking, you will reach your destination. The trick is to *never give up.*

The bomb blast put me and my family through immeasurable pain. But instead of crying, 'Why me?', I taught myself to ask, 'What can I do about the situation? How can I come out of it?' Remember that no one else can do the work for you. You have to grit your teeth and forge ahead. Love yourself. You are your best support. You are blessed to be alive and have time on your side. Time truly is precious.

Nidhi Chaphekar

While I wish to include every detail and every person who came along to help me in my recovery, the scope of this book restricts me. I sincerely apologise to you if you don't see your name or a particular event mentioned in the book. It is not intentional. There was so much love and kindness pouring in, I could not keep track of it all. Some of you came into my life after the book was submitted to the publisher, so I could not include your efforts in this book. I have changed some names to respect privacy. Whatever I have mentioned is to the best of my knowledge, and I apologise in advance if I have hurt any sentiments.

My prayer to the world is simply this: Do your best for yourself and those around you. When you sow seeds of compassion and love and water them with faith and humanity, you reap a harvest of peace and prosperity.

Part I

*'the world breaks everyone, and afterward,
some are strong at the broken places.'*
ERNEST HEMINGWAY

FEBRUARY 2016

I joined Jet Airways on 1 August 1996. In the course of my career, I had many opportunities to join other airlines, but I had fallen in love with my company and was committed to giving it my best.

On 26 March 2016, Jet Airways was to operate its last flight to the United States. It was my final chance to fly to this destination. And I was eager to do so. When I got my roster of scheduled flights on 29 February—the day I had just returned from Brussels from another flight schedule—I realised to my dismay that I had no flight to the United States in the month of March. The very next day, I requested the planning team to give me one flight to the United States, but in vain. I didn't give up. I spoke to a few of our cabin managers to swap their flight with me, since three of them had got two US-bound flights each this month. After repeated requests, one of them finally agreed. But I still needed the planning team's approval. With just a few days left for the departure of the flight, I started mailing the planning team and the roster department, but no one agreed. They had issues with our off-duty days being changed. Then I started approaching assistant base managers, the in-flight base manager, and also visited them personally in their office to convince them, yet no one agreed. But I continued to hope I would operate this flight and kept on sending emails.

❧

18 MARCH 2016

At around 2130 hrs IST (Indian Standard Time), I received a call from the cabin manager, Sofia, who was supposed to operate the 20 March US-bound flight, the very flight I had been trying to get for days now. She told me she was to do her slide drills — emergency evacuation drills that crew members have to complete once in every three years — that day, but they had been cancelled. She had been removed from the flight as her SEP (Safety & Emergency Procedures) card was not valid. So now, she said, there was a vacancy on the flight. I knew at once that it would be difficult for the rostering team to find a cabin manager for the flight at the last minute and they would agree to put me on that flight since I met the required flight time-and-rest requirements.

❧

19 MARCH 2016

I made four calls and also sent emails to my base manager and the rostering team to put me on the flight as there was a vacancy now. However, nothing came through.

In the evening, when I was at my kids' school attending the cultural annual day programme, I decided to call the rostering team again. I was sure no one had been scheduled for the flight yet. Again, they told me that I could not go, but I said I would call them back. At 2000 hrs, I called yet again and this time, Nandu from the rostering team answered my call. He said yes, there was a vacancy; so I immediately requested him to put me on the flight. He said he would have to remove me from my London flight scheduled at the end of the month because otherwise I would be exceeding my flying hours. I told him to go ahead and do that. When he confirmed he had put me on the US flight, I got so excited! I jumped with joy! I told my husband, Rupesh, that I had finally managed to get the flight I wanted. He said that for some reason, he didn't want me to go on it. I told him, never mind, it would be my last flight to this destination. He should let me do it.

❧

20 MARCH 2016

The flight pattern was Mumbai-Brussels-Newark-Brussels-Mumbai. I made so many plans about what all I would do, how I would spend my days in Brussels and New Jersey. It was time to pack, and I spent around an hour choosing the best of my dresses along with matching accessories as I intended to go out every day. I packed my favourite Louis Vuitton purse and handmade sunglasses, which I rarely use, and my black handmade jacket that I had bought in Brussels nine years ago.

Last month (February), I had also purchased a pair of shoes from the US for my son Vardaan, but they had turned out to be a size bigger, so I packed those too to exchange them for the right fit. I even packed in my husband's sports shoes—they too needed to be exchanged because he had not liked them.

Soon it was time to get ready for the flight. I wore a new Sephora lipstick that I had bought in Paris. It looked so good! I also applied my new kajal and mascara. I knew I was getting late for my scheduled reporting time, so I hurried up. For the first time in my entire flying career, I missed kissing my children goodbye. All these years I had done so religiously, although they were usually asleep when I left home just before midnight for the very early morning flights. That day, however, only when I reached the airport did I realise I'd not kissed them. I felt terrible. I thought to myself, I will apologise to them when I speak to them on the phone in the evening. I would also get them lots of gifts. I called home and told Rupesh to kiss them on my behalf.

Because it was not originally supposed to be my flight, my crew were thrilled to see me. After we finished the briefing, while walking towards the aircraft, we started making plans for all that we would do in Brussels and New Jersey. All of us were very excited about this trip. I was never fond of taking photos on my phone, but since this was one of the last flights of Jet Airways to Brussels, I decided to take lots of photos.

Most of the time, before passengers boarded, I would play one or two popular songs to set the mood. I believe listening to peppy music makes you more energetic and then you enjoy your work more. To my delight, we had two women pilots on the flight—Capt. Sangeeta Joshi and Capt. Hazel Vakaria—and they would fly us to the United States and back. Usually we had a change of captains onwards from Brussels, but this time we had them all the way. Both of them were excited to see me and said, 'After you finish your service come to the cockpit to see us often.' We decided we will make plans to go out together once the flight gets over. It was very important to make plans with them then and there because we had different sets of hotels for the cabin crew and the cockpit crew, and the two were located far from each other. So if you know what the plan is beforehand, you can set your schedule accordingly. We reserved one day for Manhattan and another for shopping in Jersey Gardens, a famous mall in New Jersey. The last day was for roaming the streets of Central Brussels, to have waffles and enjoy the local cuisine. We had great fun discussing our plans. I also shared a secret with them. Just last week, I had got my navel pierced! I told them I'd always wanted to do it but had kept procrastinating. I don't know what came over me last week, though, and I decided that if I didn't do it now, it may never happen. So I went ahead and got it done! I quickly and excitedly flaunted my crystal blue stud to them through the gap in my shirt buttons. It looked so pretty.

❧

We gave the best service as always, and as on all my flights, I got to know later that one of our guests wrote directly to the chairman expressing appreciation. On landing, I had multiple emotions swirling within me, thinking it was the last landing I would be making in Brussels from my home country, India. I made the welcome announcement, and once the door was opened, I had tears in my eyes. I saw the same feeling mirrored in the eyes of our ground-handling staff. Guests started deplaning. There were many ground-handling staff who had been there since the first day of operation (5 August 2007).

All of us planned to have a blast on our last day on the way back from the United States. We had a halt of twenty-four hours in Brussels and another of thirty hours in Newark.

After reaching the hotel in Brussels, we all decided to first visit Mini-Europe, a park located at the foot of the Atomium, in the early evening and then Brussels Central. Someone from the crew suddenly asked whether anyone had brought colours to play Holi — the Indian festival of colours that was coming up on 24 March. I remembered that last year too I had celebrated Holi in Brussels. No one had brought colours, though. I immediately checked on the system to see who would be operating the next incoming flights to Brussels from Mumbai. I found that my friend Jerri would be on the 23 March flight. So I immediately called and requested her to get some colours for us. She said, 'tell me the colours you want and I'll get them.' I remember I told her to get red and yellow — my favourite colours.

For our jaunt in the city, we split into two groups. The first group left early, and we went at 1500 hrs with my 'rakhi' brother Shabir bhai in his car. I had formed a special and very warm relationship with him — like that of siblings — and his family around nine years ago and it remains strong to this day.

I had first met him on 6 August 2007 at his store. It was my first flight to Brussels. That was the first time I had left my children behind for six days. I had been particularly worried about my daughter, Vriddhi, who was not even two years old then. She was very attached to me. Right opposite our hotel was Shabir bhai's shop named The Top Shop. I had gone there to make a call from his telephone booth to find out about my children. I had come out in tears after hearing my daughter's voice. Seeing me cry, he asked, 'Aap theek ho?' (Are you okay?) Then he offered me a glass of water and a cup of tea as well. I felt a little better, and then on every trip after that, we would have tea and cookies together. His wife, Fozia, a very good-natured lady, had invited me and my crew home many times. I would even bring gifts and Indian sweets for his family, and he would send chocolates for my kids. When we visited Europe in 2009, he met my husband and the rest of my family for the first time. Shabir bhai and Fozia baji had welcomed my family as well to their home. Their kids and our kids were of the same age, so they all got along well. Our ties became stronger when the families connected. I have always called him my 'big bro'.

On the eve of that fateful day, Shabir bhai picked us up from the hotel to take us to the Atomium, a landmark building in Brussels, and to see Mini-Europe. After enjoying the natural beauty around the Atomium, we had planned to meet the rest of the crew members at 1930 hrs at Sultan of Kebabs, my favourite food joint in Brussels. All of us gathered there and relished doner kebabs. From there we went to have the most amazing local delicacy – my favourite fresh waffles served with cream, chocolates and strawberries. Yummy! After satisfying our hunger, we headed to the Grand Palace. We saw the Manneken Pis, a famous sculpture, and Our Lady of Sorrows, a statue that is fixed horizontally on a wall just next to the Grand Palace. It is believed that when you pray there, all evils are taken away. I prayed too. On earlier visits, whenever I had touched this statue, my heart had felt heavy, but this time my tears flowed uncontrollably. I thought that this may be the last time I would touch her. In my mind, I told her – *please do take care of me.*

A while later Shabir bhai took us to Hot Spot – a new food joint he had opened, and then dropped us back to the hotel.

My friend Jerri messaged me that evening saying she had bought lots of colours for me, including my favourite red colour. She also said that she would hand it over to me at the airport as she would leave for Newark from Brussels on the morning of 24 March, and I would be returning the same day from Newark to Brussels. We decided to meet at the airport.

In the night, I packed my stuff, ironed my uniform for the morning, and went off to sleep.

❧

22 MARCH 2016

I woke up in the morning with a wake-up call at 0540 hrs. I was a little taken aback because usually I never remember my dreams. But today I could recall that I had dreamt of my guruji, a person who had inspired me—the late Shri Premvir Singh. In my dream, I asked him where he was going, and he replied, 'I have come here for very important work.' I was surprised because he is in heaven; I wondered what had brought him down to this earth again. I realised I was covered in sweat. I washed my face, made some coffee and called home. I was still a little upset for not having spoken with my children yesterday. I spoke to my husband and asked him to please tell the kids again that I was sorry and to assure them I would speak to them once I reached Newark. The kids were off to school, Rupesh said. He told me that Vriddhi had wanted to have a word with me, but she could not get through yesterday as my local number was not reachable. And earlier in the day, when I had given them a call, they had gone to play. I felt really bad. Nonetheless, I continued getting ready for the day while listening to my morning prayers. Normally, I listen to some kirtans like the 'Gurbani', the 'Hanuman Chalisa' or the divine chant 'Hare Rama Hare Krishna'. It all depends on what I feel like listening to while I get ready in the morning because I am of the opinion that at times it becomes difficult for us to thank God as we go about our busy day. With the kind of strength He has given us and the beautiful life He has gifted us, I believe it is important to thank Him regularly in whatever way we can. Especially, given the kind of profession we are in, we change time zones every day, we play with our body systems with different sleep patterns, but still He gives us a beautiful morning to see the sunrise every day.

Finally, I was ready. At 0650 hrs, I went for breakfast. And there I met a Mumbai-based reservation staff member, Melvin, who had arrived here a few days back to carry out the closure procedures for this base. Meeting him was great, but listening to why he had come made me feel low. I told him we would celebrate Holi together when I returned on this flight. He took the coach at 0715 hrs for the airport. A coach from the hotel leaves once every thirty minutes. After breakfast, I had a short brief of the flight with my crew, which normally happens before the commencement of any flight. This time I told my crew that today we would find sorrow, tears, and maybe many would hug each other as this may be their last day of work or duty for departure from Brussels and our last departure flight to New York as well. I told everyone that I had a lot of sentiments for this place, and I didn't know why, but I was feeling very low and didn't feel like going.

In response, Amit, my cabin supervisor, said, '*Don't worry, we will have a blast today.*'

I said, '*Yes, we will. We will make it so memorable and special that everyone of us will remember this flight throughout our lives.*'

At 0735 hrs, I saw the bus arrive at the port to take us to the airport. It left the hotel at 0740 hrs and reached the airport at 0755 hrs. Two sets of arrival crew were standing to take the same bus to the hotel. We alighted. I said hello to everyone. I always like to be ahead, so I quickly headed to Level Two of the airport. Most of the crew place their bags on the trolley and take the elevator. But I always took the escalator. I was carrying three bags. Behind me was Amit.

We reached Level Two and had hardly taken a few steps when a loud explosion took place a few metres away, right in front of us, towards the side of the counter where we were heading. I saw dust fly everywhere. It looked like small bits of feathery, paper-like stuff flying down. Something like a big firecracker may have exploded. At first, I thought a part of the ceiling had fallen. Then I thought perhaps an air-conditioner's pipe had burst. Finally, I thought the lithium battery of a wheelchair had exploded. Just two days ago, we had received a safety circular stating that we are not allowed to carry wheelchairs with undetachable lithium batteries as they could explode if the batteries were not stored separately and properly.

I said to Amit, 'Let's go and help.'

But he said, 'We are in a different country and we don't know the rules… we also have to operate a flight, so just wait.'

He told me this was an unusual explosion. But I wondered aloud why there was no fire. So what could it be? At that moment, everything seemed to have come to a standstill. There was no dense smoke as such, and while we were talking, within a few seconds of that first blast, people started screaming. They began running to the right, towards the exit. There was a lot of panic. We didn't know what to do. We could not turn back as there was a large crowd behind us now. Then we saw another crowd running towards us. I thought this could lead to a stampede. The fearful screams of people surrounded us, and then I heard the loud voice of a man standing just a few steps away from me—he cried out loud, a beseeching call to his god perhaps, and I felt this was the end. I told Amit, 'Bhaag!' (Run!) I thought we would be sprayed with bullets from Stenguns. I could only see a little open space to the left side of the area, so I took a left. I remember that in the hurry, while carrying my three bags, I counted about seven or eight steps in all. Whenever I feel some trouble approaching, I have this habit of automatically saying 'Jai Mata Di', and at that moment, my heart was saying it clearly.

That's when I heard another loud bang. It looked like a fireball. A second bomb had exploded. The blaze, light and heat of the explosion were extremely powerful. It was as if the sun and lightning had hit us, all at once. The sound was so deafening—it felt as though we were standing in the centre of blazing lightning. The impact of it was such that it hurled me to one end of the wall, and I went flying like a football. Due to the sheer heat of the blast, I thought I was about to melt. I assume I was thrown about fifteen to twenty feet away and had landed on my feet and then fallen down on my back. While I was falling, I remember telling myself— *Oh! It was a bomb!*

I lay unconscious for some time. At the back of my mind was a voice screaming in alarm, asking me to wake up, to get up. I was in shock as to what had just happened. The voice was continuously and desperately telling me — *Nidhi, get up, wake up, you have to inform home that you are fine, the kids have exams, the news would reach in no time! How would they come to know that you are fine? For your kids, get up!*

And suddenly I opened my eyes. I couldn't see anything because of the smoke. I wanted to get up but was fearful. What if there were more terrorists lurking somewhere? What if my movement alerted them to the fact that I was still alive? I was breathing hard, almost gasping for breath. I felt like coughing but didn't, because that too could give me away. I held my breath thinking they would shoot me now. Don't move, I told myself. I closed my eyes again, pretending to be dead. The next second I was thinking — what if there is another bomb and that explodes? It could be bigger than this one. Then how would we survive? I made up my mind to get up and help others as well to move away from this place. And that's when I realised I couldn't feel my legs.

It was as if they were no longer attached to my body! There was no pain either! I tried to lift my legs, but was unable to. I wondered, are they no longer there and is that why there's no feeling at all? I was scared. Then I moved my head to one side and saw a man whose blood was spreading all around, and I thought he had lost his life. On my other side was a lady with severe injuries, but I was not sure whether she was alive or dead as she was lying facedown. She did not respond when I tried calling out. I made an effort to sit down. There was smoke all around.

I gathered the courage to see if my legs were still in place. Yes, they were there! But they were badly injured with metal pieces stuck here and there; it looked like someone had scooped the flesh out, and I saw a glass piece sticking out halfway through my foot. My legs were losing a lot of blood. I was a little worried, but I did not let go of hope. At that moment I simply thanked God for keeping me alive. I convinced myself that since I had survived the blast, I would live. I looked behind and saw that I was lucky to have fallen on a flat surface, for behind me I could see the wreckage and destruction, the debris and remains. I felt like I was sitting all alone in a pool of blood. No one was moving and torn bodies were strewn on the ground amidst mass destruction.

I tried to lift myself up. But my legs just wouldn't move. I tried to drag myself, but there were metal pieces that had pierced my body. I lifted my arm to signal that I was there, if only someone would help me, but I couldn't see anyone who could help, and because of the smoke, I wasn't able to see much farther. I realised I was sitting alone in that debris with everyone else lying down. My heart was beating wildly. I looked at my watch—it had stopped at 0808 hrs Brussels time, and the dial had no glass over it anymore. I think I had remained in that position for almost eight minutes because normally we report at the counter around 0800 hrs. Mine was a dual-time watch. The India time was running. Actually the time was nearly 0800 hrs, but something had hit the needles, and they had shifted a little ahead. The seconds hand was missing from the dial.

The first thought that came to my mind was—*Oh God, my kids are very small and not independent, so please save me.* The next thought was that I needed to call them as they had exams. But how would I call them? I could not see the bag that contained my cell phone. As the smoke had risen a bit by then, I was feeling giddy sitting all alone in the pool of blood, with debris and dead bodies. I was feeling sick looking at the floor with chunks of flesh and other remains lying around. I closed my eyes and started chanting. My breathing became very heavy. Again I tried to push myself into an upright posture, or to roll from there, but glass and metal pieces scattered on the ground were piercing my body and causing too much pain. I thought since my arms were covered, I would try to push with my elbow, but even that did not work. I could not take it anymore and lay down then. I knew someone would come soon.

Suddenly I heard an echoing sound... tuktuk... tuktuk... as if someone was walking up to us. I lifted my head and saw the shadow of a man running towards us. I waved to him and said, 'Help, please help!' And in no time, he came up to me, a young military man (commando) fully loaded with ammunition.

He said, 'Move away, go out.'

I said, 'I can't walk. Help me.'

He said, 'I have to take my position, but I'll send someone soon, don't worry, lady.'

And in some time, another military officer arrived and asked me to get up. I told him I couldn't walk, and requested him to please help me out. He had a big rifle and was strapped with ammunition just like the previous man. I suggested to him that I would hold him with both arms and he could drag me. I asked him to put me on a nearby chair as I wanted to sit with some support and stop the bleeding. Then he almost lifted me with one hand while I grabbed him around his neck, and finally he heaved me onto the chair. While he was dragging me, a big piece of glass came out of my foot. The chair was close to the elevators and away from the area of destruction. People were helping kids, taking injured people away and climbing down the escalators that had stopped. Some were lying on the ground, screaming in pain. I tried pacifying them. I told them that we were all safe and fine now. While I sat there, I wanted to somehow stop the bleeding. I was exhausted trying to lift my leg and was unable to stop the bleeding. Unbeknown to me at the time, someone took my photo during those moments—the picture that was circulated all over the world, which the media used to spread the news of the Brussels airport attack, as if it was a promotion campaign for them. If they had sought my family's consent or mine before using the photograph, we would have asked them to crop or blur it. Basic human ethics require one to have the decency to respect others' dignity.

That picture was taken while I was trying to lift my right leg. I was trying to put pressure on my left leg and ease my foot into the hanging shoe so that I could stem the bleeding by applying pressure. I was trying to cut down blood circulation by putting pressure on the armrest, but to no avail. I couldn't apply any more pressure with my burnt hands.

During our first-aid training as flying crew, we go through the emergency-aid procedure every year. We have to clear this exam once every year, and I thank God that even in that terrible situation I was trying to implement my training and put my skills into practice. I believe my brain was working well because I was thinking I must survive for the sake of my kids. I was trying out different ways to stop the bleeding. The pressure was not adequate to stop the blood flow, and the shoe was not fitting as my foot had literally fallen open; so I thought of tying a band around my leg to stop the blood flow. I looked for some string or belt, but apart from broken and shredded material, I could not find anything. I thought of tying my pass-holder sling, and it was at that moment that I realised that I had hardly any clothes on me! My clothes had got burnt and my undergarments could be seen. Naturally, this feeling of being exposed to people around you is awful, but I had no choice and I did not care either. For a few seconds I was stunned, but for me, at that moment, my life was more important. The most challenging task at hand was to stop the bleeding. I knew if that didn't happen soon, I would lose consciousness. Excessive loss of blood from the body could lead to shock, which could cause death.

I used to wear a gold anklet and a sacred thread around both my ankles to ward off the evil eye and I instantly realised that with the explosion, these too had gone missing. I am also known as a 'diamond beauty' in my airline. At all times I would wear two diamond bangles, two solitaire rings, and single solitaire studs in my ears. And around my neck I would wear a chain with a pendant. To my surprise, all that was intact.

By now I had begun feeling dizzy and I wanted to restore some energy. I wanted to lie down to cut the blood supply to my legs. But there were pieces of metal shrapnel all over. I felt helpless. Breathing had become difficult due to the lack of oxygen supply to my internal organs. The lady sitting to my left, who was holding her phone in her hand, advised me to take deep breaths. She was a nurse by profession, I later learnt. I was requesting people passing by, even military officers, to please place me on the ground. They were all running from one end to the other. A few who understood replied that the paramedics were on their way. That gave me some hope. Finally, the lady, who was also captured in the photograph talking on the phone, helped prop me up on the ground. I asked her to help me place my legs on top of the chair that I was earlier sitting on, so that the elevation would reduce the blood flow to the legs, and to help the heart and the brain receive sufficient blood to work for a longer period of time. Another reason for lying down was that I just couldn't look at the desperate condition of the people passing by, of the people lying on the ground in pools of blood, as if they had been torn apart. I felt as though my heart was sinking as I was unable to do anything for them.

As my legs kept slipping down, the lady who had helped me got a stuffed bag and put it underneath my legs; she even got a piece of cushion from the torn chair and placed it under my neck so I would be stable (I got to know about this when I met her again much later). She had a band in her bag, which she used to tie my leg with to stop the blood flow. But just then she was asked to move from the place. The security personnel were asking everyone who could walk to leave.

News had already reached the police headquarters and the special forces had been assigned to take charge of the airport. People passing by were asking me, 'Are you okay?' I would say, 'I am fine, I hope you are good.' I was still replying to them while my eyes were almost closed. I had begun to worry that if it took a long time to reach the hospital, I would lose my life. I knew I had limited time. I was keeping my hopes high that yes, I would live. I kept saying to myself, I will make it, don't worry, all is good. I would also tell others—we are safe, so there is no need to worry, have faith in God.

I was praying to God to help us. After about fifteen minutes, I saw two men getting a stretcher towards me. While they were placing me on it, my eyes caught sight of my big purse that had my cell phone. I had kept it inside my laptop bag. It was torn. I told them that it was mine but I think they did not understand what I said. They lifted me and moved me from there. I could understand that the path for them was full of obstructions, so my stretcher kept swaying from side to side. They could not walk at the same pace. They kept talking to me and telling me not to worry. They placed me outside the airport, just opposite the Sheraton hotel where our

Nidhi Chaphekar

airline captains were staying. My hopes were revived. I thought, now in no time my captains would come and take me to a hospital and would also inform home that I was fine and alive. I would speak to my family too. I kept on looking in that direction. But no one turned up. It was so cold and breezy that I started shivering. I hardly had any clothes on, and the cold surface of the ground was killing me. I felt as if I were lying on an icy rock. My hands had become stiff.

Much later, after two months, when I spoke to my captains, they told me they had wanted to come out but were asked to stay inside the hotel by the commandos. They were also asked to show their passports as a proof of identity to them. My captain, Sangeeta, said that she told them her crew must have reported at the airport and she needed to check on them, but they didn't listen. They had sealed the hotel. She also said that when the blast took place, she was in her room, which had windows facing the airport. The blast shook the windows, shaking up the objects in her room. She realised that it was a bomb blast and, in panic, she actually screamed from her room to call out to Hazel, the other captain who was supposed to fly with her. She grabbed her passport and was running down when the commandos asked about her nationality and instructed her to stay at the reception area. She was worried about the crew as she knew we would be at the airport at this hour. She tried calling me but my number was not reachable. On the other hand, the crew who had come with me were still at ground level, all except Shrungal, who had just arrived at Level Two but was talking to a guest when the blast took place. The impact of the blast was so powerful that both her bags flew up in the air and couldn't be found later, but she was saved. The rest of the crew felt the ground shake, as if in an earthquake, and the crew members who were standing outside the lift saw broken pieces of glass falling. The crew members who were boarding the bus said the entire bus shook and the driver then drove the bus hurriedly. This bus was standing on ground level in an open area, away from the building in the parking. This should give you an idea of the sheer impact!

Almost twenty-five to thirty minutes after the blast, I was lying outside the airport and felt as though I would freeze. I started saying out loud—'Help, please help, someone please help me'. It was then that one police officer named Alain heard my voice. He later told me that the intensity in my voice had made him turn around, even though I hadn't been screaming. In fact, my voice had been quite feeble. He saw me lying on the ground, half-covered in torn clothes. He felt pity seeing me shiver. He came close to me and said hello. He started speaking in French. But I couldn't understand a word. I told him, I can't feel my legs, see if they are intact. He did not understand what I said. He called out to a friend who was handling the next casualty. 'Hey Pascal, what do you mean by *legs*?'

He replied, '*Jambes*.'

Alain turned and said to me, 'Ya, ya!' He told me my legs were there. By then I was shivering uncontrollably. He got a big blanket and covered me with it; then he started asking me questions. He said he could see my face was burnt and blood was dripping from a few spots on my face. He couldn't wipe my tears, which were streaming down continuously. He tried to give me strength to survive. He started communicating through questions. What is your name? Your country's name? You work? Married? Travelling alone? Kids? Age? Names of your children? How old are they? And many more questions. I was looking up at the sky. Tears were rolling down my cheeks. I was responding to him in single words, short sentences. I told him many times that I wanted to inform my family that I was alive. 'Please inform them or else my kids will go into shock.' Around me I could see people screaming, crying to find their loved ones, people injured, crying in pain. It was the most horrific scene I've ever witnessed in my life. The terrible blast had put everyone in extreme pain. I saw one person next to my stretcher with three holes in his thigh and his knee torn. I closed my eyes and asked God, why did you put people in such trouble?

Alain thought I would not be able to make it, so he called out my name repeatedly, 'Nidhi! Nidhi!' He was trying to make sure I stayed alive. 'Hello, wake up!' he kept saying. He wasn't well versed in English but was trying his best to communicate. I asked him if he had seen my colleague in a blue uniform or any other crew in a yellow jacket. But he said, 'I can't see anyone, but don't worry, you are saved. All fine, don't worry.'

I told him again that I couldn't feel my legs, and asked him to take me to the hospital. 'Doctor... ambulance...' I mumbled one word at a time now and then. I couldn't manage to put in more effort to yell or cry or talk. I kept thinking I would have to save my energy till I got medical attention as I knew it would take time for them to take us to the hospital. I was worried about my people back home who would be concerned about my well-being. I repeatedly told Alain that I wanted to inform people at home that I was fine. I needed to call them. I was constantly using the same words — *I can't feel my leg... ambulance... doctor... hospital... please inform my family that I am fine.* He kept thinking I wouldn't be able to make it.

By then I had started feeling the pain too. And it was increasing slowly. Some of my body parts had become numb. I lay on the ground for more than half an hour outside the airport.

After some time, my stretcher was lifted from the ground and they transferred me to a roller stretcher. By then I could hear the sirens of ambulances. I thought they were going to take me to the ambulance and then to the hospital. But they took me to the end of the road that was a 100- to 150-metre long walk, and then they took me into a shed to the left. I saw red-coloured vehicles parked inside. They placed me on the ground (later I got to know this was a room used to park a fire engine).

I saw a boy, around ten or twelve years old, to my right side. I was disappointed that they had taken me there. I took a deep breath. I told myself that when my turn came, I would also be taken to a hospital. I looked at the boy. His eyes were closed but his heart was still beating. I didn't see any injury on his body. I saw a person taking care of us in that room. I recognised him as one of the ground staff I used to meet at the screening machine when we went through security or at the counters, where he used to help with our bags. He was fair, of medium height, lean, with long blond, straight hair, bluish-green eyes, probably in his forties, and was looking after the boy and all the others in the room. He had placed his hand on the boy's head and was pacifying him. He was telling him, 'Don't worry, I am there to look after you. Doctors will arrive soon. You will be fine. Your parents are okay.'

I took a deep breath and prayed to God that his parents should be alive and fine to take care of him and get him out of this trauma. I was glad that he did not have any visible wound. His clothes had dust on them. I realised that he was in shock. Actually, we all were, and the world was in shock too.

I was watching all this to distract myself from my own pain, seeing if I could help anyone else gather strength. I started pacifying other people lying in that room, telling them not to worry as medical aid would arrive soon. We were all lucky that we had survived by God's grace. Just a few more minutes and we would be taken for hospitalisation. Thinking about others' suffering and assuring everyone that help was on its way was the only way I could keep my own situation from worsening. But by that time, I had started feeling drowsy, and the pain had begun to intensify. I still couldn't feel the lower parts of my legs. I was now sure I had damaged my nerves, and was also worried about the blood flow. So I asked the ground staff member whether he could place my legs in an upward angle. I don't know what he used, but my legs were soon in a raised position. While he was attending to me, we heard a shout from outside. I couldn't understand what it was, but it was repeated. The ground staff who was with us immediately ran to pull down the shutter. Then he lay down on the floor. I kept asking what had happened. He said, 'Sshh…' and just lay flat and still on the ground. I thought maybe some of the terrorists were roaming around with guns. My breathing became faster, but through my fear, I started chanting 'Jai Mata Di'.

My eyes were closed and I was praying to God to give strength to my kids and family, even as I wondered who among us in the room would take the first bullet. As there were around five or six of us in there and my stretcher was the farthest from the door, I was sure I'd get hit first as the bullets would most likely be shot in a downward slanting angle. I prayed that even if I lose my life, this child should live as he would not have seen the beauty of this world. After about ten to fifteen minutes, another loud, and this time, very clear voice was heard. It seemed as if the person was standing right outside the door. I made my last wish—that my kids live a healthy and loving life even if I am unable to be with them. But then I heard a reply from the ground staff member who was inside with us. He got up and opened the shutter. I asked him in my feeble voice if everything was okay, and he replied with a simple 'yes'. I asked him why he had closed the shutter and lain down. He replied that another bomb had been found, so we were asked to take safe positions and lie down on the floor to minimise the impact.

Later, we came to know that this bomb had been kept very close to the Jet Airways check-in counter and was of such massive strength that had it exploded, the whole airport would have been demolished. He added that everything was under control now as the special-forces commandos had arrived, and so had the paramedics to provide first aid.

I noticed one of the paramedical personnel entering the room. He checked my vitals, assessed my condition and tagged me. There was another lady on the first stretcher, screaming and holding the paramedic tightly. When we were asked to be calm, she became quiet, but until then she had been screaming at the top of her voice. I saw him putting tags on everyone. In the aviation industry, in case of any disaster, if there are many casualties, we prioritise them by putting tags. Red tags are for those who are severely injured, yellow for a little less injury, green for those just wounded, and black for the dead. I'm sure other national forces would also have triage patterns they follow, but being from the aviation industry, this was the pattern I had been trained to learn. I thought to myself, now in no time the ambulance will arrive as they had tagged us. I would get the best treatment soon and I would be fine. But my eyes were closing again even though I didn't want them to.

Then I saw another team of paramedics arrive and they appeared to be heading straight towards me. One of them said, 'We are from the paramedics team. Don't worry, we are here to give you first aid.' He told me he was cutting off my clothes and within a few seconds, using scissors, he opened up my shirt sleeves, and then from the foot to the abdomen, my pants were cut. My clothes were hanging in shreds from my body and there was practically nothing on me now. I got scared and asked him, 'Why are you doing this?'

He replied, 'to see if you have severe burns or wounds anywhere.' The bones in my feet could be seen, they said. They put a bandage above my thigh. I think they applied a tourniquet on top of my thigh to stop the bleeding completely. They noted down a few details about my condition. They injected an intravenous (IV) connection and suspended the pack on top of the vehicle parked next to me. I worried if they would amputate my legs in the hospital. But then I said to myself, even if they do that, I would still live and be loved by my family. At that point I actually thought I had yet to serve my people and society. I had yet to tell others about the real meaning of life. I must live to explain the most important values of life.

I noticed that the tags they had put on me had shifted to one side. Thinking they would not know which one was priority or that they would find it difficult to locate the tags, I decided to place them in the front. With great difficulty, I managed to somehow place them on top of me. My hands were swollen and becoming numb and hard.

Almost two hours had gone by after the blast, and by now, I was totally zombie-like. I was left with no energy and feeling very sleepy. I knew it would be dangerous if I slept, so I kept on asking the ground staff member questions. When would they take me out of there? What was the time? When would we reach the hospital? The lady who was screaming throughout was taken away sometime earlier, I believe, to the hospital. I even wondered whether I should shout or cry louder to draw attention to my case, but I decided not to; I can still manage somehow, I thought, but some others may not be able to. I repeated my questions about the ambulance, hospital, and doctor endlessly. I just didn't want to give up.

One of the paramedics came close to me and said, 'Some more time. It's on the way, just some more time.' I started thinking of my kids, my son Vardaan, fourteen years old, and my daughter Vriddhi, ten years old. I believe my eyes closed for a while, and in my dreams I was talking to them, feeling sorry that I didn't kiss them while leaving for the flight. I was telling them to be brave. That their mom would be fine soon and would join them. I opened my eyes when I heard someone shout in French, words that I believe meant — *lift her up*. My stretcher was lifted, but with my eyes I gave a signal to say, my IV pack is hanging. I again looked up with a smile and thanked God that I was finally being taken to the hospital.

As we neared the ambulance and the sounds of the sirens got louder, they put my stretcher down and I looked to the side. They kept my IV pack on my chest. On the right side was a police officer. At that moment, for the first time, I felt like I was losing strength and called out very loudly — 'Someone please help! Please take me to the hospital.' Then I looked at the police officer. He came near me. My eyes filled with tears. I expressed that I was losing strength and consciousness, and he should help me. I wanted to live for my children. He calmed me down. He told me that ambulances were on the way and would only take five more minutes. My eyes were burning, waiting to see the ambulance. He kept talking to me to keep me awake. I told him that I wanted to convey to my family that I was fine, that my captains were staying at the Sheraton hotel and asked him to please inform them that I am alive. I regret I didn't ask him to give a call to my family, so that at least they would have been saved from the harassment they later went through. My eyes were still searching for a familiar face, perhaps someone in uniform.

I then told the police officer: 'My name is Nidhi and if someone comes to enquire about me, please tell them that I am alive.' My sentences were short as I would say two or three words and pause for a while and again gather the courage to continue speaking. I asked him if he had seen any other injured person who was in the same uniform as mine or in a blue suit with white shirt. He replied in the negative. I thanked God and prayed that He keep all of them in a safe place.

Meanwhile, the ambulance arrived and my stretcher was lifted and placed inside. The ambulance worker could speak fluent English. The door of the ambulance hadn't been closed, though. I waited for some time and asked, 'How much longer?'

He replied, 'We are trying to find someone else less injured to take along in the ambulance as many people are injured.' Finally, he closed the door after another person was brought in. I asked him how much time it would take to reach the hospital. He said we were going to Antwerp. His words shocked me because I knew from experience that it would take us one-and-a-half hours to get there by road. I told him that was so far. He replied, 'No, high speed. Max thirty minutes. No speed limit. Just don't panic or worry. I will make sure you are awake.' And he kept on talking to me. He acquired all the basic information about me. And sometimes he had to shake me up and repeat the questions many times because I would not have registered them. I could see him, but my brain couldn't understand his voice. I would slowly blink my eyes and try to listen to him. It was becoming extremely difficult, though. By now my mouth felt very dry and my lips were not opening; at some point, I guess he too thought I wouldn't make it. I told him, don't let me sleep. He said he wouldn't. Whenever he saw my eyes closing, he would shout, 'Ma'am, wake up! We are almost there.' Finally, I asked him how much longer it would take as I couldn't bear the pain anymore. He said, 'Just ten more minutes.' I asked God to please give me grace time. Again I heard his voice, 'We are almost reaching there. Open your eyes. Ma'am, wake up. Wake up, ma'am!'

When we reached Sint-Augustinus Hospital, Antwerp, my stretcher was quickly moved into a lift. I was taken to a room where nurses and doctors were already present. One of the doctors pressed my abdomen and asked if I felt any pain there. From the chest downward to the lower abdomen, they pressed in at least twenty different places and asked the same question, 'Do you feel any pain here?' I could not feel any pain in my chest or abdomen, and kept saying no.

Just looking at the medical team gave me the confidence that I would be saved. I knew it was very important to give correct information to the team. I told them that my legs were aching, and that they had become very heavy. I couldn't feel them at all. They asked me to lift my leg, but I failed. As I was wearing diamond

Nidhi Chaphekar

bangles, the doctors asked me if I could remove them or if they should cut them. By that time my hands were swollen and had become rotten at the top. Not realising this, I pulled out the bangles. And that's when I felt for the first time immense pain in my hands as the skin there peeled off completely. My teeth clenched in pain, and my eyes rolled up. The pain was unimaginable. The doctor said, 'Don't remove the rings. We will cut them off.' He himself hadn't realised the consequences of removing the bangles (earlier they had assumed that I was dark-skinned but later realised that the dark skin was actually burnt skin on all the exposed parts of my body). A man cut open both my rings and chain, and my earrings and navel stud were removed. The nurse took a small plastic box and a bag to put all the things in. They asked me my name, family name, date of birth, passport number, and nationality as marks of identity. Then my details were written on the plastic bag and he showed it to me while he sealed the bag.

They asked me, 'Do you know someone here who could come to see you?'

I gave them my husband's number and asked them to give a call and tell him that I was fine. I told them that I was an employee of Jet Airways, but I didn't know who would come to see me here. Then I added that my brother Shabir bhai would definitely come to see me. I didn't know his number offhand, though. The nurse cut my clothes that were now hanging in shreds and said they would remove the rest in the operation theatre. Before they could take me anywhere, I asked them two questions. 'I can't feel my legs. I know they are badly wounded. Will you amputate them?'

The nurse had no answer. Then I asked, 'Is my face totally burnt?' I had by then seen what had happened to my hands.

The nurse replied simply, 'Yes.'

Instantly, I told him that I didn't want to live. *Let me die.* My mind began to get flooded with negative thoughts and fears. How would I face the world if my face was burnt? What would people think of me? How would my kids and family feel? How would I continue my job? I am an airhostess and the thing we most value in our service is being presentable — *we must look beautiful*! My company may ask me to leave. How would I run my home then? People would pity me and I would be a burden on my family.

But the nurse, Marc Hermans, consoled me gently, 'Don't worry, you will be fine soon.'

I was numb by then. They took me to the CT scan room. They asked me not to move. They strapped me down and asked me not to worry. I felt brain-dead. There was no reaction from me to anything they said. They informed me that they were going to do a full-body CT scan and it would take a few minutes. 'Do not get scared, we all are here,' they assured me. I didn't move and just lay still. But I was still complaining of my legs feeling very heavy; it was extremely painful. After that, they took me to the operation theatre.

Again, I requested them to please call my home as my kids had exams, and it was very important for my family to know that I was fine. The nurse assured me that he would do so. He placed a mask on me. In a few seconds, I was in another world. I had no idea what was happening.

In Mumbai, my husband Rupesh was having his lunch at Indian time 1245 hrs with his brother, at his workplace, when one crew member named Manish called him and asked, 'Where is Nidhi?'

'She has gone to Brussels,' replied Rupesh.

'today or yesterday?'

'today she would have left for Newark.'

When Manish said, 'Oh no!', Rupesh got a bit worried and hesitantly asked what had happened. Manish told him then about the bomb explosion at Brussels airport and added, 'But don't worry, let me check if the news is true.'

Rupesh immediately called me on WhatsApp from his workplace, but could not get through. My 'Last seen' status bar showed 0740 hrs Brussels time. That was 1210 hrs IST. He started searching for information on news feeds on his phone. He grew very restless, and after some time, he left for home. As soon as he reached home, he switched on the television to check international news channels. Every channel showed that an explosion had occurred at Brussels airport early that morning. Rupesh became more nervous.

By that time, my brother-in-law, Capt. Amarjeet Singh Toor, who was on a vacation with his family in Istanbul, had already got the news through a pilot of Jet Airways who told him, 'Your sister-in-law has been injured in the Brussels airport blast. I am sending you her picture, which I just received.'

My brother-in-law called my husband and said, 'Nidhi is fine and I have received her picture. She is injured, but fine.'

He told Rupesh that he couldn't forward the picture to him, as he didn't find it appropriate. But she is fine, he insisted. But in no time, the picture had gone viral, of course, had circulated around the whole world and was available on social media. My husband first saw the picture on the *Telegraph's* website. Later, it was on all the news channels. My sister Jolly started crying. As my brother-in-law is a pilot, many people were calling him too. There was complete chaos.

'She is not someone who would sit down helplessly. That means something major has happened to her legs,' remarked Rupesh after looking at the picture. He zoomed in to the picture many times and could make out that something was really wrong with my foot.

He called up my base manager, Priyanka; she said she knew about it and they were trying to locate me. If and when they got some information, they would inform him. She said, 'We have already got a call from Amit, and he also said that Nidhi was a little ahead of him, but now he can't see her anywhere.'

My husband then called up the Indian embassy at Belgium. He spoke to a man named Ashok in the consulate, who said they too had got the news but they were not aware of anything else. All roads were blocked there, so once they got clearance, they would send people to find me. Meanwhile, they assured my husband that they would call all hospitals to locate me.

My husband then called up the hotel I was staying in and asked if he could speak to any of the crew. In fact, he made several calls. He was thinking maybe the crew had got some information about me or could help obtain some news, but most of the time the receptionist told him, 'All crew have reported to the hotel except for two, but none of them is here at the moment.'

Unfortunately, the receptionist couldn't let him talk to anyone without permission. He gave her his number and said, 'Please ask someone to call me if they know anything about my wife Nidhi.' She said she was afraid no one would know, as Nidhi and Amit had not returned to the hotel and the rest had. But he never got a call.

After hearing the news, the Jet Airways office in India instructed their disaster management team to handle the situation and decide how to get the rest of the crew and team back. They assigned duties to locate me and instructed that someone should go and visit Amit as well. Mr Rahil Tuteja, the chief people's officer (CPO) of my company, who had joined just a few days back, said he had found my picture on Twitter and asked the others, 'Is this the woman we are looking for?' Looking at my picture, everyone felt somewhat relieved to note that I was alive and not too many injuries were visible.

My brother-in-law Amarjeet meanwhile came to know that his batchmate, Capt. Shiraz, was in Brussels and in charge of the disaster management team there. Capt. Shiraz assured him he would pass on any update on my status as soon as he got it. He said no one was allowed to move out of the hotel and the roads were blocked; the situation was very bad. He explained that it would naturally take some time before anyone could reach me.

My mother who lives near Amritsar started getting calls from friends and relatives. My sister Goldy, who lives in Delhi, was shocked to hear the news and was contacted by many relatives and friends. My family members were sitting in front of the television and praying for my well-being while continuously attending phone calls. My father, who is a lofty personality and hardly interacts with anyone, broke down when he heard the news. Everyone was in tears. I am from a very small town called Raja Sansi near Amritsar city. My mother runs a school and my father is a shopkeeper. We are among the renowned families there. People started visiting my home. My brother Rishi who had gone for a holiday with his family to Mussoorie returned the next day itself. He said he just couldn't fathom how he drove the car for nine hours. Everyone was using their contacts to locate me.

It was at 0900 hrs Brussels time that Shabir bhai came to know through a call made by my colleague Pooja that I had been injured in a bomb blast. But he said that couldn't be true, as my team and I had been with him last night and he had himself dropped us to the hotel. Pooja, however, told him that it was confirmed that I had been injured in the bomb blast that had taken place at the airport. He later told us that after his conversation with her, he ran downstairs from his bedroom and switched on the television—the first thing he saw was my picture on the screen. He said he was stunned for a while but thanked Allah because looking at my picture, he understood that I was in shock but alive. He tried calling up many hospitals, even the military hospitals, but nobody was ready to respond as they were not allowed to give out any information, and the list of the victims in each hospital would be ready only by late evening.

Back in Mumbai, Rupesh was worried as reporters flooded our residential area within three to four hours of the blast. They were taking photos of our building, the gate, ringing the doorbell, and taking photos of my family even when they were not willing to talk. Rupesh was anxious about the media reaching the kids' school. So he asked the driver to pick up our kids and bring them straight home without taking them to the club to play badminton as he normally would have done. The kids asked why they weren't going to the club today and the driver told them that their father had given instructions to get them back home. They were surprised as this had never happened before. When our kids reached the building, they were shocked to see so many media vans and press reporters. When they reached our floor, they saw a crowd and wondered what had happened at home. Why were there so many people? Once they entered the house, my husband took them to their room. He knew they would get the news soon, so he felt it was better if he conveyed it himself. He told them, 'Your mom has been injured in a bomb blast at Brussels airport. She is fine, so not to worry.'

Vriddhi fainted and Vardaan hugged Rupesh. My husband sprinkled some water on Vriddhi's face to wake her up. The moment she revived, she began howling and crying out for me. My husband knew it would be a difficult task to handle the kids, and that he needed to be strong. My in-laws were taking care of the constant inflow of people who kept coming to ask about me because of which the doorbell kept ringing continuously. Our landline, my husband's phone, his brother's phone, my sister-in-law's phone and even my kids' phones were all ringing nonstop! My husband made sure he didn't miss even one call, hoping that someone would give him information about me. At 1700 hrs India time, a passenger, Mr Jigar Joshi, called him up from Antwerp saying that they had got his number from one of the ground staff at Brussels airport as the Brussels-based Jet Airways team had got information that many injured people had been taken to nearby cities, and had requested Mr Joshi to enquire at the hospitals nearby about my whereabouts. They assured him that once they got to know something, they would inform him.

My nephew Abhimanyu called up the office of the Minister of External Affairs of India around 1600 hrs IST, after the minister had tweeted that I had been found and was alive. Despite Abhimanyu's enquiries, nobody gave any positive answer. He assumed it was because of security reasons.

My husband was in constant touch with Shabir bhai in Belgium. But he too had no clue where I was. In Belgium, the Indian Ambassador Mr M.S. Puri was delegating duties to different officers to locate me. Rupesh told me later that he doesn't even remember all the people he spoke to at the time. He also added that there were times when he was talking on two phones, holding one to each ear.

Our friend Rohit, who was on his way with his son Karan to attend the Karate US Open Championship, heard the news while boarding the flight to Houston. He too tried to gather information through his contacts in the police, the ministry, and in the intelligence. His wife was also on the job to locate me. But every effort was drawing a blank.

❧

Rupesh doesn't remember who gave him a call with this information, but it was at 2020 hrs IST or a little after when he heard the news that I was at Sint-Augustinus Hospital. Around the same time, my brother-in-law Amarjeet also got news of my whereabouts. Rupesh immediately called up the passenger at Antwerp, Mr Joshi, and requested him to visit the hospital and inform him how I was doing. He called up Shabir bhai as well and asked him to go and see me. And he urged, 'Please make her speak to me!' He also tried calling up the hospital many times but language was a problem. He even informed the embassy that he had located me and requested them to go and make me speak to him. Our friend Rohit too got news from another source about where I was.

❧

My captains, who were staying at the Sheraton hotel in Brussels, got panic-stricken on hearing the news. They also tried calling up many hospitals. But no one was giving out any information. They called up the disaster team at Mumbai, which also said they hadn't got any information. It was around 1700 hrs Brussels time when they got the news that I had been taken to Antwerp. So both of them decided to call up all the hospitals in Antwerp. They Googled the names of the hospitals and dialled each one of them. As most of the staff at hospitals there would only speak Dutch, one of my captains' Dutch friends was asked to join in on a conference call. Their first question to any hospital would be, 'Is there any Indian female victim in your hospital from the airport blast?' After calling up several hospitals, one of them said, 'Yes, we have got one case of an Indian female, but you need to tell us the date of birth for identification of the victim.' But none of them knew my date of birth. Suddenly Capt. Sangeeta realised that Capt. Hazel had a general declaration form in her bag. Any crew that flies out of the country would have their details such as date of birth, passport details, rank, origin of flight, destination, date, company and full name listed in this form, and a copy is submitted to the immigration, customs, ground handling team, security and, on arrival, to the staff. One copy each is given to the captain and the cabin manager of the flight. Capt. Hazel ran into her room to check and shouted over the phone, 'It is 28 August

1975.' And the nurse replied, 'Yes, the victim details match.' This occurred at around 2200 hrs Brussels time.

❧

Mr Joshi came with his wife to the hospital twice, but on both occasions, my surgeries were underway. The authorities at the hospital told him: 'Since she has not given your name, you cannot be allowed inside.' But on explaining that he could make them speak to my husband in India, they agreed and said they would take the necessary permission. Meanwhile, Shabir bhai left for Antwerp from Brussels.

When he reached the hospital and asked the receptionist whether they had any victims from the airport blast, she replied, 'You are Shabir, Nidhi's brother, right?' He was surprised that they knew him. She explained, 'Well, Nidhi spoke about you, and said that you would come for sure to see her, and she is the only Indian victim we have here, so we could tell that you are Shabir.' She then asked him to follow her. She told Shabir bhai that when I had arrived, I had been conscious, alert and very responsive. I was calm and composed, though. They had thought I was going into shock, but saw that I was brave. Her account made Shabir bhai think I was in good shape and he could take me back home the same day. There, outside the room, he met Nurse Marc Hermans who brought Shabir bhai into the room I was in.

All this while he kept thinking—*by now Nidhi would have got medical treatment and so I can take her back home*. When he saw me, he almost lost his balance; his limbs started shaking. He wondered how he would inform my family about my actual condition. Nurse Marc told him how I had even asked them whether my face was burnt and when I was told that it was, I'd told them to let me die instead, as I'd never be able to fly and flying was my passion. He added that I was beautiful, but he felt sad for whatever had happened with me. Shabir bhai went out and met the doctors, who assured him that I was fine; that they were doing their best to save my life, and I was out of danger. The doctors told him that they had put me in an induced coma but didn't know any further as the situation was changing every second. He asked the doctors how long I would be kept in an induced coma; they said they couldn't say anything yet. He asked how much time it would take for me to be perfectly fine and back to normal. The doctor said it would take nearly one to two years, adding that I was very lucky as my vital organs hadn't been injured and were working well. Shabir bhai took permission from the nurse to come into my room again. He came in and saw that Rupesh's name and phone number and his (Shabir bhai's) name were tagged on my bed along with other details like my passport number and date of birth. He told me later that only my eyelids could be seen and the rest of the body was covered in bandages. He took a picture of me, but didn't have the heart to send it to my family. I was on life support.

When Shabir bhai went out, he saw a few people from the Indian embassy standing around. He told them that he was a friend of the family and that Rupesh had asked him to check on me. They thanked him for being there. No one else was allowed inside because I had not given anyone else's name. It was around 2240 hrs IST when Shabir bhai called Rupesh and said, 'She has given your name, my name and her details. That's how we know she is Nidhi, but other than that, you can't make out anything as she is fully covered in bandages and only her eyelids can be seen. Doctors are saying that she is stable, but Rupesh, you must come here immediately.'

He then took my mom's number from Rupesh and informed her that I was okay, that she shouldn't worry, and that I was sleeping when he came to meet me. He then called up Amarjeet and my friend Rohit, who had been in constant touch with him, and briefed them about my situation.

Having heard from Shabir bhai, Rupesh called up Jet Airways' management personnel at 2330 hrs IST after having a discussion with my family to say that he wanted to go to Brussels. He asked the rest of the family members to take care of the children in his absence. Nobody in my family could sleep that night. My kids were horrified, but they were told that mom is absolutely fine, that she was sleeping, and that there was nothing to worry. My husband also checked with our kids whether they were okay with him going to Brussels to take care of me. He asked them, 'Will you be able to take care of yourself?' This would be the first time in their lives that they would be left at home, with neither of us around. But Rupesh just had to come to see me.

❧

23 MARCH 2016

In the early hours of the morning, Brussels time, when Rupesh called up the hospital to check how I was doing, and whether I was awake, the nurse told him that they would be airlifting me sometime soon to the best burns specialist hospital, Grand Hospital in Charleroi, as the condition of my burns had started deteriorating. Rupesh was speechless and wondered what would happen next. After the kids arrived from school, they asked Rupesh, 'How is Mom now?'

'She is still sleeping,' he told them calmly.

'When will she open her eyes, Dad?'

'Very soon.'

❧

Someone from the Jet Airways management informed Rupesh that they were working on the visa formalities. Ms Jayshree, deputy general manager, HR, Mr Rahil Tuteja, the CPO and Ms Gita, the assistant base in-charge, arrived home at 0830 hrs and said they would provide him with a visa and manage all his travel arrangements. Mr Tuteja said, 'Please take someone along with you as a source of support.'

So Rupesh's younger brother Nilesh was asked to travel along. The visa was sanctioned on the spot for a month's stay from the French embassy on humanitarian grounds. An Air France flight to Paris was booked for them.

❧

Nidhi Chaphekar

At home, some of the media persons were creating a nuisance with their continuous phone calls. Now I know it's their job, but they should be sensitive to the condition of the family too, I believe. I don't know how they had procured the telephone numbers of my family members. My family was trying to arrange things for Rupesh's travel while managing other complications, and was not in a state to give the media any information.

When my kids were going to school, at the traffic signals on the road, newspaper vendors were handing out the paper that carried my photo on the front page. 'Aaj ki taaza khabar' (today's latest news), they said, not knowing that these are the children of the lady in the photograph! My kids stayed silent in the car with their eyes closed, praying to God. I can't imagine how they must have felt facing this frightful situation on a regular basis during those days. This happened not once, but many times. To this day, I can never express in words how sorry I feel for them.

When my kids walked into their school, teachers hugged my daughter, as she was visibly unable to take the stress. She didn't know how to face the situation. She went to the washroom and cried. Parents came forward to support the children. The school principal called my son and told him that they were there for them. Vardaan told her, 'My father and uncle are going to Brussels today.'

'You may stay with us till your family comes back,' the principal kindly offered.

'We have our aunt and grandmother to take care of us. So we are fine,' he assured her.

Prayers were performed by all the children and teachers of the school for my well-being. It was all so unreal for them — just two days ago, I had met all of them during the annual day programme. I had told them that I would be going to the United States on one of the last flights to that destination.

The school was supposed to celebrate Holi today, as the next day, 24 March, would be a national holiday. But it was not celebrated; instead, the assembly gathered to pray for me and all those who were injured. An announcement was made: 'We will celebrate the festival of colours when Vardaan and Vriddhi's mom is back; we will all play Holi together with her.'

❧

When the Indian ambassador got to know that I was being shifted to another hospital and that my family was taking the night's flight, he called for an urgent meeting in the office. He asked his team whether anyone amongst them stayed close to Charleroi and could take care of me until my family arrived. He also said he wanted round-the-clock updates on my case. A staff member named Sumita Sharma volunteered to take care of me. Immediately, she was given a driver, Gurmail, to bring her to the hospital. At the hospital, when she showed the letter stating that she was on duty as deputed by the embassy to look after me, the nurse brought her to the window of the ICCU room to have a look at me. She was so stunned that she started crying. She was offered some water. She had to report back to the ambassador, but she didn't know what to tell him. She took my pictures and sent them to him. She told me later that she deleted the pictures immediately after sending them, so that in case she became emotional, or even by mistake, she wouldn't forward them to anyone else. When she went downstairs and the driver saw her face and asked how I was doing, Sumita di replied, 'I don't know, but she needs everyone's prayers.' She later told me about how she kept chanting prayers for hours till midnight.

From my company, my in-flight Mumbai Base Manager Priyanka accompanied Rupesh and Nilesh. My injured colleague Amit's brother and cousin were also travelling with them, and were accompanied by another cabin manager, on the same flight to Paris.

While my husband was about to board the aircraft, Mr Tuteja (the CPO) called him to let him know that he had checked with the hospital and they had said, 'Nidhi is stable and she is in an induced coma and on a ventilator.' Rupesh was not aware of this. Mr Tuteja explained that I was severely injured and that was the reason they had to keep me in a state of induced coma. Otherwise, the pain could be fatal. My husband was not satisfied with this explanation.

He thought a ventilator was the last stage. Throughout the flight, he was worried and hoped that on arrival he wouldn't hear any more bad news. All kinds of negative thoughts were flooding his mind. He was praying continuously and couldn't sleep throughout the flight.

⚜

24 MARCH 2016

When Sumita di arrived at the hospital, the window was closed as dressing was in progress. Gurmail asked whether he could see me as well. She told him to pray for me. She told me, 'After waiting for about two hours, the window opened and we saw you fully covered in bandages, without the sheet covering you. I took another picture of you then, to send it to the ambassador. You looked like a body wrapped in white, like a mummy.' Gurmail couldn't stop his tears because he kept wondering what my children would be going through as they couldn't even see the condition I was in. He is a Radha Soami devotee and he too prayed for me.

Sumita di and Gurmail could only see instruments, pipes and a nurse standing next to me. They knew that in some time, my husband would arrive. Sumita di started praying to God to give her the strength to handle my family when she would meet them.

When my family reached Paris, Duty Manager Ms Shalaka, Airport Manager Mr Paters and staff member Sami received them. A car had been arranged to take them to Grand Hospital, Charleroi. One of the Jet staff was waiting outside the hospital to receive my family. He took them to the room where Sumita di was waiting. To comfort Rupesh she assured him, that I was fine and would open my eyes soon.

Rupesh first spoke to the doctors, Dr Peeters and Dr Hans. They explained my condition to him and told him they were doing their best but the rest was in God's hands. No assurance was given at that time as my condition was stable for the moment but kept changing from time to time. The doctors told Rupesh that he could see me, but he stepped back, thinking it may not be safe as he had travelled a long way, first by flight and then by car for almost sixteen hours. Any infection from the germs he may have been carrying could affect my recovery. He said he would take a shower and come back but the doctors told him that since I was in the ICCU, he wouldn't be able to go inside the room in any case but could still see me from the glass window.

Head Nurse John guided them to the ICCU room's glass window area where three chairs had been placed already. Sumita di held my husband's hand and asked him to hold Nilesh's hand and then Nilesh held Priyanka's hand. She said, 'All will be good, just take God's name.' When they reached the window and saw me, Rupesh sat down on the chair and burst out crying. Soon all of them were crying aloud, and it was difficult for Sumita di and Nurse John to manage them. It took a while to get them out of the shock and trauma of seeing me in that condition. Sumita di tried to console them, 'Don't worry, she is in the best hospital and being treated by excellent doctors. God is with her and we are all praying for her.'

She told me later that she made a promise to Rupesh, when he first saw me through the ICCU window—'*Dilwale dulhaniya le jayenge*! Have faith in God.' She asked Rupesh to say something to me on the speaker that was outside the window, which would play his voice inside the room.

Rupesh kept saying, 'I have come, baby. Don't worry, all will be good... And the doctors are saying you are fine. Nothing will happen to you. I will take you back soon.' Later, he burst out crying again. At that time, I was in a shared ICCU room, Room No 2.

The doctors had offered the facility to play any music or sounds that I may like, so Sumita di had brought a pen drive with chants of the Gayatri mantra, Gurbani, and Hanuman Chalisa to be played 24/7 in my room. These were played continuously from that day onwards.

❦

In the morning, Rupesh came to see me, but the situation was the same. Reluctantly, Sumita di asked if it was okay if her husband came to see me. Rupesh told her he didn't mind and requested her: 'Please ask your husband to pray for her.' Her husband, Madan, prayed for my well-being.

After some time, the Indian Ambassador Mr M.S. Puri, and his wife visited. They too were shocked to see the condition I was in. Mr Puri said he had no words after he saw the initial photograph that Sumita di had sent him. He didn't know what to tell my family, but he did manage to say: 'Have faith in God. Things will improve soon.'

Rupesh had nightmares about me that whole night. He was not able to talk to anyone on the phone either, although every single member of the family was calling him. He asked his brother Nilesh to attend to all the calls. My sister Jolly was eager to come see me, but Rupesh told her that her presence would be needed later when I regain consciousness. While talking to the kids, he would try to sound confident. They kept asking him, 'Show us how Mom is, just once...' But he told them that even he wasn't allowed inside the room where I was resting, which is why he wouldn't be able to connect me with them on a video call. Rupesh's day passed looking through the ICCU room window. Later, Shabir bhai came to meet my family.

Rupesh knew that no one could ever force me to do anything, so he started talking to me via the speaker in a very pleasing, imploring manner, the way a small child would beg his mother for something. He would say, 'Baby, you are very strong, nothing has happened to you. Just get up. I know you are angry, okay, I am sorry.' And with that, he left with tears in his eyes. That night, my heart started pumping irregularly and at midnight, they had to call the cardiologist. Later, we came to know that I had got a cardiac arrest. I had been given four shocks of 100 to 200 joules in a span of a few minutes to revive me. This showed that the first three attempts had failed but I was lucky to finally be brought back to life.

❧

When Rupesh came to the hospital the next morning, he was horrified to hear about what had happened the previous night. Around midnight, Rupesh had actually felt as though he had lost me. He had told me that his heart felt cramped as if he had lost his soul. But the doctors assured him I was stable. So after visiting me, Rupesh, Nilesh and Priyanka went to Antwerp to meet Amit. He was injured but in his senses. He explained in detail what exactly had happened. We had just reached Level Two of the airport using escalators and had walked a few steps, when we witnessed the first blast. He told them that I wanted to go and help, whereas he sensed that something was wrong and insisted that I stay put as we were in a different country and we had the duty of operating a flight. We realised something was wrong when people started screaming and running towards the exits, and then towards us, as the lifts and stairs were behind us.

He said that we had sensed the danger of getting caught in a stampede, and that's when I screamed, 'Bhaag!' I'd moved towards the left but a moment later, the second blast took place. Within a second, he was flung flat on the ground. 'I don't know where my bags went, but I was searching for a ray of light. It was too dark and smoky and I was looking for a single ray of light there,' recalled Amit. He then started crawling towards one side and saw a glimmer in the distance. His eyes were injured and he was unable to open them. He said he had to forcefully open one eye with his hand. It was so painful but there was no other option. Then he realised that his other eye was bleeding. He was gasping for breath in the smoke. Finally, he found a place, a food joint set a little far away from everything, and thought that would be the safest place to be in at that moment. He remembered that he had his phone in his pocket, and called up Jet Airways' base. Deep (the assistant base in-charge) answered. On hearing the news, Deep was stunned into silence. When Amit repeated that a bomb blast had happened at the airport, that I had been with him but he couldn't see me anymore, Deep asked, 'Are you fine?' Deep then handed over the phone to the base manager, Priyanka, who tried to assure him, 'Don't worry, you are fine. We will find Nidhi. Move out of that place.' The whole base had come to a standstill. Now the question was, *where was the rest of the crew*? Amit told them that we had both been ahead of everyone else, so he believed that all the others might be safe.

Meanwhile, the police came and asked him to move towards the exit that led to the tarmac. Amit said he called up his family members. He also marked himself 'safe' on his Facebook page. He said he tried to look for me, but couldn't find me. He had to be helped by others as he had an injury on his leg and was crawling.

He remarked to Rupesh, 'What an irony... because Nidhi was on the flight and this would have been our last flight to the United States, I had updated my status on Facebook with the words, "We will have a blast". I can't believe we literally experienced a blast...'

Amit clicked his own pictures to update his near and dear ones of the news. Then, one by one, the authorities started sending casualties to the hospital. On hearing Amit's narration of the incident, my husband started feeling restless. Rupesh thanked Amit for narrating the sequence of events and wished him a quick recovery.

❦

That day, the ambassador was to visit Amit. Everyone was waiting for him to arrive so that they could leave thereafter. Knowing my nature, about how I never bothered with small injuries, Nilesh remarked he was confident that once I regained consciousness, I'd recover so fast that everyone would be amazed at my strength. My husband agreed and said, 'I have faith in God and I am very sure about that. Yes, we are waiting for her to just open her eyes.'

After meeting the ambassador, Nilesh and Rupesh came back to the hospital and found me sleeping, just the way I had been when they left. A doctor informed them, 'She is stable as of now.' Rupesh said he could see uncountable pipes inserted in my body, in my mouth, and noticed a brown fluid being secreted. It was too much for him to bear and he got worried. He checked with the head nurse who assured him that this was common in such cases and asked him not to worry. He prayed to God and went back to the hotel. His angst and helplessness was clearly visible to everyone around.

❧

27 MARCH 2016

Today the chairman of Jet Airways with his wife, and our company head doctor, Dr Kharam, accompanied by a few others, came to see me. Everyone was astonished on seeing my condition. The chairman had a word with the doctors and said, 'I don't know where God exists, but for me, you are God and I want my Nidhi back.' This was conveyed to me by Roopa, the duty manager at Brussels. I was told that he even called out my name on the speaker and said, 'You will be fine, Nidhi.' He also assured my husband that they would leave no stone unturned in getting me back. Jeet, an assistant base in-charge, was asked to stay with my husband for a few days and to keep updating the chairman. He asked Roopa to stay back in Brussels from 1 April until I was fit to get back to India.

❧

Rupesh recounted later how for him the days were never-ending and the nights were like long nightmares. All he could do was look at the machine's screen and pray to God. He was surprised when they shifted me to another ICCU room, which was exclusively for me (a single occupancy room). So now I was in Room No. 3.

❧

27 MARCH 2016

I had a slight fever today. Rupesh was anxious; the doctors said there was nothing to worry. But knowing what had happened two days ago, Rupesh was worried. My lungs had caught an infection. The doctors said it was normal in such cases. When Rupesh asked the doctors why they had shifted me to another room, one of them explained: 'As she has more than twenty percent burns with many open injuries, chances of getting an infection are very high, so it's better to shift her as the burns look affected.' Then another doctor added, 'Don't worry, we are taking all precautionary measures to keep her out of danger.'

Rupesh wanted to know how the burns would heal, as three-fourths of my back was burnt. I also had burns on my chest, stomach and thighs. Dr Peeters told him mine was a special bed. He said, 'It is very expensive, more expensive than the car we drive. The medicine passes through the bed's holes. Air is also passed through its pores — it will distribute the weight of the body evenly with air pressure, and this would help the burns dry faster. It doesn't matter if the burns are on the front or back. This way they will heal faster than usual.'

❦

28 MARCH 2016

There was a lot of pressure on my husband as no one else from the family had seen me apart from his brother. He would respond to the calls that came in keeping in mind the caller's age, and inform them about my state accordingly. It disturbed him more when people asked, 'Is there any improvement in her?' Eventually he started saying that once there was some improvement, he would inform them. My kids were another task to handle. They were told that Mom had been given a high dose of medicines, so she was sleeping continuously. But of course, they came to know about my condition through the news.

My younger brother-in-law, Ashish, also arrived from San Francisco today.

❦

29 MARCH 2016

My lungs had been further affected and the fever was not coming down either. The doctors were changing the medicine every day to check which antibiotic suited me best. Rupesh noticed that the secretion from my mouth was very dark that day. But, like the doctors said, this was expected. Rupesh told me later, 'Every moment I looked at you, I would speak to you in my mind—"Stop it and get up now, Nidhi. Let's go back. It's too much."' He just didn't feel like talking to anyone.

❧

Today, all the men—Rupesh, Nilesh, Ashish and Jeet—were there at the hospital but no one spoke to each other. Looking at Rupesh's condition, the others decided that at no point of time should he be left alone. Someone would be present with him 24/7, as he had lost his appetite and had become very quiet and aloof. In Mumbai, at my home today, my sister-in-law Madhuri had called up my elder sister Jolly to ask her to speak to my son as he had not yet cried or expressed his emotions and had grown quiet. He was totally broken and seemed very confused. Jolly di tried to speak to Vardaan, but he didn't utter a word. The kids said that they know Mom would come back home soon. The only thing gnawing the kids was why their dad wasn't showing Mom via a video call from the hospital. My sister told them, 'Papa himself isn't allowed to see Mom.'

My sister realised that at such an age, any child, when disturbed, would always want to consult his or her parents. But here, both parents were away and this made her feel even more worried. Jolly di later told me that she felt he had many questions in his mind but wasn't willing to share his thoughts. On the other hand, Vriddhi was howling continuously. My sister told them, 'God listens to children, so pray to God that Mom should be fine and be able to come back home soon.'

❧

30 MARCH 2016

My fever had not come down and the infection level had risen. My blood pressure was also on the higher side. Today, the doctors who were treating me, specifically Dr Peeters and Dr Saidane, were going on a holiday for ten days. My husband was already worried as he had been informed by the doctors that I would be woken up today. This meant that they had stopped the sedation dose, and would now watch for my reaction. They would try to wake me up in the afternoon, Brussels time. They requested Rupesh, 'We want you in the room, next to her, and we want her family members to speak to her. Brief your family, including your children and Nidhi's parents, to speak with her.'

Rupesh informed everyone in the family and asked the kids to be ready to talk when he called later in the day. He briefed them that they should speak even if they didn't get any response. 'Keep talking to her because your voice will be heard inside the ICCU room through the speaker. She will not be able to speak as she has a tight bandage on her jaw. We want your voice to be heard by her so that she can feel nice. This is an exercise the doctors would like to conduct today to wake Mom up from her deep sleep.'

In the afternoon, the doctors called Rupesh into the ICCU room where he was provided with special clothes to change into. This was the first time he went inside the room. Apart from my eyelids, he couldn't see anything and he stood frozen for a while. He did not touch me because he didn't know where it would be okay to touch, as I had bandages all over. Later, he told me, 'I was controlling myself. I was asked to speak, but all I wanted to do was hug you.' He was on the verge of tears but knew he needed to gather strength and control his emotions. The doctors urged him to speak. He said he kept on speaking, holding my bandaged hand, but his voice started trembling. He stopped speaking and saw that the doctors were moving my head a bit, calling out my name and tapping my cheeks, but there was no response from me. Rupesh then asked Nilesh to call up my parents and ask my family to speak. One by one, my mom, brother, sisters, and everyone else spoke to me, and still there was no reaction.

Nilesh called out to me while he was standing outside, 'Bhabhi, get up, we are waiting.' Ashish, my younger brother-in-law who had reached the hospital by then, tried his luck too. But in vain.

Rupesh said, 'I couldn't control myself and was crying, but

the doctors said you would take some time, so I should relax.' He thought that perhaps the brain may have been affected and that is why I wasn't reacting.

Then they were asked to call up the kids. My son spoke to me. 'Mom, I am doing a great job in school. I have given my best for my Cambridge checkpoint tests. So don't worry. I know you will be fine soon. Papa is there and don't worry about us. We are waiting for you to come back. Get my shoes, please don't forget them! I need them.' Still no reaction from me. 'Arre! Mom, speak na! I miss your scolding. I don't like it when you are not around,' and saying that, he handed over the phone to my brother-in-law's daughters, Sakshi and Snigdha.

'Nidhi mamma, we are missing you and your Punjabi parathas. Come back, we want to have them soon.'

Hearing no response, my sister-in-law Madhuri and my mom-in-law tried their best too, but all in vain. Finally, the phone was handed over to Vriddhi. She said, 'Mom, hi! How are you? We are good. Waiting for you and, you know, I am actually finishing my tiffin every day. We have not missed school for even one day, see what a good girl I am! I promise I won't waste food from now onwards. (Earlier, she would never finish her tiffin.) I am missing your cooking, Mom. All my friends miss your pasta. I have an event coming up, but who will buy me new costumes and get me ready? I am playing badminton with dedication and I promise you I will get a gold medal in the upcoming events, but I need you. Come home. I love you, my tigress.' Vriddhi stopped speaking at that point, but my husband saw a little movement in my eyes, so he shouted out to Nilesh, 'telling him to request Vriddhi to speak more. Vriddhi controlled her tears and took a while, but started again. 'Mom, do you know, in your absence I am taking care of Bhaiya. Don't forget to get waffles and chocolates… there are none left. I will come to the airport to receive you.'

She was asked to keep talking, so she started with an update on the only serial I used to watch — *Parvarish*. Rupesh told me later that my eyelids fluttered a bit at that point, and the fingers on my right hand shook. Then suddenly my leg, and then my whole body, started shivering and my parameters began fluctuating. The doctors immediately instructed: 'Stop it!' My hands and legs were strapped.

Rupesh kept on saying, 'Baby, don't worry, I am with you. I will take you back. The doctors are saying you are fine. Nothing is wrong with you. Just relax... relax... relax...' And all the while, my body was jerking.

My daughter kept asking Nilesh what was happening to Mommy. 'Has she gotten up?'

Nilesh told her, 'She can hear you and will get up soon.' Vriddhi was overjoyed on hearing this.

On the other hand, the doctors told my husband that my body was not ready for this and they couldn't take this risk so soon as my parameters were also fluctuating; I was tired and they would try this later, some other day. They gave me a sedative again. Everybody was watching from the window of the ICCU room, and through the speaker, voices were wafting into the room. Rupesh was satisfied about one thing, though—the fact that I could hear showed that my brain was working and responding. All my body parts were moving and not paralysed. Gurmail too had watched as they were trying to wake me up. He felt bad that apart from shedding tears and praying to God, he could do nothing. He realised how true it is that kids are always connected so strongly with their mother, as she is the only one who can relate to them in the worst of situations. She can even fight with God for them.

❦

Today was the first day when only Rupesh and Ashish were at the hospital, as all the others had gone back to India. Even Sumita di was to report back to the embassy the next day.

I believe at that time I surely saw my husband in the light-blue-coloured clothes he was wearing and a cap, and I could hear them all, but I was unable to respond or even open my eyes fully. I remember when I heard my parents' voices, my mom's voice was trembling. I could hear my husband talking to me, and in my dreams I was telling him, 'Someone hold me tight. My body is leaving me. Witches are waiting to eat me up, you go away from here, don't leave the kids alone.' Then when I heard the kids, I thought someone had thrown me into a pool of sharks and they would eat me in no time. As I don't know how to swim, my kids jumped into the pool to save me. I was trying to save myself too and was asking my kids to get out of the pool, to stay away from those witches and sharks.

❧

Dr Saidane believed it would be very dangerous to reduce the dosage of the sedatives. He also told the rest of my family who were present that I could hear. He said, 'So whenever you come to the window, make sure you speak to her. Tell her she is fine. That she will be well soon and will go back to her kids.' Everyone went back today thinking I would open my eyes soon and would be fine in a couple of days.

By the afternoon, our friend Rohit had come with Shabir bhai from Brussels. He hadn't expected me to be in such a bad condition. He requested the doctors to provide him with the full case study as he had many good friends who were doctors in different countries, and whose opinion he could seek. He said he'd been briefed about today's incident too. He prayed to God and said he had full faith that I would fight all odds and come back soon. He spoke to his friends and they confirmed that the doctors here were following the right method of treatment. With a heavy heart he told Rupesh not to worry and assured him that everything would be fine.

❧

Roopa was asked to join my husband from 1 April to keep my company updated about who our daily visitors were and to periodically report on my medical status. This was important as it had become a very high-profile case because of wide media coverage.

❧

My condition remained the same. There was a lot of panic, stress and confusion among my family members and they had doubts about the competence of the doctors and the efficacy of my treatment. Rupesh was dealing with a lot of pressure and sometimes he would wonder if the treatment was working on me. But he had to pacify himself by thinking of the other victims of the blast who had been discharged from the hospital. He was hoping that his wife too would be discharged soon. But my health had worsened. Ashish said he had seen Rupesh talking to himself many times as if he had gone mad, and that would worry him. Many a time Rupesh had to be shaken up and he would feel embarrassed. Ashish said later, 'I don't remember if we had a proper meal during those days.'

❦

1 APRIL 2016

A new month began, but there was nothing new for my family except the determination to keep their thoughts positive. My situation started changing. The infection in my lungs worsened and the fever spiked a bit. My blood pressure was 165, higher than normal. Now I was under the care of Dr Nadine Hans and Dr Robert Van der Horst. Dr Hans had already been treating me. So when my husband spoke to the doctors, they said these changes were very common in such cases. The oxygen level from my ventilator was increased to fifty percent now.

Rupesh spoke to me for a long time through the speaker, hoping that I would hear his words and recall memories from before the incident, which could help improve the situation, but there was no response from my end. The whole day passed without any improvement; Rupesh and Ashish left for the hotel in the evening as usual. A few people we didn't know had come to see me after hearing about my situation, to perform prayers for me. Rupesh never turned away or prevented anyone from doing this—'You never know whose prayers will work,' he would say.

Much later, I got to know that his appetite had disappeared completely. He had to be forced to have a meal and he would skip his dinner every day. At lunchtime, he had to be forced to have a bite. He had already lost about six to seven kilograms.

❦

2 APRIL 2016

The king of Belgium, King Philippe visited me. When he arrived, Rupesh was in the visiting room. Before the king could enter my room, the chief of protocol of the Royal Household, Alain Gerardy, walked in. He had entered the hospital first and the king had followed. The king shook hands with Rupesh and took his permission to take a look at me in the ICCU room. Rupesh told me later that being the king, he could have simply visited me at will, but it was so nice of him to ask first. King Philipe asked all the doctors treating me about my health. He was very concerned. He shook hands with my family, assuring them that the Belgium authorities would personally leave no stone unturned in my treatment, and that he felt sorry for all the suffering they were going through. Later, he had a long meeting with the other victims and their families and said he was very sorry for all that had happened, and promised that all support would be provided without hesitation. The mayor of Charleroi also came to pay a visit.

My situation remained the same. The doctors changed my medicines and put me on another antibiotic. More tests were being done. Rupesh felt so perplexed; my fever was rising day by day and the doctors said it was because of the lung infection, but Rupesh kept thinking that it could be because of him. He felt that the day he had entered my room to try and talk to me, perhaps he had passed on some kind of infection to me while he was in the ICCU room. The doctors asked him to sit in the room and talk to me again, but he was now hesitant. He felt guilty and continued to talk to me only through the speaker phone. Seeing my health deteriorate, he became numb, his mind full of negative thoughts. My family in India was planning to come now. But he asked them, 'What will you all do here? There is nothing to do apart from looking at her from the window. It is really depressing. So please don't come.' But my sister Jolly was adamant. My parents on the other hand are quite old—it was difficult for them to travel all the way.

❧

3 APRIL 2016

There was no improvement, and my lungs were still infected. My oxygen requirement was more than before. My temperature was not returning to normal. Many people from different religions and nationalities started visiting the hospital as word had spread around the world. My husband, in the last two days, had received a pandit from a temple in Brussels as Sumita di had asked the pandit to perform special prayers; a maulvi from the mosque as Shabir bhai had informed the maulvi to conduct namaz for my recovery; and a head from the Nirankari Samaj, as my sister in Delhi had visited Babaji, who in turn had asked one of the followers to come to Brussels and perform prayers for me here. Someone from the Radha Soami organisation too had come to offer prayers—perhaps Gurmail, the driver, had informed them. Rupesh also met a priest from a church, sent by local citizens, to pray for me. They all prayed for my recovery. But things were only getting worse. Rupesh wouldn't stop anyone from visiting or praying there. He would take them to the window, believing that God may listen to them. Every evening, he would return to the hotel room, his mind racked with all the complications and flooded with bleak thoughts.

❧

4 APRIL 2016

My body temperature was 101.3 degrees Fahrenheit. Rupesh received a call from the kids—they wanted to see me. He simply told them that I had fever, and so they should pray to God for my recovery. The truth was, the whole world was praying for me. Rupesh tried to analyse what had gone wrong, why things weren't improving in spite of the doctors doing their best. Every day, he would speak to the doctors, and they would always thank him for his patience and confidence in them. Even though they were trying their best to save me, Rupesh was considering taking another opinion as my condition seemed to be deteriorating.

᪄

5 APRIL 2016

The infection level was very very high. The situation was really tense for everyone, including the doctors who were treating me. They kept trying their best, changing my antibiotics day after day, but all efforts were proving to be unsuccessful. They urged Rupesh to keep motivating me, as despite all odds, I was fighting to be alive. Rohit visited again with Shabir bhai. He too was worried about the situation and spoke to other friends of his who were doctors. They opined that the treatment was fine, but the lung infection had to be brought under control soon, otherwise it would lead to organ failure, and then reversing the situation would be difficult. Rohit had consulted an astrologer friend who had advised him a few *upaays* to make my condition stable. He had brought the 'charan padukas' (old-style slippers) of Shri Sai Baba and joss sticks on his last visit. He had asked Rupesh to light the joss sticks in the eastern direction every morning, and to keep the charan padukas too, to be worshipped, in the same direction. My mom was already chanting mantras, doing paath, donations and prayers at different holy sites. Donations were going to gurudwaras and temples. Eleven pandits were requested to do eleven days' puja continuously in the temple near my mom's home. For several days, many people, including family and friends, performed various rituals of worship for my quick recovery.

Rohit said a few prayers standing by the window today. He was very sad and asked God—*Why did you do this to her*? He had brought with him a laminated picture of Lord Vishnu with Goddess Lakshmi and Lord Krishna with Radha, as advised by the astrologer, to be kept near me inside the ICCU room. He requested the nurse to place these next to my bed, and left with a heavy heart.

Back home, there was a lot of tension building up, as Ashish had to go back to San Francisco on 7 April. The question was — who would come to stay with me now? It was decided that my sister Jolly would. Everyone who had been to Charleroi was aware that Rupesh was not to be left alone at any point of time. He really needed support. My jiju (Jolly's husband) said he would accompany her as my condition might prove to be too unnerving for her, and then both of them would need someone's support. But getting the visa would take two days, so they were booked on a 9 April flight. In the meantime, Abhimanyu, Jolly's elder son who lives in London, said he would keep Rupesh company. Rupesh called up Ajay, from the Indian embassy, informing him that my condition was getting worse day by day, so he wanted another medical opinion.

❦

6 APRIL 2016

In the morning, my nephew Abhimanyu arrived from London. When my husband came, the window of my room was closed. He waited for some time and then went to speak to the doctors. The doctors said there had been no improvement but they were doing all they could. They told him to pray to God and keep boosting my morale. Rupesh sat in the visiting room for hours as many people would come to ask after me and enquire if he needed anything. Later, our In-Flight Services Vice President Ms Pom Warakorn arrived to meet my husband. When Abhimanyu, Ms Pom and Rupesh saw me, they were both taken aback. A nurse was standing next to me and I was covered in wet sheets. Ice slabs were kept in the room. Blowers had been placed on both sides and the parameters raised to the extreme. My body temperature had risen to 104 degrees Fahrenheit and wasn't showing signs of receding. The supply of oxygen that was being given to me was turned to one hundred percent, the blood pressure had shot up and the infection level was dangerously high. After having a conversation with Dr Robert Van der Horst, Rupesh wondered how the doctors were going to handle the situation. He also felt that perhaps they were scared to tell him the truth. This was not a multispecialty hospital and so they would be capable of handling only burns patients, he thought. All this came to his mind more so because Amit was in a multispecialty hospital, which was huge, located in a big city, equipped with all kinds of facilities, whereas I was in a hospital located in a forested area and perhaps not on par with the other hospital. Rupesh was filled with doubt, just as anybody would have been in such a situation.

Meanwhile, Ms Pom called the chairman and briefed him on the whole scenario. She took a picture of my parameters to send it to him. She concluded the call saying she would do her best, and after some time, left to meet Amit in Antwerp.

Rupesh, his brother and my nephew were all very nervous. Rupesh said that standing next to the window was agonising, but at the same time, leaving the place made them feel very insecure. He stood next to the speaker and spoke his heart out to me that day. He said, 'Don't you dare go anywhere... we would all be incomplete. I will not go home without you, Nidhi. You are so brave. We look up to you and you know how weak I am. It's time to get up, because I can't take it any more now. Your kids are waiting for you and your love.'

❦

7 APRIL 2016

My situation had worsened considerably. Doctors were surprised as to why no medicine was effective. They told my family to keep encouraging me. But my husband couldn't see me in that condition anymore. He thought he had almost lost me. When he received a conference call from Mr Tuteja and our chairman, Rupesh admitted that he wanted to take me to another hospital. Dr J.D. Sunavala from India's famous Breach Candy Hospital was also on the call. After listening to everything, he replied that it was very difficult to say anything at that moment. Apart from the reports, there are many other things they need to look at, he said. Dr Sunavala said he would have a word with Dr Peeters as well. Dr Peeters said he was aware of the situation, and it was worrying him too. He would visit me in the hospital the next day and would try to figure out what was wrong.

In the hospital, looking at my worsening condition, Dr Hans, who had been treating me from day one, decided that they would do a full-body CT scan again. They had done several CT scans for many parts of my body but hadn't done a 3D CT scan till date. So they now decided to do a 3D CT scan for me. She took this decision because in spite of high doses of antibiotics, infection levels were increasing and the fever was not subsiding. In fact, it had now shot up to almost 105 degrees Fahrenheit. This meant there was something else bothering the body. The ultimate danger in such high-level complications was that there could be a complete failure of the system at any time.

❧

8 APRIL 2016

In the morning, they did the full-body 3D CT scan and found that there were many metal pieces, like bullets, lodged inside the bones. They found that my right ankle bone had big metal pieces that looked like bones but were not bones at all! There was a huge piece of metal inside the bone shell. In my left elbow joint, a large piece was lodged entirely inside the bone and a lot of metallic shrapnel and foreign bodies were found. They immediately took me into the operation theatre. By then, Dr Peeters had arrived as well. They reopened my grafted foot and removed as many pieces as they could. The biggest piece was about two inches long. They had to cut my skin deep from the elbow joint to remove the piece stuck inside the bone. The metal piece was so big that they had to cut it into two pieces and pull each one out from either end. They even had to cut the bone of my right heel to remove a metal piece that was stuck in such a way that it almost seemed to be a part of the skeletal structure! The procedures were successful. My family was so tense throughout, my husband and nephew prayed nonstop. The doctor believed I would be fine now. 'the situation will improve,' one of them said.

❧

9 APRIL 2016

My sister Jolly and her husband Amarjeet arrived from India. When Rupesh reached the hospital, I was a little better than before. All the parameters were improving though they were still at a dangerous level. When my sister saw me, she couldn't stop crying as nobody in my family had ever seen me lying helpless on a bed; they knew me as someone who was always on her toes. Rupesh comforted her that I was in fact much better than before. Since there were no wet sheets and ice slabs covering me, he felt I would be fine soon and said, 'Let's keep our fingers crossed.' He told my sister to speak to me through the speaker.

I heard her say something like, 'Nidhi, utth jaa ab,' which means 'get up now'. She continued, 'It's been so long since you've been sleeping, look what I got for you from Istanbul. Arre, I need tea, chalo let's make some!' She has always been very fond of the tea I make. She also confessed, 'Everyone in the family has decided never to ask you to keep quiet, we promise you, so please speak.' (This was because when I am with my family, I don't allow anyone else to speak, and they always have to ask me to be quiet!)

In my dreams, I was telling my sister, *'I am on a water bed and I am very tired after the long and hectic flight, so I can't get up. Let me sleep. You give chocolates to the kids. I have no energy to get up. See you later.'* It was as though I felt very bad that she had come to give me a surprise at night and I just couldn't get up. I was cursing myself and telling her, '*I won't be able to get up early in the morning to make lunch for the kids to take to school, so you make it for them.*' After that, I was lost again in my own zombie-like world. Abhimanyu (her elder son) left for London that evening.

After trying to talk to me for a long time, Jolly di sat down. My family spoke to the doctors; the doctors were hopeful too. But they emphasised: 'Keep talking to her. Boost her morale, motivate her.' In the background, Hare Rama Hare Krishna, the Gayatri mantra and Gurbani chants were played 24/7.

❧

10 APRIL 2016

My situation improved a little. Everyone was praying. My family members would talk to me through the speaker phone. They would attend to the people coming to see me and pray for me.

My husband was not able to relax as he had seen the situation go from good to bad in no time. He prayed to God to give him strength because it was very depressing to continue seeing me like that through the window all day and get back to the hotel in the night without any sign of even a movement. Almost every day, Shabir bhai would visit. Sumita di's husband Madan bhai would also drop in three to four times a week.

❧

11 APRIL 2016

I was much, much better than yesterday. The bandages from my arms and forehead were removed, so everyone could see more than just my eyelids. They asked the doctors when I would open my eyes. 'Very soon,' they said. Rupesh saw a ray of hope. He said it was very tough to accept the present situation. Every day on the phone, he would tell the family and kids that I was still in deep sleep. Of course, they must have wondered whether he was telling the truth or hiding things from them. That was the reason why he would hand over the phone to the others, whoever was around at the time. Many times, my family back home had pleaded with him to send them at least one picture of me, but he would deny their request.

❧

12 APRIL 2016

Things were looking better than before. The infection level came down and my fever was subsiding. The doctors said, 'Maybe tomorrow she will open her eyes, as we are going to decrease the sedation dose today and will stop it by tomorrow.' Everyone was waiting for the sun to rise.

❧

13 APRIL 2016

When my family reached the hospital this morning, the doctors said, 'today she is looking medically stable. We will inform you when she opens her eyes.'

All of them were sitting in the visiting room, waiting anxiously for me to wake up. In the afternoon, I opened my eyes and after a while, Rupesh was asked to come into the ICCU room. At that time, my family was in the visiting area and not at the ICCU room's window gallery. When they had gone to the window earlier, they had found it closed as my bandages were being removed. To go to this window gallery, one had to cross the entire length of the hospital and then climb up from the rear. My husband wore antibacterial clothes and came into my room. He had always seen my face wrapped in bandages, but when he entered the room today and saw an old lady sitting, leaning forward on the bed almost lifeless, with very short grey and black hair, lean, burnt, he got scared and ran out of the room and told the nurse outside—'I have come to see Nidhi, my wife. Where is she?'

The nurse replied calmly, 'that is your wife.'

He was so shocked he didn't know what to do or where to look. He stood there for a few minutes just to gather the energy to face the truth because, he told me later, he wanted to be strong enough to handle me and my questions.

At no point of time did Rupesh want to look weak. He came near me but I was frail and could barely look around. He said he loved me, kissed my forehead and placed his hand on my head, as that was the only place where he could rest his fingers, but he received no response from me. By that time my sister and brother-in-law too reached the window and my sister, again, couldn't stop crying seeing my condition. It was tough to control her, my brother-in-law later said.

I could barely move my eyes. I was very, very weak, because for twenty-three days I'd been on only liquids and heavy doses of medicines. Holding my hand, Rupesh started talking to me. 'Baby, you are fine now. How are you feeling? I am your husband, why are you not responding...?' He spoke about the kids and told me that they were missing me. 'Vardaan and Vriddhi wanted to come here, they want their mom back home soon.'

But he got no response at all from me; it was as if I didn't know him or could not hear him. I didn't even look at him. He was so tense. He went out and spoke to the doctors. One of them said, 'We have already briefed you that she may take a few days to recollect her past. What she speaks may not be relevant, and she won't even remember it the next moment. You may have to keep on reminding her about things that happened in her past. She may speak about what she saw in her dreams while she was in a state of induced coma. For her, that was the truth.' Now everyone was worried and started wondering if I would remember the past at all. No one was allowed inside the room after that.

In the Punjabi calendar, 13 April is Baisakhi, which marks the new year for Punjabis, so everybody said this was my rebirth. The doctors said I was too weak to respond, and they may have to wait for days, but all would be fine. My sister said she waved at me from outside; she smiled and blew kisses to me through the window. She also spoke through the speaker. 'Nidhi, *o meri beti,*

Nidhu. Darna nahi… (Don't be scared.) We are with you. Look here, we are standing at the window.'

Immediately afterwards, all the family members were informed — *Nidhi has opened her eyes.* They all wanted to speak to me then, but were told that I was too weak to utter a word. The good news was shared around with everyone. My family asked Rupesh to share my picture on WhatsApp, but he refused, as he thought I might be disturbed if I chance upon such pictures in the future. He had instructed the family not to take my photo. He was not even aware of the picture Shabir bhai had taken at Sint-Augustinus Hospital.

My sister-in-law Madhuri went to Mataji's temple to thank the goddess for answering their prayers. She had told my kids, 'We will eat the first mango of the season when your mom opens her eyes,' and as promised, she got it for them! My kids folded their hands and thanked God with tears of joy streaming down their faces. My eldest sister Goldy went to Nirankari Baba Sri Hardev Singh ji's house to thank him for his blessings. My sister Meenu went to pay her gratitude at Mataji's temple. My mom went to the Krishna temple and my brother went to the gurudwara. My father stood in front of Lord Shiva and thanked him; he actually lay down on the floor to offer the 'dandwat pranam' to pay his regards. Rohit too went to a Krishna temple. Shabir bhai performed special namaz that day. My friends in the United States and in Australia lit candles in churches. My Guru (late) Sri Premvir Singhji's devotees held a special assembly at the Buddhist temple in London. I also call him my godfather and he had named me 'Nidhi the Dabang' because I was never scared of anything but God. Prayers were conducted at a Buddhist temple in Delhi as well.

There were many strangers who had prayed for me. I would say humanity prayed for me. And everyone's prayers counted.

❧

Rupesh came inside the room around noon. He noticed that I seemed to be moving my head a bit. He kissed my forehead and stood next to me to watch for any further movement, but there was nothing more after that. He again reminded me of what he had said yesterday. But I did not utter a word. He was there with me for two to three hours and then he went out. My sister insisted on meeting me and came into my room late in the afternoon. She too kissed my forehead. She told me later, 'the room was so silent... seeing you in the room like that was unbearable.'

She could hear my strained breathing, an unpleasant, eerie sort of sound, and it started haunting her, so she broke the silence and began talking to me. She kept talking to me about what the kids did in my absence. How much they missed me. How Mom and Dad wanted to come, but she had told them that I would fly back soon. She spoke nonstop, but there was not a word from me in response. She even asked me, 'Do you know me?' She told me later that I just gave a small smile in response to that question.

She continued, 'I am your elder sister Jolly. We are four sisters and one brother.' She mentioned everyone's names, and around 1730 hrs Belgium time, when she was about to leave, I spoke these words looking at her—'*Inhone mujhe paani nahi diya,*' meaning, they have not given me water.

At the point, she couldn't control her emotions and broke down. She replied, 'they will give you water very soon.'

After a pause, I told her, '*Mere par bahut goliya chali...*' (Many bullets were fired at me.)

'But now you are fine. All the bullets have been removed,' she spoke gently.

The nurses told my sister that they would soon give me a few drops of water. Everyone was so happy as I spoke my first sentence today after all these days of silence. Head Nurse John urged my sister to ask me whether I had nightmares, and when she did, I gave her a blank look. She explained later, 'We asked you this question

daily for at least fifteen days after that first day you spoke, and
sometimes you would nod your head as if to say yes.'

※

15 APRIL 2016

Around 1100 hrs Brussels time, the nurses used a patient-lift
device to shift me from the bed to a chair. They wrapped big
bands around my thighs and back, supporting my shoulders. The
bands were hooked to a small operating machine controlled by an
attendant. The device lifted me from the bed and placed me on a
reclining chair. (This was done for a few days and I used to love
being suspended in air for a few seconds. It was just like being
in a swinging wheel.)

The physiotherapist introduced himself. But I just gave him a
blank stare as I still couldn't process what was happening around me.
He started with physiotherapy for my legs and hands. He lifted my
leg slowly, then brought it down, and moved it a little sideways and
inward. He was trying to fold the fingers of my hands and suddenly
I cried. He thought he hurt me. He apologised immediately.

'Oh, I am sorry, where does it hurt?'

I asked him, 'Where am I?'

He told me I was in Grand Hospital, Charleroi. Filled with fear
and surprise, my next words were, 'I have to call up home and
inform my family that I am here and I am alive and fine. They
must be worried.'

He replied, 'they are already here.'

I was astonished. 'Who informed them? When did they arrive?'

He told me they had been here for almost a month now. I
was stunned and confused because I didn't remember a thing. I
told him I needed to speak to them. He assured me they would
come soon, but I was howling by then. I pleaded with him to
let me speak to my family. He asked me, 'Do you know your
husband's number?'

I said, 'No, I am not sure.'

He fished out Rupesh's local number from my file and got a cordless phone and dialled the number. My husband answered right away, but there was fear in his voice as till then he had never received a call from the hospital. He heard me crying. He kept on saying, 'Hello, hello, baby, what happened?'

'Where are you?' I managed to ask.

He told me that he was in a bus and would arrive soon.

I said, 'Come fast. I want to meet you.'

He kept saying, 'Yes, yes, I am reaching soon. I will be there in the next fifteen minutes.'

Rupesh and my sister had been told to come after 1100 hrs every day because my bandage dressing would take about two hours to complete and the window would be closed all the while.

Once at the hospital, Rupesh rushed to change into antibacterial clothes and came into my room. He held me in his arms while I sat on a chair. I couldn't hug him as I was very weak, so I rested my head on his chest. Words can never express what Rupesh and I felt for that brief period of time. Rupesh experienced immense relief. It was a moment he had been waiting for. For me, his warm, loving embrace gave me some sense of who I am and where I was. But by that time I was so thirsty that I started coughing. For Rupesh, it was the first time in twenty-six days that he had seen me sitting on a chair! I was very tired as the hospital staff lifted me again with the mechanical contraption to put me back on the bed. I saw my sister and brother-in-law through the glass window. They started waving at me, blowing kisses, and then my sister said on the speaker, 'We love you.'

I wanted water. The nurse came in with two sticks of sponge that looked like lollypops, and dipping them in about twenty millilitres of blue water in a glass, she started wetting my lips. I said, 'I want to drink water.'

'For at least two days, we can only wet your lips with this, and if all goes well, we will give you water after two days,' she replied.

They kept that glass in the refrigerator. My lips felt so dry, I felt like a dried-up orange. I had become like a shell. I was unable to swallow my own saliva. My throat felt so parched. Feeling exhausted, I slept.

When I opened my eyes, it was late afternoon and I saw my sister sitting next to me. Both Rupesh and my brother-in-law were sitting at the window. Jolly spoke to me for some time. She told me she loved me and asked me if I wanted to speak to the kids, but I refused. She assumed I had refused out of weakness. (In actuality, I was simply unable to figure out what she had told me!)

I told her I needed water. My lips were sponged again but this time, I caught hold of the sponge with my lips and sucked on it like a dog holds on to a bone. It tasted so sweet! (The nurse smiled and started shaking the stick as if asking me to let go of it.) Everyone was waiting for me to ask some questions about my condition, but I didn't ask them a single one in those two days. So they got worried: Does she remember her past? What happened to her? Rupesh, Jolly and my brother-in-law left late in the evening and I slept like a log because the day had been quite stressful for the delicate condition that I was in.

There was something very strange I did, though. I kept asking about the date every few hours. Rupesh told me it was 15 April. I asked him, '2015?' He replied in the negative and told me it's 2016. I wondered how time had jumped ahead by one year. He painstakingly narrated all the incidents that had taken place during this one year and how we had celebrated our kids' birthdays. I had no clue at all; I was blank. Again, a few hours later, I asked my sister, what is the day today? I got the same answer, but my brain couldn't comprehend anything. I felt so confused!

❧

16 APRIL 2016

I was better than before. The doctors decided that my family should talk to me today about the blast. So when Rupesh asked me, 'Are you aware that you were injured in a blast?'

I replied, 'Yes. There were two blasts that took place. I was standing near the border between two countries when the blasts happened. One bomb exploded in one country and I escaped, and another exploded in the other country. This time too I was lucky and saved by the grace of God. So I asked them, "Why do you do such things and trouble people, kill them? What do you get out of it?" And then there was a third bomb that exploded on me, but I managed to run and escape, but I got a little injured.' I also told them that I knew who had planned this and who had bribed people to sacrifice their lives in the name of religion.

Everyone in the room stared at me. Then Rupesh explained it all to me. 'You are a flight attendant. You were at Brussels airport and on your way to Newark when the blast took place, and you were injured. Do you remember that your colleagues were with you?' Looking at him with surprise, I said no. He explained all the events in their correct sequence, the things I had done at home before the flight. How I had managed to get the flight in the first place. How I was with our kids in their school when I got news that this flight had finally been assigned to me. How I took Vardaan's shoes and even Rupesh's shoes to get them exchanged. I recollected a bit like a flashback scene in a black-and-white movie.

He spoke again. 'On 22 March, you saw the first blast and wanted to help, when your colleague Amit asked you to hold on as he had sensed something was wrong. There was panic all around you and then you ran. You got injured in the second blast...' By now I had recollected much of the scene. He continued, 'Do you remember anybody clicking your picture?' I moved my head a bit to gesture a 'no'. Then he asked me, 'Do you know how we came to know that you are injured?'

I was clueless and he said, 'through a picture of yours that went viral all around the world. It was on all TV channels, printed in all the newspapers worldwide.' I told him I wanted to see the picture. He typed my name into his phone then and my picture came up on the screen.

I stared at the picture. I was shocked and wondered when the photo was taken. I could see the pain and agony I was in. I could see how traumatised and thunderstruck I looked. At that moment, I felt it all over again—that feeling of utter helplessness I had experienced that day. I asked aloud, 'Oh God! Is that me?' The incident had left such a deep impact on me. Rather than my body, my face spoke the truth. The whole scene now flashed in my mind. I recollected the moments right after the blast.

'Do you remember who was with you?' asked Rupesh. But I had no clue. 'Do you remember your crew?' Again I drew a blank. That memory flashback had occurred only because of the picture shown to me. My mind was in a whirl; I couldn't get the image out of my head.

I asked Rupesh whether the people lying next to me were doing okay. He said, 'No, a few ended up losing their lives. You are really lucky to get your life back, and so are we.'

Later that evening, he asked me whether it was okay if he went back to India as his visa was going to expire in a few days and it had been almost a month since he had been away from the kids. He said the kids would feel comfortable seeing him for a while, and then he would be back here in five days, as soon as he got his visa. He added, 'Didi and Jiju are here with you.' I told him I was okay with it.

Then I asked my sister again, 'What is the date today?'

She replied, 'It is the 16th.' But my brain simply could not assimilate this fact.

After some time, I asked her, 'Which 16th?'

'16 April.'

'Did we celebrate New Year last year?'

'Yes, we all did,' she said simply.

I nearly went into shock because according to me, it was 2012 and she said it was 2016. 'I can't remember anything from the years that have passed,' I panicked.

She calmed me down. 'Don't worry, you will remember everything soon. This is just the effect of the strong medication.'

Today again I didn't speak to anybody on the phone because talking would easily tire me out. I kept on asking for water and this time, instead of two, I got four lollypops and about thirty millilitres of syrup for the entire day. I would ask either my husband or sister or nurse to wet my lips with it. I slept the instant they left.

It became a challenge to ask me every day whether I recalled the dates and days. But they didn't give up and kept talking to me about it every day. At times I would feel I had gone mad because I would not be aware of certain times of the year and sometimes, the years would also fluctuate in my memory. There were times when I couldn't remember a single thing I had done the day before. It was all very depressing for me.

❧

17 APRIL 2016

I was surprised to see Rupesh back in the hospital in the morning. He had told me he would be leaving in the afternoon as his flight from Paris was in the evening. He stayed till the afternoon. I asked him whether he had spoken to our kids today. He told them that Mom is fine and that he is coming to India

The kids had asked him to 'Please get Mom along!'

Rupesh told them I'd come back, but it would take some more time. They were very happy. They kept asking for a video call but he told them we would try that some other day. Before leaving for India, he discussed with me his plan to shift our kids to another ICSE (Indian Certificate of Secondary Education) board school, as their present IGCSE (International General Certificate of Secondary Education) board school was very expensive. He added that now we would have to think about managing the financial challenges that the medical treatment would entail. He was more concerned about my health and said he wanted to provide me with the best treatment back home. At that time, I was wearing my oxygen mask and asked him to remove it. It was a huge struggle for me but there were vehement thoughts in my head that I needed to convey to him somehow. I shook my head to say no and spoke in short bursts. Rupesh listened to me patiently.

'We will see what has to be done but till the time I am alive, I will not let that happen.'

I also told him that I had a lot of diamonds with me; I'd kept them safely underground. We would sell them and get a good price. He smiled at me, knowing this was another dream of mine talking. Holding my hand, he said, 'Your wish is my command, madam.'

❧

Today too I asked my sister about the date, day and year, but again I could not comprehend the details. I was getting confused about where I'd spent the year that passed by. How come it is the 17th today? How could I be sleeping for days together and not know what was happening! Sometimes I used to think they were lying to me.

I did not speak much, but over the next few days, I shared with them certain things that surprised them all. I was very confident that all that I said had actually happened. Seeing my conviction, sometimes, they had no choice but to agree with me.

I told Jolly di, 'I had gone with Rupesh on a beach holiday. And I was standing in shallow waters with half my body in the water. A rare species of fish carried me away. They ate my legs when no one was around. And they are actually hiding somewhere here.'

My sister explained to me calmly that this was all a part of my dream. She called Head Nurse John. He explained that because of the high dose of medication, I was bound to have many such thoughts and feelings, but they were all just dreams. After a few minutes, I started telling them again about how the fish went hiding when I saw them. I complained to them that the doctors gave me medicines; they would take samples of my blood every few hours to see whether the medicine was having the required effect, but it was of no use. I said to Jolly di, 'I know you are planning to take me to Germany, but the fish will fly. They will not spare me and will eat me up in your absence. I will be no more. They are stuck on my back.'

After listening to my ramblings, she grew quite anxious, wondering how long I would speak like this and if I would utter such nonsense for the rest of my life! Actually, I used to get these thoughts in my dreams or maybe when I'd been in a coma, and I believed it to be the reality. It would all start with me hearing a familiar voice calling out my name — *Nidhi... Nidhi...*

Whenever I heard my sister's voice calling out — 'Nidhi, get up now... we have got so many gifts for you and the kids...' — the dreams would begin. In the dream, my sister had gone abroad. Her flight was to land at midnight. I had told her to see me before she left as it was my birthday, so she had come home with gifts. She was trying hard to wake me up, but I would not open my eyes. She thought I was fooling her. She even sprinkled water on my face, but I was floating in that water. She asked the kids to make a lot of noise and opened my favourite pack of chocolates. But still there was no reaction from me. She then told my family, 'She feels she hasn't slept for days as she was on a five-day flight pattern to the United States and had made a lot of plans, so let her rest now. If she doesn't get up in the morning, we'll call a doctor.' They had to call the doctor in the morning, and he said I was brain-dead, and in my mind, I did not agree with him. I kept thinking, I can feel you, I can hear you. Listen to my heartbeat, don't bury me, I want to live. Nobody believed the doctor. I was cursing myself for sleeping so much, and kept hoping someone would wake me up.

I remember seeing Rupesh on the day they woke me up — 30 March. I had a glimpse of him in blue-coloured clothes and a cap. He was wearing an antibacterial suit as is required of anyone who enters the ICCU room. I had a vivid dream that day. While he was saying, 'Don't worry, you will be fine, I am there to take care of you...' I dreamt that I'd gone to my hairstylist to get a different hairstyle, and she inserted a drug in the machine she used, which prompted me to perform some killer stunts! So I was standing against the wall of a dam, calling out to my family. Or I would stand on the topmost floor of a hundred-storey building and jump down from that height. In the dream, the doctors found that I had been injected with some bad drug and the only way to get rid of it was to make me bald, but for that I had to first stand at a bridge railing. While someone was shaving my head, I fell onto a glass surface and got stuck on it; luckily, nothing broke. Now how would they help me come unstuck from the glass? So they had to call a glass cutter.

After cutting away for a while, only my chest and face remained stuck. He took a break and said he would continue the next day as he needed to concentrate better. The next day, he only worked on the chest, and now while my face was still stuck to the glass, suddenly I opened my eyes. The guy got scared. He asked me to comply with his instructions and assured me that all would be fine. He was an expert and I would be saved, nothing would happen to my face. And he finally prised me free completely. I thanked God.

While listening to my husband talk to me, I would dream that we had grown old and were in an old age home in a remote part of Europe. It used to be extremely cold and our beds were next to each other's. Everyone else had left, and I would tell Rupesh what was the use of this life when no one was there to give their time and concern. What was the use of this money when children can't take care of their parents? Children must look after their parents; it should be their foremost duty. He diverted my attention and asked me to look outside the window, at the beautiful scenery in the middle of the mountains. He asked me not to worry. I used to crawl as I couldn't walk. The next morning, I was no more. And he was left alone.

In yet another dream, I was taken to a big house full of holes made by a dangerous species. They were to sacrifice a human being there to become more powerful. So they put me to death. I actually saw the light of my soul moving upwards. But my grandfather and grandmother, who had devoted their entire lives to prayers and preaching God's might, stood in front of God and said, 'We never asked you for anything, but today we ask You to let her live. Her kids need her.'

And then I found my body lying outside a gurudwara. God sat next to me and said to me, 'I am offering you another life. Make sure you do good like before, and never be arrogant. Teach others how to be humane.'

I promised God, 'I will do my best to further unite this beautiful creation of yours.' He put a white sheet over me. I saw a spark of light descending and entering my heart. I got a sudden jerk as if I was being given an electric shock.

I had so many such dreams that didn't match up to any situation in reality but were so strange that sometimes I felt I would go mad just recalling them. I was fighting an inner battle with myself. Because I remember I met God. I actually spoke to Him. It came to me like a light fragrance. The divine experience stayed with me for days. I would be so confident about my dreams and would recall in vivid detail what I saw in them. I used to narrate each of them like a story to my family and friends. The weirdest thing was on the day I talked to my mom on the phone, I asked her why my cousin gave one million dollars to plant the bombs and that too, on the eve of the festival of Eid. And in return, we were bombarded by the other nation on the eve of Deepawali. And no one could celebrate the festivals. I cried that people were suffering because of all this hatred.

I told my mom that I was saved because I got stuck to a wall due to the impact of the blast. 'Mom, tell them to stop it!' I would implore her.

Next, I would tell Jolly di to call up my brother. I would ask him, 'Have you seen my story in the news? I saved so many kids. Aren't you proud of me? We must kill that gang, or give me the gun. I want to shoot them!' He, in turn, would pacify me by saying that he had shot all of them the previous night. I would feel so relieved that now no criminal remained in this world and the world had become a wonderful, safe place to live in. No more wars, no more bomb blasts. I had many more dreams like these.

❧

18 APRIL 2016

I was given water in a glass to drink, but my hands could barely reach my mouth. I wanted to scratch my nose but was unable to do so. I scratched my nose on the pillow and the oxygen cannula came out. After some time, the machine started beeping. My oxygen levels being low, the device had to be kept running all the time.

❧

Sumita di and Madan bhai came to see me. Shabir bhai got his wife along. She asked my sister if she could come inside my room to meet me. She came in and spoke to me, '*Shukar hai Allah ka ki aap ko zindagi bakshi.*' (Allah is merciful, your life was saved.) She kissed my forehead and left after spending about fifteen minutes with me. I had recognised her and she felt so good about that. I could see a smile on everyone's face as they sat in the balcony and watched me from the window. Everybody left one by one. I was exhausted. Jolly di came to see if I needed anything. I asked for some water. She said everyone in the family was anxiously waiting to speak to me, and asked if I could try and talk to them for a bit. So I spoke with everyone, one by one. The conversation was brief, but it brought so much reassurance to them and made me feel peaceful too. I didn't even realise when my sister had left. I must have dozed off at some point. But I know I slept contentedly.

Another thing that happened today was that the doctors announced they wanted me to start eating; so they wanted to know which soup I would prefer. I told them any vegetarian soup would do. After a very long time, I was going to have something to eat or drink. The nurse fed me some broccoli cream soup. I enjoyed it! The doctors had also advised my sister to prepare something bland (avoiding anything spicy or oily) and vegetarian, just in case I didn't like the hospital's vegetarian food, which was too bland really, consisting mostly of boiled vegetables. My sister asked me what I would like to have and I promptly said, 'Khichdi' (a sumptuous traditional Indian dish made of rice and lentils cooked together).

In the night, when the nurses came, I started talking. One of them told me, 'We love your family... they are so attached to you. Your sister is very loving and down to earth.'

I said, 'Do you know, her eldest son is married to Queen Elizabeth's granddaughter?'

They were surprised and asked if that was really true. I said, yes. This news spread like wildfire.

Nurse Fredric came to my room at ten in the night. On seeing that he had more than six tablets, I asked him why I had to take so many. He patiently explained that one was for pain, another one for itching, then vitamins, calcium, and so on, and the last one was for sleep. I said I didn't want to take the sleeping pill. I slept more than required anyway.

He told me, 'It is for the weakness you have. Sleep and rest are very important for you and it is essential to have this medicine at night, otherwise you will have nightmares and get scared. Then you would be awake the whole night.'

'But I want to try.' I was adamant.

'Okay, ' he reluctantly agreed. 'In case you don't get sleep, call me. I am just outside.'

The reception area was a big square in the centre with the rooms lined up on all sides, so they were easily visible. Later, he came to give me an injection in the stomach. Afterwards, he switched off the lights in my room. I could see the big glass window on my left. It was huge, maybe six feet by twelve feet. I thought to myself, terrorists know that I am in this hospital and I am alive, so they will come to shoot me. The witches know that I am here; they will come and suck my blood. I could even see a person holding a gun, sitting on a big tree branch. I closed my eyes tight and told myself that nothing would go wrong. I chanted 'Jai Mata Di' again and again. I even imagined that the fish had entered my room to sting me, that they would now fly me to their hiding place, where no one would be able to find me. I would not stay alive there. How do I hide from these fish... Myriad thoughts filled my head. My body started shivering with fear and my mouth dried up. But my hands could not reach the bottle of water kept by my side.

My eyes were glued to the tree outside, and next to it was a lamppost. I kept looking at the tree until my eyes closed around midnight. Fredric had told me to press the bell whenever I felt uncomfortable or in case I needed anything. He had placed it next to my hand on the bed itself. But pressing the bell was a mighty task in itself. When Fredric came in, I told him I was scared and not able to sleep. He was really worried to see my face so full of fear. He kept talking to me, inspiring me and boosting my spirits by saying good things about me. He told me I was a fighter and I had come out of grave danger. That he respected my decision and courage. He also told me, 'You may continue to get these dreams for a while. I cannot say how long, but if you stay strong, they will eventually vanish. Don't worry, the first step is always hard.' He spoke to me for more than two hours like that. I grew tired and slept. I don't know when he put my bed in a reclining position and left, but I woke up again after a nightmare at 0430 hrs and called out to him. He told me to take half a tablet, but I refused.

'No, you keep the small light on, the way we do for our kids,' I insisted.

This became my routine for the next two weeks. To keep me busy, they provided me with a portable WiFi television, which was a touchscreen device. It was like a big iPad and was fixed upright onto a pole on the table with a spring to adjust the height and distance. It looked just like a portable X-ray machine.

❧

19 APRIL 2016

While my dressing was going on, I told the nurses I wanted to see my face. One of the nurses, Laurence Depraetere, said, 'Oh my God. You have not seen yourself yet!' She called for a mirror and promised to show it to me after the dressing. She got me a big mirror and told me, 'You look very good. Much, much better than what we had seen when you first arrived. All these wounds and scars will heal with time. So don't worry.' With these words, she held up the mirror to my face. And I got the shock of my life! I couldn't recognise myself. I had patches and scars all over. There were wounds, burns, cuts and discolouration. My right eye was smaller than the left. I didn't know how to react. I went numb.

Laurence asked with concern, 'Nidhi, are you okay?' I said yes, and managed a smile. But my mind was flooded with negative thoughts. How would I face the world? What would people think of me? How would my kids react on seeing me? I felt distressed.

At that moment, I didn't want to live anymore. Now I realised why my family would make excuses whenever I asked them to take my photo and show it to me. They said that the doctors had strictly forbidden them from taking any photos of me. They would add that the astrologer had advised them not to click or post any photos of mine for the next few months as that could invite the evil eye.

Some time later, Jolly di entered the room and saw me looking low and stressed. She thought I must have seen another nightmare. She asked me over and over: 'What happened? Are you in pain? Is there something troubling you?'

I blurted out finally, 'How horrible I look! I don't want to live... no one will like me...' I burst out crying.

She understood what I must have been going through. She explained how important I was to my family, and how these things didn't matter and shouldn't bother me. She talked about the meaning of life, the importance of being alive. She had to make me mentally and emotionally strong, so she told me, 'You are alive because of your children. After so much has happened, they still have a smile on their face because they are looking forward to getting your love and affection again. They need you the most. No one else but your children called to ask, "How is Mom doing today?" They pray to God each day and have the guts to face the difficult questions raised by many. Looking at you, they have become stronger and you say you want to leave them alone in this whirlpool?'

She kept on bombarding me with examples of true courage and vitality. 'Beauty is not what you see in the mirror, but what lies within you. It is what you feel for yourself.' I asked her to take a photo of me, and she did.

She then came up with an idea. 'In the afternoon, let us do a video call with the kids and family and see how happy they will be to see you for the first time as so far nobody has seen you.'

❧

A funny thing happened today. Since I had very confidently told the hospital staff that my sister's eldest son was married to Queen

Elizabeth's daughter, everyone started congratulating Jolly di as soon as she entered the hospital in the morning. At first she was confused, but when she learnt the reason, she apologised and explained that it was just one of my dreams, and that her son was still a bachelor who lived in London. She came in and looked at me with a strange expression. When she told me that no such thing had happened, I told her, 'I know you just don't want to show it.'

She said, 'But nothing like that took place!'

So I questioned her. 'Don't you remember, we took a selfie in that black-and-gold salwar suit? I was standing on the sofa while clicking the picture. I even presented two solitaire earrings to your daughter-in-law, two diamond bangles to the queen and a solitaire to you too.'

She continued to look at me with disbelief and denied it all.

Oh, I was so confused and bewildered about events (imagined and real), days, dates and years!

Every day, my sister would ask the doctor how long it would take for me to register reality. The doctor would say that sometimes it took months and, in some cases, years. But he would assure her that I was doing fine. She worried, but she never stopped hoping. She kept trying every day. The moment she entered the room, she would say, 'Nidhi, good morning. What is the date today? And today is which day?' But I would take so much time to recollect and would fail to remember correctly every day. In fact, I still have a hard time remembering specific dates, months and years.

❧

Later in the day, I got somewhat irritated with the cannula providing oxygen as it seemed to be stuck in my nostrils. I desperately tried to get rid of it, but I couldn't reach it. So I asked my sister to lower the bed into a flat position, and using both hands, I managed to pull out the cannula. She warned me that I wasn't allowed to do this, but I complained that it felt irritating. So the nurse agreed to remove it for some time, assuring my sister that it would be okay as I was doing much better than before.

In the evening, I asked the doctor why I had big black spots along the jawline and above my upper lips. They said they had done a surgery on my face and had taken skin from the skin bank to cover and protect my face as well as my foot. This was done to help in healing faster, but sometimes those cells (in the skin taken from the skin bank) end up matching a person's original skin cells and form scabs. So they had to operate again to remove this. They also briefed me that earlier they had done a blood transfusion for me. My sister told them about how terrible I felt looking at myself in the mirror. Dr Peeters assured us that there was nothing to worry as the scars would eventually become light. He added, 'You know, the whole world admires your courage. You have actually set an example for them, that the show must go on. The whole world is praying for you... and are you saying you want to run away now?'

I managed to understand what they were trying to tell me. But a new question sprang to my mind—*would my legs be fine*? My right leg was almost without sensation. I used to bang my legs to the left and right despite being warned against doing this multiple times by the nurses, as it could damage my nerves further. They would tell me, 'If you don't understand and stop this behaviour, we will have to strap your legs.'

Late in the afternoon, Brussels time, when it was evening in India, we did a video call with my family. It was the first time my family was seeing me after the incident. Vardaan spoke to me first. He blew me kisses and asked how I was feeling. He said, 'You are our brave mom. We love you the most. Come back quickly as we are waiting for you here.'

I spoke to the rest of the family members at home and could see the immense happiness and joy on their faces. Vriddhi too talked to me. She saw me, but somehow, she seemed indifferent and casual. And after saying a few words, she said bye and hung up. The amount of love showered on me by my family was incredible. I felt even stronger when I heard my son say that he was sorry he couldn't come here to see me because he wanted to give his best in the upcoming exams to cheer me up. Everybody praised me and prayed for my well-being. I was repeatedly told, 'Come back home soon. We are eagerly waiting for you.'

I wondered why Vriddhi didn't use the word 'mom' while talking to me. Why she was so formal. She had said, 'How are you? Don't worry, you will be fine soon. Get well soon, okay.' Later, I found out that she had just returned from her badminton class and was asked to speak to Mom. But after she looked at me she thought she was speaking to one of the victims. She was very disturbed after the phone call. She felt concerned but was also confused and asked someone, 'Why was that aunty calling and asking me—"Baby, how are you?" Mom will be back soon I know, but where was Mom?' When she was told that the person she had seen and spoken to was her mom, she couldn't control her tears and cried for hours. She hadn't recognised me. She called me up again and apologised.

On calling my parents, I saw their tears of joy and satisfaction. They kept looking at me as though I was some phenomenal sight. Sometimes, our expressions say more than a million words. After a video call with my parents and everyone else in the family, I felt I had no regrets. Everyone said, 'We are thankful to God that you are back.' I realised that it is not our looks but our presence that counts in life.

❦

Today I was given two different protein shakes to finish. I was so thirsty that I drank them up in no time, but I found it difficult to eat solid food. I had soup instead. Jolly di had also prepared khichdi, which she forced me to have. Every two to three minutes, she would feed me a small spoonful while keeping me engrossed with stories, just the way a mother does with her child. I had no taste for it though, and she would go out every few minutes to reheat it. Finally, I finished one-fourth of a bowl of khichdi.

❦

The doctors also analysed the fact that my right toe was touching the bed—which meant it lacked stability because of the fractures and bone loss. The right ankle bones had been almost crushed. So they decided to tie my foot in a crepe bandage and suspend it upright against the wall opposite me, with my toe pointing towards my head and stretched at an angle of fifty degrees for at least six hours in a day. There was no sensation in my legs, especially in my right foot to begin with, and now having my leg suspended in the air like that was even more irritating and depressing.

I then asked the doctors when it would be possible for me to go back home.

'Your system is not yet balanced and you are very weak. There are many parameters to keep in mind, so it will take some time,' one of them explained. I insisted on knowing how many days it would take. 'At least a month and a half more,' was the reply. But I promised myself that I would go back as soon as possible. With determination coursing through my veins, I started working towards this. I started willing myself into thinking positive thoughts and decided I would motivate myself every time I got a chance. I would comply with everything they say or ask me to do.

❧

20 APRIL 2016

Dr Hans and Dr Peeters came into my room at around ten in the morning and asked me, 'Are you ready for the surgery, or do you want to wait for your family to come?'

I said, 'I am ready, let's go.' (They had done so many surgeries on me but during all those surgeries I had been in a coma.)

They briefed me that they would perform three surgeries—one on my face, the second on my right foot and the third behind the knee of my right leg. When I reached the operation theatre, it was very cold. It was as big as a badminton court. I started shivering. I was reminded of the shivering I had experienced outside the airport just after the blast. They switched on a warm air blast machine. It had a cover attached to the blower that fills warm air in the sheet that was covering me. It felt so nice and cosy. I was almost enjoying it! I told them I wanted to see what they were doing. I believe they gave local anaesthesia for my leg and foot, and I kept talking to them. Obviously I couldn't see what they were doing but I could feel something rolling on my thighs. Actually, they were removing the skin from there for grafting. Then I was put to sleep.

❄

I don't know when I closed my eyes, but when I woke up, it was afternoon. I was in my ICCU room, and a tight bandage covered my jaw. It looked like a white beard and moustache up to my ears. It was so difficult for me to eat because I could hardly open my mouth. I could barely talk. In the evening, I asked the doctors when they would remove the bandage. They said it would take three days. I saw my right thigh, where two big patches of skin had been removed — filled with blood, covered with a transparent plastic sheet... they looked like two cricket pitches. Six such patches of skin had been removed earlier too but had healed by now. I was in excruciating pain. I touched my thigh in the centre and it felt as if my finger was touching a floating bed of blood! The doctors told me it would dry by itself and warned me not to scratch it. It felt as though my body wanted to scream but had no voice.

❄

Today, I was given soup, potatoes, and protein milk to drink. My sister had prepared a little lemon juice for me. We call it 'shikanji'. I loved it. I told her, 'tomorrow onwards, get a full bottle of this!' I used to feel so thirsty that I used to consume at least four to five litres of water in a day.

In the evening, somebody called up the hospital to enquire about my health; my brother-in-law was asked to speak to him. He later came up to me and said that a policeman wanted to meet me. Apparently, he was the first person to come to help me before

I could receive any first-aid right after the blast. I said I would love to meet him.

❧

21 APRIL 2016

Late in the afternoon, the policeman arrived. I was asked if I would like to go to the visiting room. I was happy at the opportunity and said, 'If it is possible for you to take me there, it would be great!' The hospital staff readily agreed.

This was the first time I was taken to the visiting room with all my machines attached. I felt nice. The policeman came and presented me with a card and a bouquet. 'Do you recognise me?' he asked.

'Are you the person who helped me sit on the chair?'

'No, I am Alain, from the Belgium Federal Police squad. I helped you when you were brought outside the airport.'

I told him, 'Sorry, I can't recognise you. But yes, I remember vaguely that I spoke to you.'

He told me that on the day of the blast, when he arrived at the airport, he heard a voice in the crowd call out, 'Please help, help me, please!' And when he saw me, he immediately responded. He recalled our conversation.

'the first thing you said to me was, "I can't feel my legs", and I couldn't understand what *legs* meant. So I asked my friend Pascale, "What do you mean by *legs*?" Pascale replied, "*Jambes*" (in French). He told me to reply with the words, "Ya, it is there." Pascale translated for me all that you were asking—ambulance, doctor, hospital.' Alain then shared that he had asked me many questions, but I gave him only one-word replies. 'You were telling me that you wanted to inform your family in India that you were fine because the news would reach them in no time. You even told me that your pilots were staying in that hotel nearby, that I should call them to inform that you were okay. And till today, I regret that I didn't give you my phone to make a call or call your family myself, but in that situation, my mind had stopped working!'

In his service of nearly forty years, never had he seen such a disaster. He told me about how I had been shivering uncontrollably because it was windy and cold, that I was hardly covered. Later, he got me a blanket and covered me with it. He said, 'You were continuously looking up at the sky silently, with tears rolling down your face. You were traumatised, but you were not wailing. You were not even blinking. It was as if you were talking to God.'

He had thought I would not be able to make it and would go into shock in no time. He remembered how he put his hand on my head as that was the only area on my body that he had found safe. And he told me, *don't give up*. Whenever he felt that I was losing consciousness, he would call out—'Nidhi, hello, hello, Nidhi...' and then I would roll my eyes in response. My eyes were half open, he said. He recalled that despite the serious injuries, I didn't scream or cry loudly.

I listened to him and said, 'I was saving my energy, and secondly, I was horrified by the wailing cries of people all around me. It was killing me.'

'You were looking to the right and were telling me someone would come.' He expressed how he had fallen in love with the courage and strength I had shown. That my behaviour was commendable and I was one of the strongest women he had ever met. About twenty minutes after our first encounter, I was put on a rolling stretcher (trolley) and was taken away from there. But he decided then that he would meet me again for sure. He saw my picture later on social media and my words haunted him all over again... about how I'd kept saying that I wanted to inform my family that I was alive. He didn't know at the time whether my family members were aware of the news, about where and in what condition I was in. The words I kept repeating—*ambulance, doctor, hospital*—were tearing him apart. He remembered thinking then, *she can't feel her legs, hope her legs are fine.*

Listening to him revived all my memories, and I was quiet for some time. He took my permission to tie a lucky charm around my wrist, something he had brought especially for me. Till date, except during my surgeries, I have never removed it. He and my brother-in-law exchanged contact details so they could stay in touch. Alain said he felt really sorry and ashamed for whatever happened to me in his country. And he still felt bad about how it hadn't struck him then to dial my Indian telephone number and inform my family at that time. He asked me to forgive him. I thanked him sincerely and told him, 'Your presence proved that we have humanity and love in this world. I hope such incidents never happen again.'

I continued, 'Your team did a wonderful job and I hope your team and you are fine after seeing so much.'

Hearing this, Alain looked overwhelmed. 'I wish every person could think the way you think, then we won't have hatred in this world.' He told me that he didn't feel hatred for anyone because he could feel the love in my eyes.

I smiled, 'Yes, be the symbol of love, peace and humanity.'

Ever since that day, he calls me the queen of humanity, love and peace.

I asked him, 'How did you find out I am in this hospital?'

He told me that it was a long story.

'Along with you, there was another lady there that day—Stefanie De Loof. A few days later, her interview was published. Actually, she is the lady sitting in that picture with you, holding her phone and talking to her mom. Her hand was injured. She explained how she had helped you before she left the place. So through the reporter who interviewed her, I got in touch with her and explained that I wanted to find you. She knew you were a flight attendant with Jet Airways. At my request, she sent out emails to Jet, and Benat Guisset, a manager from the Europe region, who helped her with the hospital address, which she forwarded to me. And she did this because she too was curious to know if you were okay, and since I'm not that good in English, she did the homework for me. That's how I got the address and came to meet you.'

I felt really nice listening to Alain. I felt so touched by his gesture. A person who had spoken to me for just about half an hour, and that too in an emergency situation, was here to meet me again! A lady who was with me for only a few minutes took such pains to find out about my whereabouts and my health. This truly shows how much care and love we can all have for each other, how beautiful this world is. My sister served him masala tea with some snacks. It was the first time he had ever tasted Indian chai. He said he loved it.

Alain left shortly after. Throughout the night, I kept thinking about this man's great gesture. I shared this story with my nurses and later with the doctors too. Flowers were not allowed inside the ICCU room, but they were placed either in the gallery or in the visiting room. The staff were so nice to accommodate people's sentiments. They wouldn't do anything without our permission. Head Nurse John came to insert a small crystal pipe into my nose, as they needed to measure the amount of protein intake in my diet. And I had to keep this pipe in my nose for two days, or even more if they found that the food intake was not up to the mark, as appropriate diet regulation was absolutely necessary for my healing. I found the pipe slightly painful and very irritating. It was fixed with a tape. I wanted to remove it the next day, but they threatened that they would tie my hands if I tried that. They said that even if it came out by mistake, they would fix it again and would count out two days all over again. This scared me and successfully stopped me from thinking of ways to get rid of it!

❧

Shabir bhai called me today and told me about how he used to come every day to visit after I got admitted. Last month, he was due to go to Pakistan to meet his ageing parents, whom he hadn't seen in a long time, but seeing my condition, he'd cancelled his tickets. Now that I seemed stable, he said he would leave for Pakistan tomorrow, and would be back in three weeks—to see me before I left for India, as the doctors had said I'd take some more time to be well enough to travel.

I said, 'Mera salaam kehna ammi jaan aur abba jaan ko, yeh unki duaon ka aasar hai.' (Please convey my regards to your parents, this improvement is thanks to their blessings.) He told me to call his younger brother Baber, or his sister-in-law in case I needed anything.

The doctors informed me today that they would be sending me to another hospital for an eye checkup — there was metal shrapnel in the upper side of the left eye orbit and they wanted to seek the opinion of an eye specialist. My brother-in-law and sister were asked to reach the other hospital directly from the hotel because the appointment was early, at 1000 hrs. All night, I was awake, wondering what they were going to do. What if I lost my eyesight…

Ultimately, I knew it was best left to the Almighty.

❧

22 APRIL 2016

As I had been speaking too much, my bandage had come off from one side. The nurse fixed it again. She made it tighter than before. I had my protein milk. My nurse, Carine Joue, who loved me like a mother loves her kid, for a change put butter on the toast and fed me. It was delicious but it was very difficult for me to chew. The small pipe inserted in my nose to measure the protein intake did not allow me to sleep properly. It was so irritating, yet I had no choice but to keep it on. John came to check if it was fitted properly and I remember I made a very sour face. I was feeling a bit heavy in the stomach, but was hesitant to tell them about it and kept quiet. They did my bandages, wiped me clean, and I was fully dressed to go. We were ready by 0900 hrs. I was the first one to be dressed as I had to go out. I asked the nurse why a patient should have to go to another hospital. She told me that this was a burns speciality hospital. 'If we find a patient has any other problem that needs specialists' opinions, either we call the doctor here or send the patient to the other hospitals.' She also added that when I was in a state of induced coma, they had called specialists such as an infectiologist, ophthalmologist, cardiologist, bone specialist and many more.'

I was taken on a wheelchair (commonly shortened to WCHL) with my machines, IV drip, and my urine bag. I felt awkward as my bowels were full by now. The driver opened the ambulance door, and I was wheeled in. My WCHL was later strapped down on all sides. The nurse sat in front with the driver, holding my IV stand.

There were two windows in the front. I tried to peep out, but it was difficult. It took us about twenty minutes to reach the hospital.

Once there, I saw my sister and brother-in-law already waiting for me. I was parked outside the doctor's room for a bit, and then called in. The doctor asked me a few questions. He made me read and examined me with some machines. He told me that he would like to examine me again after seven days. He added that the metal piece was in the eye orbit and very deeply embedded. So as of now they couldn't do anything, but in case it irritated me, shifted or affected my eyesight, they would operate it. Else it would just be left as it was. I asked why my right eye seemed smaller than the left but the doctor said nothing could be done about it. I was wheeled into the ambulance from the garage room and brought back, so I couldn't even feel the fresh air. My sister and brother-in-law sat in the same ambulance.

❦

Today Madan bhai was bringing us food. We had asked him to cook some light khichdi for me. I had been feeling very heavy since morning and not even a wee bit hungry; rather, I was scared. I told my sister that since yesterday, I had been controlling my bowel movements, but now I couldn't hold it in anymore and needed to use the washroom. She said she would call the nurse right away. I told her not to, and that it could wait a while. While we were talking, Madan bhai arrived and so I gave her a pleading look, requesting her to please wait. We went to the visiting room, enjoyed a little khichdi and I also had homemade tea for the first time. I then requested to be taken back to my room. I thanked Madan bhai for the delicious food and for all the love.

I told my sister that now I can't control myself any longer, and I pressed the bell. This was the second time we had pressed the bell in the eight or nine days since I regained consciousness. The nurse came running. I explained my situation as best as I could, but the nurse didn't understand. At many times, language was truly a big problem we faced. The nurse called another person in. I was almost

Nidhi Chaphekar

in tears with the pressure building up. My sister tried to explain. They said, 'Yes, peepee... urine? The pipe is attached.'

Then I played dumb charades to actually make them understand and it worked! Finally they exclaimed—'Ooh *kaka!*' Then she got a pan with the help of three other nurses. They placed it on my bed, right under my pelvis. I felt as if my upper body was disconnected from my lower limbs. I tried my best, but I couldn't manage to do it for nearly twenty minutes. They raised the bed level for me to put more pressure, but in vain. Then I told them that I would do it in private in the washroom. Their instant reaction was 'No, no!' But Christopher, a male nurse who could understand English very well, said, 'Okay, we can try on the chair.'

He got a chair that had a pan below the seat. They placed me on the chair and I asked them to give me a lot of tissues and a room freshener, and to leave me alone after that. 'But what if you fall?' They were anxious.

I said, 'Okay, you can keep an eye on me from the glass door, but I won't feel nice if you stand here. I don't want you to smell my shit!'

Finally I emptied my bowels, and sprayed half the bottle of air freshener. They were asking me from the outside whether they could come in, but I was still hesitating. After about fifteen minutes, they all came in. I emptied the tissue roll into the pot. I couldn't look them in the eye though. The nurse told me, 'We are really very happy. It's good you emptied your bowels, otherwise we would have had to give you a tablet as advised by the doctor.'

Oh, what a relief!

I was really tired but was unable to sleep. My brother-in-law was to leave the next day and Rupesh would arrive on the morning of 24 April. So to give company to my sister, her son Abhimanyu would arrive from London early that morning. The day passed peacefully. I thanked my brother-in-law for spending so many days with us, and especially for taking good care of me. He told me to come home soon.

My face bandage had come off again, but the nurse said it was fine now, they would apply lotion. I told Carine I wanted to brush my teeth. She got a sponge brush, gave me a mouth freshener and asked me to use that. It was so tough to hold the brush as I couldn't close my fist, but somehow I managed. For the first time in a month, I rinsed my mouth. I felt so fresh!

I was surprised to see my brother-in-law again, but he said he had been asked to stay for one more day as Ms Pom was coming in the evening to see me. Abhimanyu also arrived at the hospital after a while. He smiled at me from the window first. I asked him to join me inside the room. He told me how his mom had sobbed when she'd heard the news while in Istanbul and how they'd tried so hard to get in touch with me after that. Their entire trip had been so stressful. They did not visit any place in the city; all the time was spent in the hotel contacting people and making decisions. He asked me to watch good movies online and helped me become a pro at operating my portable TV.

Since it was a Saturday, I had many visitors. During my physiotherapy, I saw Ms Pom enter my room. She took one look, got confused, and went out to ask the nurse which room was mine! When the nurse confirmed this was indeed me in the room, Ms Pom was stunned. She was dressed in blue antibacterial clothes. She came in and hugged me. She said she couldn't believe her eyes. The woman who had been lying in bed completely wrapped in bandages, just a few days ago, was today doing physiotherapy all by herself! She said she was really happy to see me like this. I finished my exercises and spoke to her for some time. She had got so much for us—a huge carton full of goodies! I believe that was the biggest box of chocolates I've ever received! I opened it and had one and asked her to put away the rest in the refrigerator so that I could share it with everyone else later on.

I talked to her about how concerned I was about my job security. She told me not to worry, and that they would take care of it. I was also worried about my kids' education and their future, and she guessed that this distress could be a reason for the delay in my recovery.

I assume to lighten my heart she said, 'You don't have to worry about money because you will receive a huge amount.' Then she added that she had heard someone was keen to make a film on my story, so I don't really have to worry about my finances. She said my kids would be able to study abroad.

I was overjoyed to hear this. She then handed over a letter from our HR department, which had to be signed by me. I could barely hold the letter. After reading it fully, I was not satisfied with the contents so I expressed my thoughts to her frankly. She is such a kind-hearted person – she apologized and said she was not aware of the contents of the letter but would surely convey my message to the HR department. She hugged me tight.

'We all are praying for both of you (me and Amit) to come back home safe.' She also asked me to let her know if something was disturbing me. I was so glad to meet such a pure soul.

Then I was taken to the visiting room. There I met many others, including Shalaka, the duty manager at the Paris airport. She was in Mumbai earlier, but had been shifted to Paris as they had started operations to this destination a while ago. She felt so good to see me. She cried a lot and I found myself consoling her! I told her that we must never ask why something happened. We must instead think about how things could have been much worse, and that God had been kind. I asked her why she'd come all the way. She said she just knew she had to, but hadn't found the courage to come to see me earlier. She talked about how she could empathise with what my family must have gone through when they first arrived in the hospital to see me and said she had been speechless when she heard about it. 'We could only provide every type of logistical support to your family, like arranging for tickets and an easy pass through customs and immigration without delays, etc. Your family had been so anxious and worried, but this time when your husband came to the airport to head back to Mumbai after being with you here, I could see a sense of satisfaction, relief and joy on his face.' She had asked him about my health, and then decided to visit me herself. She had to gather all her courage to come and wondered whether I would like it or feel depressed meeting people who were coming to see me. She told me it was unbelievable how the incident had failed to change the smile on my face. She was proud to know me, she said warmly.

Soon, I was called back to my room to see another patient who had suffered deep burns and was due to arrive by a helicopter in two minutes. The helipad was visible from my room. I saw the helicopter landing and the nurses taking him out on a stretcher, then placing the stretcher on the rolling trolley. I prayed for his well-being. They had called me because many a time, I had asked them whether they got a lot of patients via the helicopter. It was a rare occurrence, I was informed. They had even shown me the video of how I'd arrived in a helicopter — wrapped in silver protective sheet. And now to give me a live demonstration, they had called me.

Later I spoke to my kids on the phone and they asked me whether they should send something with Papa. I said, 'No, I am good.'

'But we are sending you something special made by us,' they continued. As I was to discover later, it was a handmade card!

We didn't realise how the day turned into evening. Sumita di arrived. She was so happy to meet me and talked about how she'd taken care of my husband and the family. She said she was sure my health would return to normalcy very soon, and she always prayed to God for my quick recovery. She had tears in her eyes as she spoke. She asked me what I would like to eat so that she could make it and bring it for me tomorrow. This was actually the first time I met her personally. I told her I felt like having dal, rice and halwa. All of them left in the evening and had dinner together to celebrate the improvement in my condition. I apologised to the nurses and even thanked them for allowing so many people in today, one by one. Visiting hours were actually restricted from 1500 hrs to 1700 hrs, but it was only for my family that they had relaxed the rules for — they could come any time.

I humbly requested one of the nurses to remove the small pipe

Nidhi Chaphekar

attached to my nose as it was irritating me a lot, but she said they had been instructed not to remove it today. I felt like pricking my nose hard so that it would automatically come out!

As Abhimanyu had shown me how to find movies on the Internet, I watched an Amol Palekar film at night and slept very late.

❧

24 APRIL 2016

I got up early in the morning at 0600 hrs. I put on the Gurbani first, followed by Hare Rama Hare Krishna chants on YouTube. The nurses liked it too and one of them said, 'What you are playing is very nice. It's very soothing and melodious.' They had heard it before, but at that time, there had been no one to explain to them what it was. I did my best to tell them all about it.

I finished *kaka* and brushing on my own, but when it came to dressing and sponging, I had to wait for a long time. Two nurses came; it being a Sunday, there were not as many staff members around. The nurses removed my clothes and went away to attend to another burns patient who had arrived as an emergency case. I was nude for a considerable period of time. They had already filled the tub of water and the washcloth was placed on the side along with the medicinal bathing solution. I thought, why not try it myself. Having watched them do it for so many days, I did exactly what they had been doing. First, dip the washcloth in water and apply some solution over it. Rub it on the upper limbs, thighs and on the body. Then clean the body with another sponge dipped in water, and finally, dry it with a towel. The only thing I couldn't do was reach around and clean my back. I was careful not to let water enter my wounds, especially on my legs. It was tough, as my hands were unable to squeeze and wring the washcloth dry completely, so it remained more wet than usual. But I was satisfied with what I did.

When the nurses came back, I told them to only clean my back. They saw what I had done and said, 'Fabulous work!' They patted my shoulder and told me, 'You are the first patient to do this by yourself.' I told them to take some of the chocolates my company's in-flight vice-president had brought the previous day, and this became a reason to party for everyone! For every action, they would say, 'Hup-hup!' And I would join in too. They enjoyed watching me say it. They asked me to teach them a few Hindi words. I made them learn words like dhanyawad, namaskar, suprabhat, chalo, etc.

A while later, I saw Head Nurse John enter my room. After the colour examination of my pipe, he smiled, and finally the pipe was removed! I was so happy and asked him if the measurement of protein was fine, and he said, 'Yes, it is.'

Then Rupesh arrived with so many gifts, sweets and other goodies sent for me by my family and kids. I liked the card made by the kids the best. It had beautiful lines written by them. It explained how much they were missing me. Now I wanted to fly back home sooner. I called them, thanked them and promised that I would be back soon by God's grace.

We got a call informing us that the Indian ambassador, Mr Puri, would come to meet me around 1600 hrs. Mr Puri arrived and I was called into the visiting room. Going to the visiting room was an outing for me; I loved it! Mr Puri couldn't believe that this was the same person whom he had seen just a few days ago! He poured his heart out to me. He asked me if I could narrate that day's events to him. I told him whatever I could remember. After hearing my story, he confessed that he had come wondering how and what he would say to me when he saw me. He had felt sure that I would cry. His wife too praised me a lot. She said, 'You are a true hero!'

Mr Puri added, 'After going through so much, you still hold such a beautiful smile... it's commendable! I can gauge you are a very positive person. What got you back is your karma, the prayers of your family and your will to survive. I am going back knowing that I have met a pure soul. God has been kind to you. I could never believe that a person can revive so fast! You are a true inspiration for us.'

To his surprise, nurse Carine, my so-called mom in the hospital, called out loud—'Nidhi! Nidhi, where are you?' Then on hearing my response, she came to the visiting room along with two other nurses. They asked me to open a bottle of champagne because it was one of the nurses' wedding anniversary and she wanted to celebrate it with me! So I held on to the cork and someone helped me uncork the bottle. Carine poured out glasses of champagne for everyone present. I too had a sip to reciprocate her love. Mr Puri was surprised to see the relationship I shared with the nurses, the love and bonding we had. He said, 'From today onwards, I will call you a superstar!' He felt as if he had come here not to visit a patient but to attend a friend's party. We all enjoyed the snacks and sweets Rupesh had brought from India.

Later, Sumita di came and brought along food for all of us. I was really tired by then, having sat on the WCHL for over three hours. I was taken back to my room and Sumita di came inside along with my sister. They got my food served on a plate, and as always, Jolly di fed me. Sumita di expressed that today she too wished to feed me, and was delighted when we granted her request. As if she were tending to a small baby, she sat next to me and fed me small bites. I could only have one chapatti, but my favourite halwa was yet to be served. So she fed me the halwa with her delicate little fingers. I had a good seven or eight bites of the lovely sweet dish. I felt filled with her love.

She hugged me and told me that today she really believed that I was her younger sister. She would always say, 'We have got you back from very, very far, from where no one comes back…' She told me that she was only too aware how many of them were fighting with the Almighty to give me back my life. That she used to tell God to take her away and bless me instead with a new life. 'It's a special life that has been given to you, always be thankful to Him. I am lucky to have you in my life.' Her words struck a deep chord with me.

❦

My guests and family left late, around 1930 hrs. I was so tired that I slept in that half-sitting posture. I never told anyone when I felt tired because I believe everyone was taking time out specially for me, so naturally it was my duty to give them a little time too.

I woke up abruptly at midnight since I had slept early. I think I slept so deeply that I didn't even realise when my evening injection was administered. All the lights were off and even the window was covered. It was pitch dark and I got so scared that I began pressing the bell furiously. Fredric came running and asked me what had happened. I asked him to switch on one light for me and open the blinds on one window. Then to distract myself, I switched on the TV and started watching some videos. I don't know why but I looked for videos of that day's disaster, videos that showed how many people had lost their lives and how many were injured. And then I read that a third blast had taken place at Maalbeek metro station. I just couldn't sleep after that. I kept thinking, *what is wrong with them*! I said an earnest prayer — God, please give them wisdom to understand that committing such acts shows their weakness, and not their strength. Bless their hearts with Your light, dear God, and give me the strength to educate my fellow human beings, and to spread the message of love and humanity.

❦

25 APRIL 2016

I underwent another surgery. I had to empty my stomach before going to the operation theatre. More shrapnel was removed from my body and given to me in a box. The hospital staff told me I should keep it as a souvenir!

The surgery was carried out on my right foot and it went very well. Clips like staple pins had been put around the foot. I asked them how many more surgeries I needed and they said hopefully this would be the last one for now. I was not worried about the surgeries as such, but I did worry about how soon I would be able to go home.

❦

Nidhi Chaphekar

Today, I was feeling very uncomfortable because there was hardly any sensation in my feet and my right foot felt as heavy as a log. I used to lift my legs and shake them a bit, but I couldn't hold up my right foot, so it always came banging down on the bed—the nurses had told me quite strictly not to do this. When my sister saw this, she called the nurse, who then strapped my legs. Sudden jerks could cause more problems—I could lose more sensation, which would create many other issues. I promised the nurse I wouldn't do it again. She explained to me again the consequences of doing this.

'I know,' I nodded, 'but it is so irritating, it feels as if your legs are being eaten by ants. Such an awful feeling!'

I loved doing physiotherapy because immediately after doing it, I would go off to sleep. But on waking up, I would feel pathetic again, looking at my right foot tied up and hanging in the air. The best part of the day was going to the visiting room.

In the evening, the nurse came and said she was putting a clamp on the urine pipe and asked me to call out to them whenever I felt like peeing so that they could unclamp the pipe for me. 'From today onwards, you have to sense when you want to pee because we want to remove this catheter in a day or two.'

I was glad to hear that they would remove it but was worried about how I would manage because now I was drinking at least six to seven litres of water a day—I would have to call them every hour! How awful! Fearful of wetting my bed, every fifteen minutes, I would feel the urge to pee and call them, and then later realise that only a few drops had passed. I would think I was peeing a lot because looking at the catheter bag, it seemed filled to capacity and I would worry that it would now spill on the bed. And so I would try to hold it in for some time.

I think in two hours, I must have called them five times. I apologised to the nurse, but she said this was normal and this is why they wanted me to practise for a while first and only then could they remove it. Finally, I had my soup and slept.

Before sleeping, I would always place four 500-millilitre water bottles next to me and would finish them before sunrise. I asked them the reason for my thirst. They told me that the room I was in filtered the air three times, so that no moisture got in. And then because of the high dose of medicines I was given, my body felt dehydrated. Moreover, I was a burns patient. They assured me that it was a good thing I drank a lot of water because it cleaned up my system.

❧

26 APRIL 2016

When I woke up at 0630 hrs, I felt like my stomach would burst! I pressed the bell frantically. Since they were busy, it took the nurse more than two minutes to come in. By that time my eyes were brimming with tears. The moment she unclamped the bag, it filled up and she actually told me to stop. But I couldn't. She immediately placed a tub underneath. I felt very embarrassed, but I was helpless.

Nurse Carine came in and asked me if I wanted to have tea. I asked her to make lemon tea for me, as I don't really like dip tea. It was really bright outside today, so I requested the nurses to take me out. I wanted to breathe in the fresh air. But at first no one said they would. Then Nurse Depraetere promised to take me out on Thursday. It was her day off the next day.

Little things would make me happy, like when they shifted me from the bed to the visiting room. Even if no one came to visit, I'd feel like going there just for a change of scene. It entailed a lot of hassle because to move me from the bed to the chair, at least three people were required, and then to push my WCHL with the instruments attached was also a tough job as all the tubes were connected. But they would do it happily every time I asked them to. I had told my sister to get me more lemon water. She told me 1.5 litres was good enough, as too much of lemon and sugar may not be good for me. I started putting around 200 millilitres of it in my water bottle for a change of taste, as my mouth would always feel bitter and tasteless because of the strong medicines.

Soon, I had learnt the technique of holding in urine for some time. In the afternoon, I called the nurses but all of them were busy either in the operation theatre or attending to the patient in the next room. I tried to unclamp the pipe myself. I didn't have enough strength to do it, but Rupesh did it for me.

In the evening, when the physiotherapist arrived, he told me, 'Now we want you to gain more strength in your arms, as in your case, it is very important for moving, shifting and lifting your body. All the weight has to be borne by your arms.'

I said, 'I can't fold my fingers after a certain point, can't make a fist. So how can I possibly do this?'

'But shifting yourself, taking the weight on your arms would ease your difficulty,' explained the physiotherapist.

And so we started. Within five minutes of exercise, I was tired. I asked the physiotherapist when it would be possible for me to close my fist completely. He said it would take a long time, perhaps a year or more, and that it differed from person to person. My skin would resist stretching due to the grafts and my hands were still swollen.

The only thing I didn't like in the hospital was the vegetarian food served at night. Soup, boiled veggies, bread and butter. So I would ask my sister to feed me a little khichdi before she left, so that I could enjoy the bland soup and the little milkshake the nurse fed me afterwards. Of course, they used to take my meal preference for the next day, every day. But then we Indians do enjoy eating a little oily food with spices!

❧

27 APRIL 2016

In the morning, Carine got a toothbrush for me, with a tray, a bowl to spit in and a glass of water. After I finished, I realised my tongue actually made a sound while rubbing over the teeth. It was a crisp sound. I felt really good. Even holding a glass for a short period of time was a task; my hands would start shaking. Carine made me eat breakfast, and made lemon tea without my asking her. Another nurse came to remove the urine pipe. I told her to come back a little later as I was scared of peeing on the bed. She explained that if the urine pipe remained inside my body for a long period of time, I could get an infection. I was ready instantly and asked her to do it. As she was about to remove the pipe, she said, 'Hold your breath.' And just like that, it was out. I felt like a part of my body had been removed! They cleaned me and put an adult diaper on me. I felt like a baby. But the question was—would the diaper hold urine? She told me it was only in case of an emergency, and asked me to call them when I felt like peeing.

I always felt a strong itching sensation all over my body. I would feel like scratching my body even after taking the medicine that was supposed to get rid of the itching. So to ease my suffering, today they got three different types of lotion and asked me to apply these on different parts of my body so that I could tell them which one suited me best (the one I was using earlier was not proving to be very effective). By the evening, one of them gave me much more relief, and that lotion was ordered for me.

Soon, my sister and husband arrived. I told them how I could constantly hear a strange sound in both ears—like an aircraft engine running—and also that I heard a little less in the left ear as compared to the right. When they conveyed this to the doctors, I was asked why I hadn't mentioned this earlier. I said, 'I did not realise what it is and why it is happening. I thought maybe it is a side effect of the blast or medicines and would go away. Or maybe because I am in room where hardly any sounds from the outside could be heard.'

Rupesh said they would take an appointment with an ENT specialist who would analyse the problem.

I wanted to pee, so we called the nurses for help. To my surprise, they placed a pan underneath me and asked me to pee in that. I tried for almost fifteen minutes. My face turned red and tears started streaming down my face, but I just couldn't pee.

They said, 'Okay, do it in the diaper then.'

But even that didn't happen. This went on for over half an hour!

I finally requested them, 'Please help me sit on the chair with the tub where I do *kaka*?'

While they were placing me on the chair, a nurse tripped on

the tube of the IV cannula that was fitted around my neck, and it got pulled quite hard. We got really scared; even the nurse turned pale. Eventually I did manage to pee. The head nurse arrived shortly and ordered the other staff to immediately put me on the bed first. The nurse removed all the tapes. She felt the area with her hands and said it was fine but she would wait to see if it swells up. If that happened, they would do something about it. I kept my mouth shut and closed my eyes. All this while, I used to think that the cannula had a needle inside and that was the reason why I never turned on my right side while sleeping. Much later, on the day the cannula was removed, I got to know that there was no needle inside. I would only sleep ramrod straight on my back or on my left side, facing the big window. By God's grace, all was fine and the nurse taped back the cannula.

My immobility was a big problem for me and for others too. I required manual support every time I had to shift from the bed to the chair to attend to nature's call or to go to the visiting room. I searched my mind for a solution to overcome this soon. I played the Hare Rama Hare Krishna chant to change my frame of mind and I saw a few nurses dancing to its tune. They asked me—'Is this the god you pray to?'

I told them, 'I believe in all gods.'

I opened the Google tab on my TV screen and showed them images of the different gods Indians believed in and they found it all very interesting. I told them, 'For me, even you are God, as you are helping me during such hard times.'

On my portable TV, I showed them different kinds of temples, churches, dargahs, mosques, gurudwaras, and monasteries where we worship our gods. I told them, 'I believe being human is the best kind of devotion you can ever preach.' They appreciated my thoughts.

Then they started enquiring about my birthplace, the city I belonged to, where I lived. One of them would listen carefully and then translate my words to the others; by now we had also mastered the art of translating things using their phone or on my touchscreen TV.

I told them that I was planning to go back. All of them went quiet, and their faces suddenly fell. One nurse said, 'But your treatment is going to take a long time. How can you go?'

I told them that I would take the rest of the treatment in my own country.

'But why?' another asked.

'I need to meet my kids. They are waiting for me.'

'Call them here. We will take care of them. They can stay along with our kids.'

I had no words to express my emotions.

After some time, a nurse came and took me to the adjacent building. There I saw Dr Hans come running towards us. She told the nurse, 'Get her left hand and thumb X-ray done.' I used to feel a lot of pain if someone even touched the top of my left hand. If the upper side of my hand came in contact with anything, I would actually scream. Dr Hans always wondered whether there was a metal fragment there that was hurting me.

Then the ENT specialist called me into her cabin. She examined my ears and said they were perforated. I asked, 'What about the noise I hear all the time?'

'It's too late to do anything now. You will hear this throughout your life,' she announced.

Later, I was taken for an audiometric test. As I was on a WCHL, my legs were in a straight position and it was not possible for me to get inside the room. So the instrument was shifted and the test was done outside the soundproof room. The reports showed a slight decline in my hearing. The doctor said the results may have been better if the test had been done in the soundproof room. Then I was taken to the X-ray room where two X-rays of my left hand were taken.

Today I disturbed the nurses aplenty, as I felt the urge to use the loo a number of times. I wondered how I would travel back to India at this rate. Every time they helped me, I would say thank you and apologise for bothering them. It became so frequent that now whenever I pressed the bell, they would say with a smile in their language—'Yes, we know you want to pee-pee and you are sorry to bother us,' and they would laugh. I loved them for their good cheer.

❦

28 APRIL 2016

After the morning routine of freshening up and eating breakfast, the nurses came to my room with soap, washcloths, water and the medicinal solution, kept it all on my table and asked me to do the needful myself as they had seen me doing it once. I was very excited and felt good about being independent. They instructed me not to go below the thighs. My body used to itch all over and I would usually end up scratching a lot, but I was told strictly not to scratch my skin. Now that I was going to do the cleaning myself, I thought this would be the right time for me to scratch wherever I felt an itching sensation, especially since the nurses were busy with other duties. Though they gave me anti-itching tablets, plus creams and sprays to apply, the itching remained because of my burns, grafts and dried skin. While rubbing, I saw the skin peeling at the side of the tape from where the grafts were taken. I believe it was because I would frequently scratch and rub the area. I requested the nurse to change the tape since it had become slightly dirty and rough at the edges. On my insistence, she removed the tape from one end but instantly, blood started oozing out. She immediately sprayed the affected area with some medicine to stop the blood flow and then taped the area again. She asked me not to fiddle with the skin in that area, else, it would not heal.

For the first time, they washed my legs by pouring Betadine-like water. Bandaging was a very time-consuming session. The whole process took two hours, maybe more. But I felt so good after my legs were cleaned. The oxygen mask on my side was removed, as it was only kept there for an emergency and I wasn't really using it anymore. I was also made to use a nebulizer for nearly half an hour every day. Today was the last day to do that as well. I thanked God for His mercy.

As all this took more time than usual, my family had to wait outside. When my sister arrived, Carine told her that I didn't need a diaper now and she could get me a fresh pair of underwear tomorrow. This excited me so much that I exclaimed aloud—'Wow! I will wear underwear now!'

❧

Daily, I would eagerly wait for my sister to bring me lemon juice. The nurses were always curious about this drink, so today Jolly di made an extra bottle for them. Everyone enjoyed it and asked for the recipe. After lunch, Jolly informed me that they would leave early today to buy some underwear for me because all the stores closed by 1730 hrs. I asked her why I couldn't use the ones I had as my layover bag had plenty.

That's when she shared information that saddened me. 'We received your bag nearly a month after the attack. It was in a pathetic shape. Water was still dripping from it and it smelt really bad. And except for the pair of shoes you were carrying to be exchanged, we couldn't retrieve anything else from the bag, and those shoes were damaged too, but Rupesh has preserved them. We managed to take out your passport, flight license (SEP card) and a few other documents from your purse and stroller even though they were more or less burnt or torn, as they would be required in the future.'

I asked whether they had taken a picture of the bag, but she replied in the negative. I felt miserable because I had so many memories of all the things I had kept in that bag. She explained that Rupesh didn't allow anyone to take pictures while I was in a coma because he didn't want me to get disturbed by any photograph I may see in the future that may recall the horrific memory of the blast. 'And we were not in the state of mind to do so either,' she added.

I told her I would still have liked to see what condition the bag

With Shabir bhai (extreme left) and my crew at Hot Spot,
a day before the blast

The watch I had worn on the day of the blast. It stopped at 8.08 Brussels time and lost its glass casing.

The ring I wore on that day. It had to be cut off my finger.

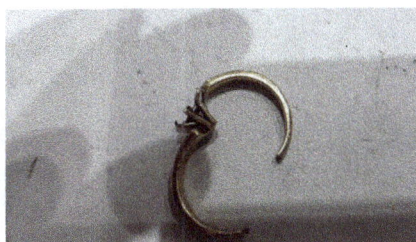

Vardaan's shoe — the one I had to get exchanged — recovered from my suitcase, damaged by the blast

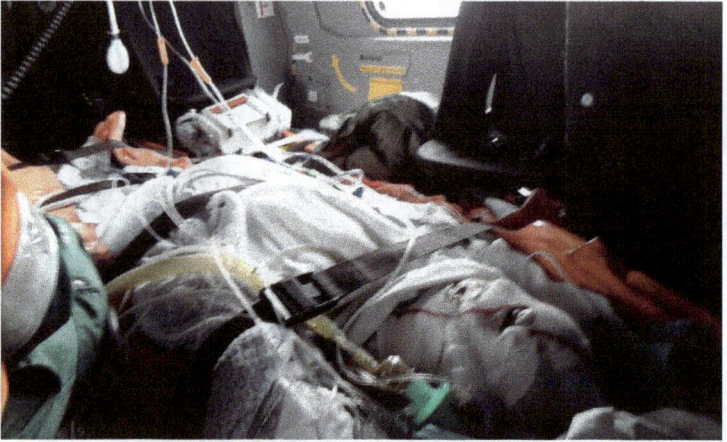

This is me being transported from Sint-Augustinus Hospital to Grand Hospital, Charleroi, in a helicopter

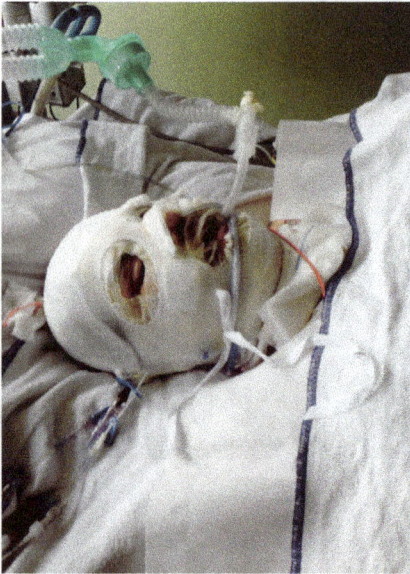

The photo taken by Shabir bhai the first time he saw me in Sint-Augustinus Hospital

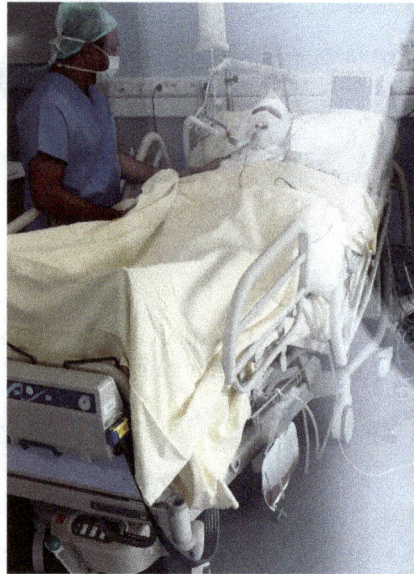

A photo taken when Rupesh entered the ICCU room and held my hand for the first time after the blast

King Philippe of Belgium meeting Rupesh. This is the day
the king visited us for the first time in the hospital.

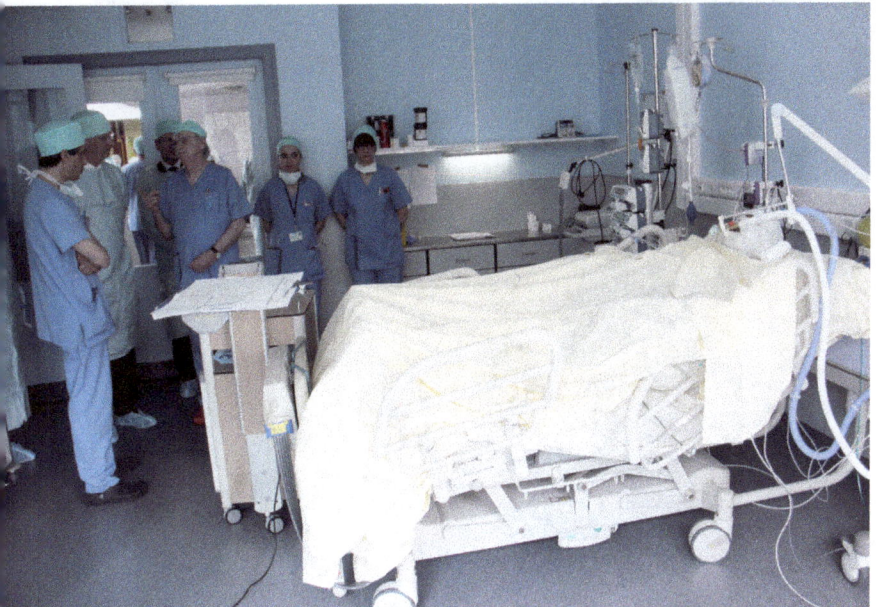

King Philippe talking to the doctors and enquiring
about my condition

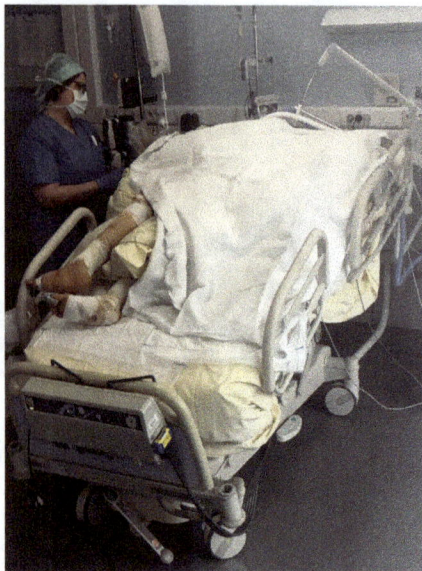

The photo taken by Ms Pom and sent to the chairman of Jet Airways to let him know the condition I was in

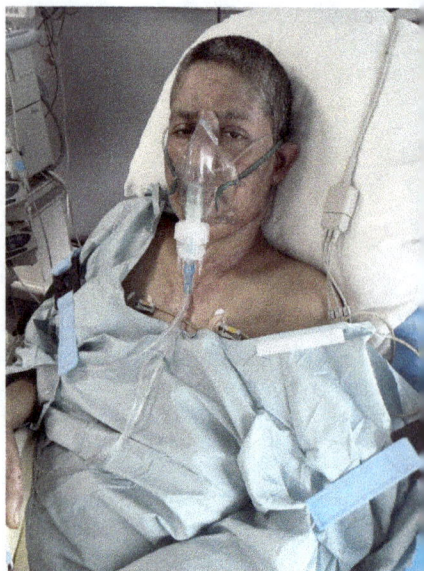

A photo taken at Grand Hospital when I was still on oxygen

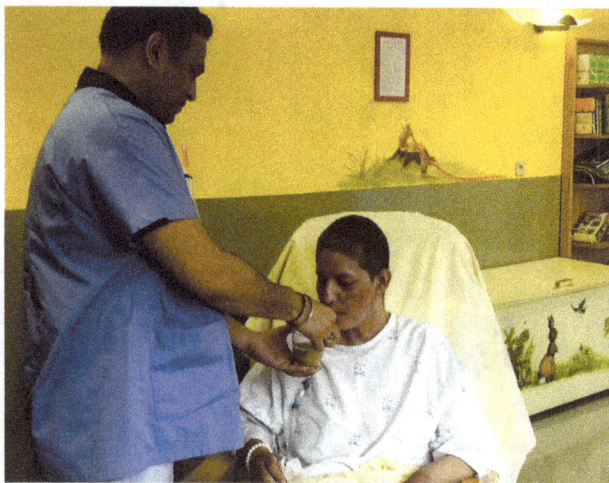

Rupesh helping me drink tea as I couldn't even hold a glass at this point of time

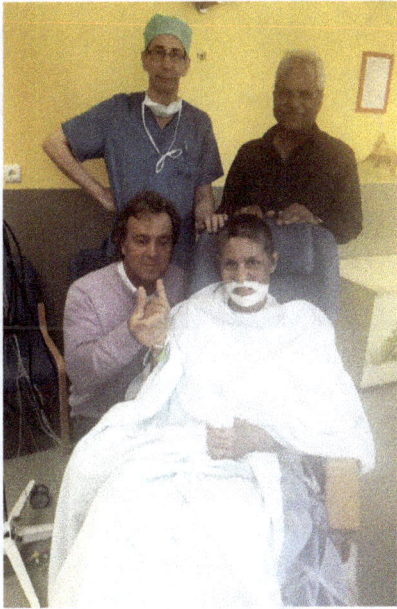

With Alain, wearing the lucky charm bracelet he had gifted me. Behind us are Head Nurse John and Amarjeet jiju.

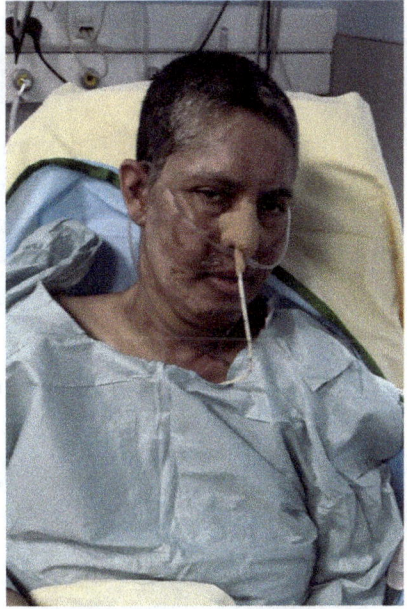

A small pipe had been inserted in my nose to measure protein intake

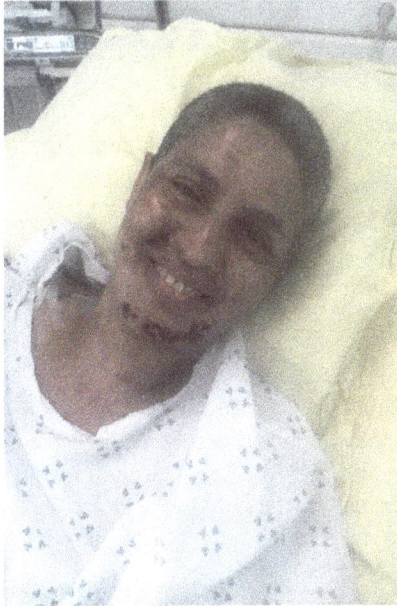

Big black spots erupted on my skin after a surgery in which a layer of artificial skin was used to cover my original skin to help it heal faster.

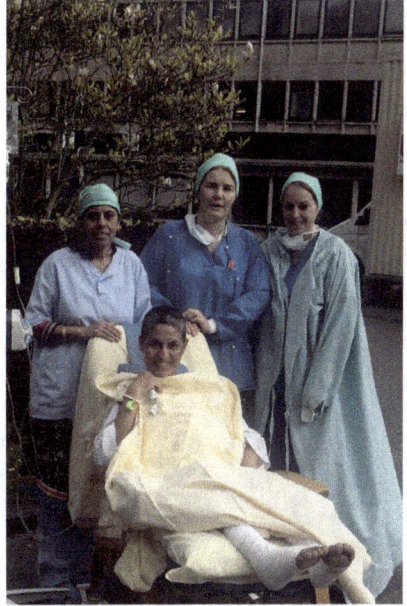

The first time I was taken out for a dose of fresh air. With me are Jolly di and the nurses Laurence Depraetere and Amélie Ferrari.

Mr M.S. Puri, the Indian Ambassador to Belgium at the time, along with Rupesh, my sister Jolly, and me

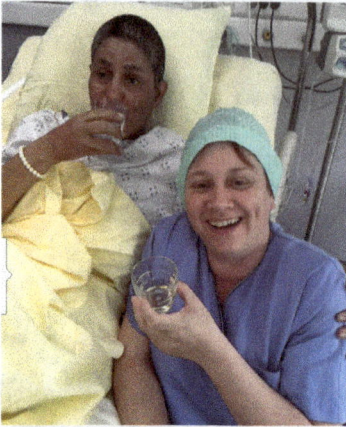
With Nurse Carine, who loved and treated me like her daughter

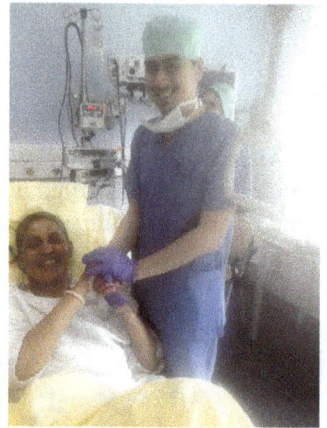
With my physiotherapist in Belgium

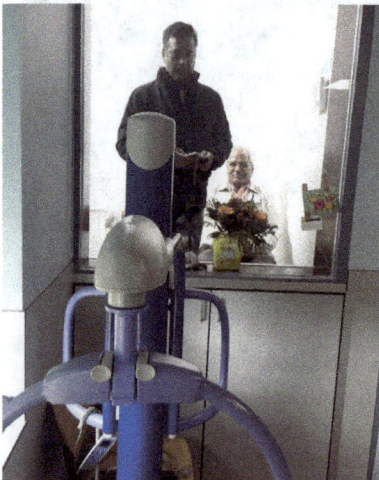
The visiting window – on the right side is the small speaker through which communication used to happen between visitors and me. And the blue contraption is the crane which could be extended, and used to shift me from the bed to the WCHL and vice versa.

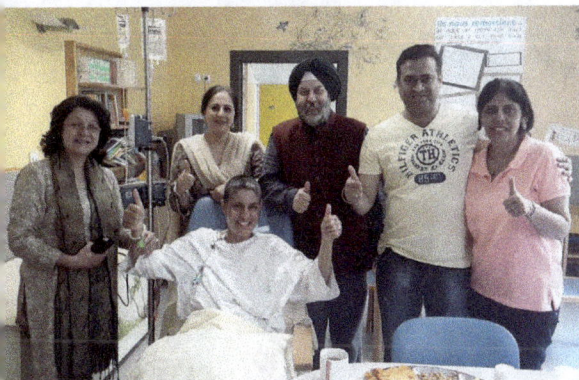

In high spirits during one of the last few days at the hospital. (L-R) Sumita di, Mrs and Mr Puri, Rupesh and Jolly di

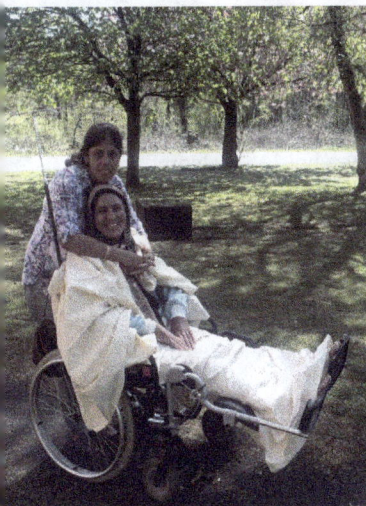

Being wheeled around the premises of the hospital by Jolly di during the last few days of my stay there

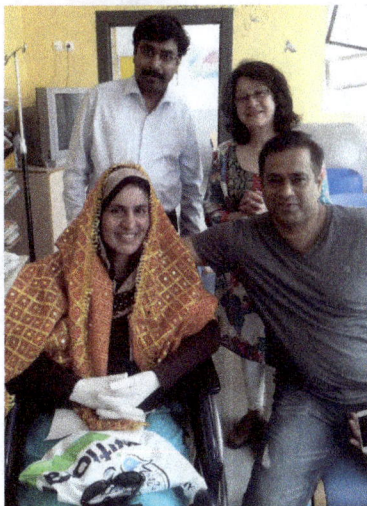

With Sumita di, after she performed a small puja right before I left the hospital to go back to India

An article about me in a Brussels newspaper. The photo (extreme right) was taken by reporters when I was about to leave the hospital and get into an ambulance that would take me to the Paris airport, from where I boarded my flight to Mumbai.

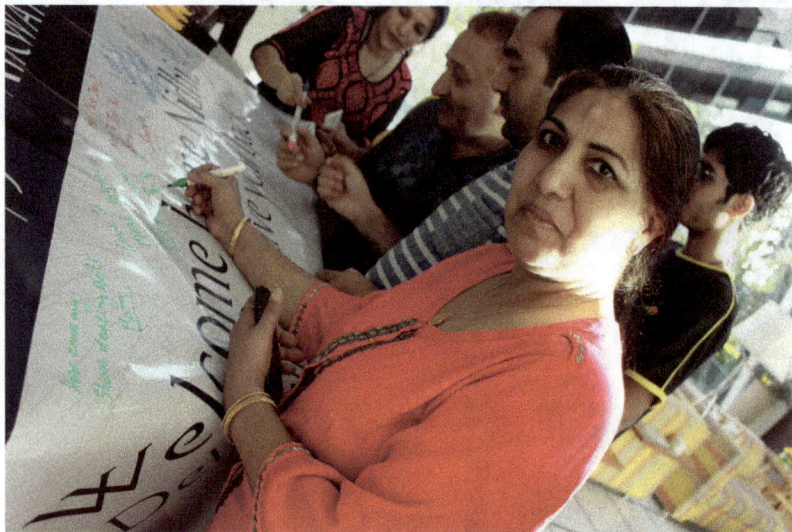
My family preparing the banner that they held to welcome me when I landed in Mumbai

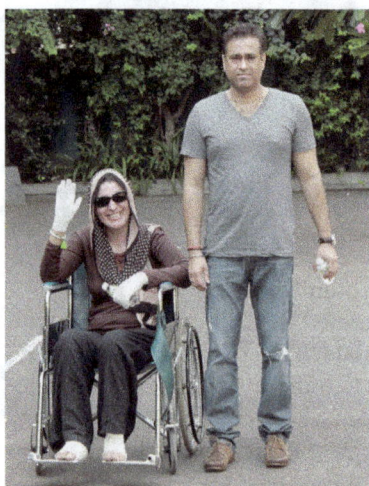
A photo taken after I landed in India. The wheelchair didn't allow me to place my legs in an elevated position—something that was a must for me. However, in all the excitement, I managed to smile through it all.

Meeting my mother-in-law after I arrived in India

With my mother and Vriddhi

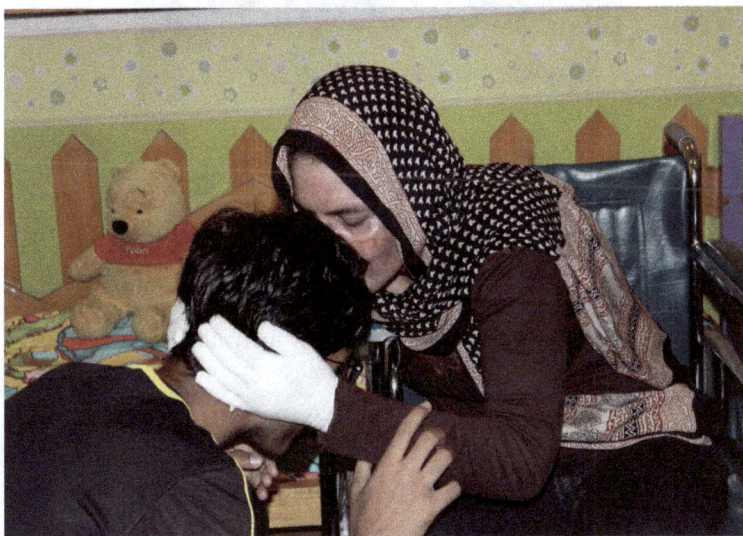

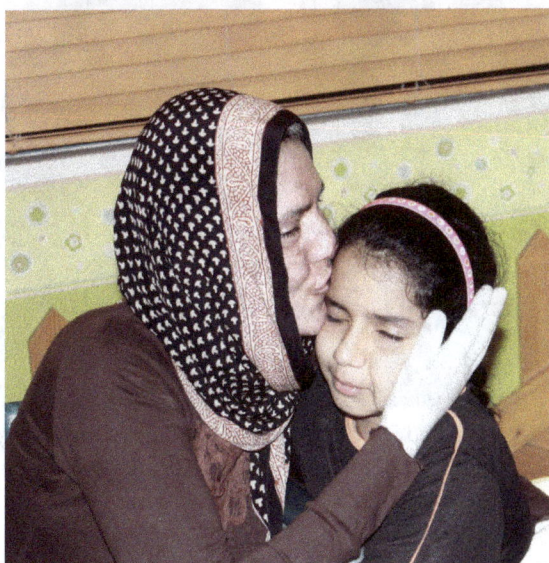

A very emotional moment – meeting my children
Vardaan and Vriddhi for the first time after the blast

Being welcomed by my mother while entering Jolly di's house, where I stayed for the first few months after my arrival in India

The day I walked for the first time without help, wearing the special shoe

Photo taken before going out for dinner one evening after arriving back in Mumbai. On this day I coloured my hair for the first time after the blast. You can see that at this stage the size of my right eye is much smaller than my left.

An extra special welcome by the children of our house — Vardaan, Vriddhi, Sakshi and Snigdha

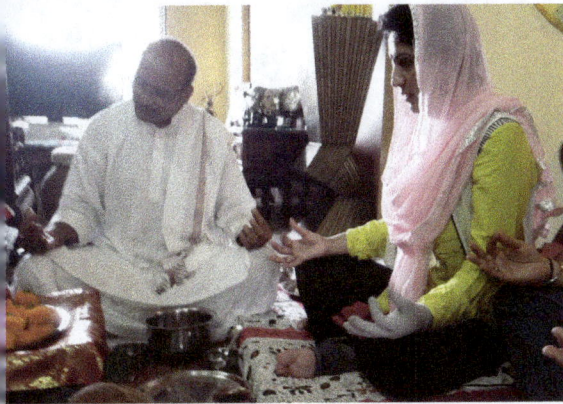

Despite the condition of my legs, I was able to sit for the special puja that had been organised on my birthday.

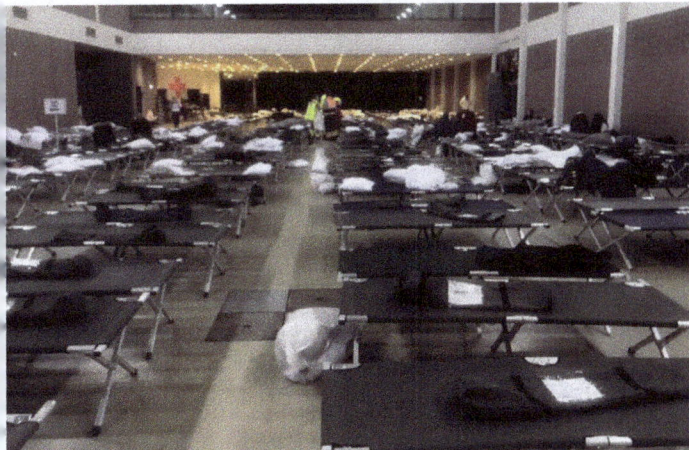

A photo shown to me by my colleagues Josimas and Rampal. When the blast happened, thousands of passengers were stranded. Hotels were full. The national forces and the government of Belgium made alternate arrangements, like this hall with 1000 makeshift beds for stranded passengers.

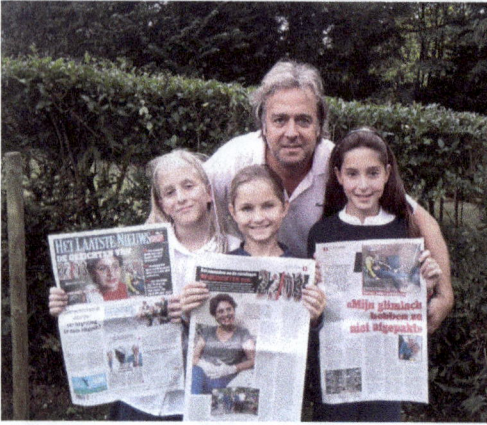

Alain with his daughters Victoria, Camille and Elisabeth, holding newspaper pages that had articles on me

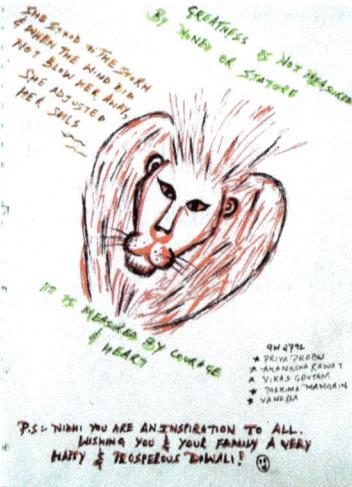

A beautiful and heartwarming card presented to me by my colleagues after I landed in Amritsar to celebrate Diwali with my family

Meeting my father for the first time after the blast

was in. She said it had holes, although it was supposedly made of unbreakable material. The handle was twisted and the clothes and shoes in the bag either had holes in them or were burnt. My makeup kit, which was in a smaller bag inside it, was filled with water. The undergarments made of nylon were stuck to each other. All my ready-to-eat snacks were spoilt. The whole bag was a mess.

'But what about my favourite jacket and purse?' I insisted on knowing. Every single thing had been spoilt. I felt quite dejected and stayed quiet after that. In my mind, I thanked God, though, for maybe my legs were saved because of my bag, which had acted like a shield and absorbed the impact of the explosion.

❧

29 APRIL 2016

I had completely forgotten about my appointment at 0930 hrs with the eye surgeon again. We had to leave by 0900 hrs to be there on time. One thing I really like about this place is punctuality. People show respect for time; everything would be on time. My sister and Rupesh arrived early and came with me in the ambulance. The doctor examined me and repeated what he had said on our previous visit.

'Don't try to do anything. But if it irritates, aches, or shifts, or your eye starts watering, then you should contact the eye specialist immediately. Get your eye checkup done every three months. Never do any MRI in your life, as you may lose your eyesight.'

I thanked him and left. I saw Rupesh parking my WCHL and sensed that both my sister and Rupesh were feeling low. Just to revive their spirits, I said, 'Don't you think we should wait for some time and then consult another doctor in Mumbai?'

I was happy about two things though—one, I had visited the other hospital without a urine bag today, and two, God had saved me from having yet another surgery. The only thing I needed to tell my family was about the MRI warning the doctor gave—even in the case of an emergency I shouldn't get an MRI done.

Once back in my hospital room, I was changed from the diaper to an underwear. I felt so light. When I gave them a surprised look as the underwear size was a bit too big for me, they said they had brought a larger size deliberately—they wanted to ensure ease of wearing the underwear as there were so many bandages on my legs.

❦

A while later, on seeing Nurse Laurence walk in, I asked her, 'You were supposed to take me out yesterday, but you didn't!'

She smiled, 'Okay, we will go when you are in the visiting area today.'

I was so looking forward to this. I was readied around noon. I asked them to take pictures before we went out. They had to wear the antibacterial coat over their uniform. The nurse carried four extra sheets to cover me as it was windy and cold outside. And what a beautiful moment that was—to be out in fresh air! We never realise the value of God's beautiful creation until we miss it...

I wanted to spend more time outside, but soon I started feeling cold. I began shivering; they wrapped me in several sheets, and even then I couldn't stay there for more than a few minutes. They consoled me, 'Never mind, we will bring you out again tomorrow when you go to the visiting room.'

Back in the visiting room, I enjoyed a hot cup of tea made by my sister. Many others joined me too. For lunch, we had food ordered from a restaurant. It was a big treat for me. The restaurant had been instructed to cook the food the way we make it at home, using less oil and spice.

Some time ago Roopa had told me that my close friends Vishwanathan, Ashutosh, Rampal and Josimus were expected in the late afternoon. They too worked for Jet Airways at the Brussels base. Only Vishwanathan and Ashutosh had seen me when I was in an induced coma, but the rest would be seeing me for the first time. I waited for them eagerly.

They arrived a little late by when I had to be back in my ICCU room. I could only see them through my window and spoke to them through the speaker phone. They were very happy to see me. Both

Rampal and Josimus were going back to India to resume their duties at different airports as managers. As they waved goodbye, they told me, 'Once you are fine, we will come again and celebrate in a big way.'

❧

We decided to ask the doctor when I could be discharged. Although this had been under discussion since long, they said it would depend on many factors and even if everything seemed fine, they wanted to keep me under observation for at least forty-eight hours after taking me off the IV and antibiotics. So the question was, how much longer would the IV be retained. The exact date hadn't been finalised yet.

Late in the afternoon, Dr Peeters announced that some reporters wanted to interview me. I'd not been feeling too well earlier, so they hadn't allowed the reporters in then. I told the doctor, 'But please ask my company if I can do this.'

Dr Peeters checked with the concerned authorities in my company; they denied permission. So I asked Dr Peeters if he could give the interview on my behalf. He said he'd do it later; for now, he was quite worried about my leg. He would keep thinking of different ways to deal with the complications I was going through. He asked me, 'Why are you in a hurry to go?'

I told him, 'It's been a long time… my kids are waiting for me.'

Finally, the doctor advised that if all went well, then I could leave by the next weekend. So I fixed the date—5 May, my airline's anniversary date. The day my airline began its journey, I would also start a new journey in my life, I thought. So we sent a message on the family WhatsApp group announcing our tentative landing in Mumbai on 6 May 2016. Instantly, we started getting messages and calls from everyone. My sister in Delhi, Goldy di, had been planning to come and replace Jolly di here in Charleroi. I told Jolly di that it was just a matter of a week now, so let's not trouble Goldy di. Her ticket had been booked for 2 May 2016 and she was supposed to get her visa today or tomorrow. We asked her to wait.

In the evening, Rupesh asked me about Amit. I could only vaguely remember him. I could not recollect his appearance. I could not remember the names or faces of my operating crew either. Rupesh made me speak to Amit. I managed to remember what he had said on the day of the incident and even the notes we had shared the previous day, yet I couldn't remember any of the crew members, nor could I remember Amit's face. Then Rupesh showed me his picture, and that helped me recollect some more. I was very disturbed on realising that I was unable to recall my past. Rupesh shared this with the doctors and they explained that this did happen at times in cases such as mine, and it was possible that I would not be able to recollect most past events and maybe not even recognise faces. It could be a tough fight in that sense.

❧

30 APRIL 2016

I played the Hare Rama Hare Krishna bhajans as usual in the morning, and saw most of my nurses enjoying the ambience it created. It was their everyday routine to wish me good morning and ask me how I was doing. Today they came and kissed me. When it came to sponging me, they asked me to do it on my own. They said they would remove the staple pins that were used during the surgery on my right foot while the bandages were being tied. A nurse first cleaned the wound. I asked her to let me raise my back a bit, so that I could watch her do it. By now I could operate the bed controls myself, just as I would have operated premier or first class seats in an aircraft. I asked them whether it would be painful, but they said I wouldn't feel any pain because of the numbness in my foot.

Today, I learnt to shift from chair to chair by holding and twisting the lower abdomen. I felt good about managing this on my own. I had to make a habit of calling the nurses less frequently; so I would finish my ablutions in the morning, and when they came by around 1000 hrs to change the sheet, I would simply ask them to place me on the chair. Whenever I needed to pee, I'd heave my body from the WCHL to the urine chair. I would now go to the visiting room in the afternoon for lunch and return to my room by late afternoon. Apart from that, I would ring for the nurses only twice or thrice—once before dinner at around 2000 hrs and then sometimes at midnight. They became familiar with my timings and the best part was that soon, I didn't even need to call them; they would themselves come and ask me if I needed help.

I learned many things from them, but probably the best things I learned were their efficiency along with their warm care and empathy. I felt some of them actually enjoyed my company so much that they looked for reasons to spend some time in my room. Even though I was heavily dependent on them, they never made it seem like a hassle. I made it a point to give them a feeling of space and comfort too. My smile would bring a smile on their faces. My laugh would get the best of their smiles. Sometimes I would pull their legs, other times I would be a good friend and offer a patient ear. We would crack jokes and I'd share stories of amusing things I had done in the past, which would always surprise them. I knew everyone's shift timings, whether they come by car or bike, who among them was married, and how many kids they had. But somehow, I would not be able to remember some of their names.

We would have such a lot of fun. Some of them had told me that they began enjoying their work more from the time I started speaking. I was so touched to hear that. They never made me feel that I was in a hospital. The kind of care, love and attention they lavished on me, their level of involvement with me, was so deep and sincere that my condition never irritated me. Sometimes, I would be a bit hesitant to mingle with them, but they were never cold or clinical. For them work was worship and they were like family to me and loved to see me smile. I honestly love them all from the bottom of my heart.

❦

I began a new exercise. I was asked to hold a pen or say, the physiotherapist's finger, with my toes by folding them. I did this for nearly ten minutes with each foot, and at the end of the forty-minute session, I was so tired that I slept soundly and woke up only for dinner. I was so upset when I got up, and to make it worse, Jolly di and Rupesh had left for the hotel without saying goodbye. I lost my appetite. I felt so tired, as though I had not slept for days. I woke up again when Nurse Christopher came to give me an injection. He was on night-shift duty with another male nurse. I told them that I needed to pee. Christopher said he would teach me how to shift my position on my own, by holding the railing fitted at the top of the bed. This would give me confidence to move a bit on the bed on my own. There was a technique involved, but it required me to use the strength in my arms. Somehow I managed to lift myself thirty to forty percent of the way. I was very happy Christopher taught me how to do this because I knew nothing would progress without building muscle strength in my arms.

I asked Christopher and his colleague to help themselves to the chocolates in the refrigerator. They loved that, and told me, 'If you don't mind, we'll take some more after you sleep.'

'All yours,' I smiled.

❦

A few days ago, Sophie, the dermatologist and skin specialist, had taken the measurements of my face for a silicone mask that I was required to put on. When Christopher placed the mask on my face for the first time that night, he said, 'You look scary!' I told him to switch off all the lights.

Every night, I would pull the TV screen up to my bed so I could check the time as there was no clock in my room. The light from the screen was enough to provide sufficient illumination. I would tilt the screen a little upwards so that the light wouldn't disturb me during my sleep. That night, I felt very uncomfortable. Every now and then I looked at the window with fear. After a while, I removed the mask and kept it aside. For the first time that night, I didn't finish the bottle of water that was kept at my bedside.

When Christopher came to change the injection at 0400 hrs, I told him about it. He said, 'Okay, I'll keep the mask aside. It won't bother you.' Sophie had instructed me to wear the mask every night for at least ten to twelve hours; I had to continue doing so for at least eight to ten months to let my skin heal properly. I was given a pair of compression gloves to wear, of the size available with them at the time, and they had also ordered a new pair for me.

The number of things to be done on a mandatory basis was increasing day by day.

❦

1 MAY 2016

It had been a very restless night for me. So I found it difficult to cope during the day and had to actually drag myself through the normal routine.

Today was the first day they didn't take my morning blood sample. This confirmed that my condition had improved. I had also asked Dr Peeters about the need for the IV — he said that if all went well, they would remove it by Sunday or Monday. But the nurse told me she had been instructed not to remove it today. I was quite disappointed because I had felt so confident they would take it off today as I had been religiously following all their detailed instructions.

❦

In the afternoon, I suddenly noticed a mobile phone being slid from underneath the door and into my room; the Hare Rama Hare Krishna song was playing on it. I was surprised; whose phone could it be? My room had two entrances, one through which the WCHL and beds were moved in and out, and the other door through which the nurses would enter. I looked at both the doors, which had see-through glass, and saw someone hiding between the walls. Then the nurses entered the room, one behind the other, snaking like a train through my room. That's when I understood that the phone belonged to Nurse Arnaud. He was very fond of this song. He came and held my hand and said, 'We will miss you.' One by one, all the six nurses stood by my side and said, 'Call your kids here. Go when you are fully ready and fit. Please stay for a few more days with us.'

I didn't know what to say, but I promised to come back soon one day.

I felt so moved. The compassion and the warm smiles with which they always treated me were a constant morale booster for me. Their positive attitude, their love for me was incredible.

To change their mood, I started cracking jokes and made funny faces. We all laughed heartily and everyone danced for a while before they left. I would keep looking forward to such moments. They were like a second family to me. They used to take such good care of my needs. They had asked me which fruits I liked, and I'd told them that strawberries, apples and bananas were my all-time favourites. Carine, Fredric and a third nurse had brought me these fruits every day for the last ten days even though I had not asked for any. Carine would get strawberries from her organic garden at home and Fredric would bring bananas.

I often felt that the nurses must be thinking, *she should have finished her treatment and then gone back, instead of leaving halfway through it like this.* And I would hope that they understood my feelings too, about how I wanted to be with my family again.

It struck me that there were just three more days to go for my tentative date of travel and so many things were still to be done! Among other things, we needed to arrange a vehicle to take me to the airport. The doctors said I could only go in an ambulance. The stitches in my left foot, however, hadn't been removed yet; so I decided to ask the doctor about this tomorrow.

❧

Many people came to meet and bless me. They saw me through the window and spoke to me through the speaker. I was so glad to see their big smiles and warm gestures, I felt like going out and thanking them. In the evening, our base manager for engineering at the Brussels base, Arun, paid a visit. As soon as he saw me, he hugged me and presented the flowers he had brought, but after that he was speechless. He couldn't utter a word. After a long pause, he blurted out, 'Why you?' And with that, he burst out crying. Rupesh offered him a glass of water. He cried uncontrollably for a while and with great difficulty we managed to calm him down. Looking at him crying, I couldn't control my own tears. I couldn't help wondering what they all must have gone through as well. I had no answer to his question. He finally said, 'Sorry, I know being a man, I should control my emotions, but first, I'm a human being. Why did such a chirpy and loving person like you get injured so badly?'

Actually, many times, many others too had raised this question. I told him, 'We should think of it this way. God has given me a second life and I should be thankful to Him. He is really being kind to me.'

He talked a while about the incident. About how he saw my picture on social media within minutes of the blast and was shocked to see me like that. He said he fought with the police and security guards to allow him to go to the departure hall to look for me but they had not been allowed to even leave the tarmac.

'But why did you want to come to the departure area?' I quizzed.

'Because I knew that was where your picture had been taken, so I wanted to be sure that you are out and have been taken to the hospital. Your picture showed that you were traumatised. I wanted to give you support. But after that, you went missing.'

Fresh tears flowed as he spoke and his voice had trembled. I tried to make him feel better. 'Forget what happened... enjoy and celebrate this moment of togetherness now.'

We had tea and snacks. He was amazed to see Indian tea in the hospital. In fact, many from the staff were in love with the tea my sister prepared and served along with snacks (cookies, namkeens and sweets). For them, this was the snack corner. And the surprising thing was that other patients were allowed to take a walk in and around the hospital, and they would also come have tea and snacks with us at times. Especially two boys, who had been injured in a bike accident, would eagerly wait for the flask to be opened. It was a daily routine for many of them to have tea around 1500 hrs in the visiting room. There was a cupboard in which the hospital staff kept toys for children; my sister would use the cupboard to stow away the washed glasses and plates. She would make tea every day before leaving the hotel. Though the hotel guests were not allowed to cook in their rooms, she would make khichdi and tea in the small balcony of her room using a hot plate. She said she was always scared of the fire alarm, so she would keep the big windows open all day to air the room.

In the evening, at about 1900 hrs, a trainee doctor came by. I can't recall her name, but she was very sweet. She was usually on duty in the daytime, but she told me she would be on night shift for a few days. Her husband was a dermatologist, and the previous day, he had attended a conference for the launch of new products in Europe. He had brought back a certain Swiss face cream, SPF 60+ (which had just been launched then). He claimed it was the best product, and when he gave it to her, she had thought of me and thus, brought the cream for me. She had tears in her eyes when she told me all this. She said, 'I heard you are going back. And in India it is very hot and sunny, and as you are not allowed to go out in the sun, you can apply this cream. This would remind you of me. Don't forget us. We will miss you.'

As D-day neared, I started becoming more emotional about things. I would shed copious tears; I wanted to make everyone around me happy. The trainee doctor hugged and kissed me and said, 'I'm around in case you need anything.'

I held her hand and said, 'thank you for your love and concern. I will miss you too.' My heart felt heavy.

I saw the nurse preparing two more injections for my machine. I knew one would be used at night. She informed me, 'We have to prepare both and start them by night. The final decision will be taken by the doctor on seeing the report.'

I was tense, sad and confused. I closed my eyes; I was experiencing so many different feelings. I wanted the IV to be removed. But I was sure they would do it in the morning.

❦

At 0500 hrs, when the nurse came in to do a routine check-up, she found that my BP was a little low. She asked me about it. I told her it was because of the pain of leaving them all. She smiled. During bandaging, I asked the nurse to show me a picture of the sole of my left foot as I had until then not seen my foot from below. She took a photo on her mobile phone and showed it to me. I could see the skin on the inside. In places, the stitches were two-inches long, and in other places they were only one centimetre long. I asked her why this was so, why they hadn't clamped it with pins like they had done for my other foot. She explained, 'Your foot had totally opened up and was in a terrible state, so we had to put stitches like these. You are lucky... if the cut had been more severe, your foot would not have been there at all.'

Her words made me realise that I had been truly lucky. I looked up and thanked the Almighty.

There were only two days to go now and the stitches were still there. The IV drip was also running. I asked her, 'When will you open the stitches?'

She was not sure. 'I don't think it would be done today, but I shall call the doctor.'

Dr Peeters came with Dr Saidane and they both declared that the drip would have to continue for today. They explained that my antibacterial and antibiotic courses were done but I needed to take more as my foot was not healing too well. The nurse readied two more injections and stored them in the refrigerator. I was anxious because the doctor had said when they discontinue the IV, they would keep me under observation for at least forty-eight hours.

When my family arrived, discussions on the transfer procedures were in full swing. All the hospital staff seemed busy preparing my documentation papers, especially Head Nurse John. Dr Peeters had already briefed Roopa, my point of contact with Jet Airways, that he also wanted a doctor to accompany me from Charleroi to Paris in the ambulance. I was then told that the head of our company's medical services department, Dr Kharam, along with an aviation specialist and a paramedic, would accompany me from Paris to Mumbai.

My hand gloves finally arrived. These were special gloves that would give total compression to my grafts and provide protection from the sun. I was asked to wear them for at least twelve months, 24/7. I tried them on. They had taken measurements two weeks ago; it took that much time to have them custom-made for me. I asked them to make me an extra pair as I would need at least two pairs if I were to wear them all the time. They agreed and told me to let them know by email if I needed more in the future, in which case they would courier them. I asked them if I could remove the gloves whenever I'd need to freshen up or during a bath. They said yes, but not for more than an hour a day.

For the itchy burn marks on my body, I was given sprays, creams and liquid drops, but was strictly ordered not to scratch the area. I was instructed not to go out in the sun for one to two years, and if I absolutely had to, then I must cover my face. I was told to wear a cap, to apply SPF 60+ cream and protect myself from getting exposed to direct sunlight. The same person who had got the gloves for me was asked to issue a special shoe to protect my foot from hitting any surface while sleeping and to provide stability to my right foot. I was asked to wear it all night as it would keep my leg upright with the foot positioned in a right angle. The speciality of the shoe was that it would safeguard the heel even if I were to accidentally place my foot on the ground. It would work for me just like a plaster would, allowing me to keep my foot fixed at a right angle to the leg and help hold the foot in that position. He also said it would give me comfort in the future. Along with the shoe, I was provided with a U-shaped stand. I had to place my foot at its centre; this was to stabilise the foot in the correct position. But when my foot was placed in it for the first time, I screamed as the fractures caused immense pain. I was then asked to place a pillow or something for support so that my leg wouldn't bend to the right and the foot would stay upright always. I needed to wear this shoe till the time my foot gained full stability. It was such a heavy shoe and it covered my leg right up to the calf.

Nidhi Chaphekar

I was busy with all this while Rupesh collected CDs and scanned copies of all the required documents and papers. A letter had to be arranged from the embassy as my passport was damaged. In the midst of it all, we got a call from Mr Jigar Joshi asking whether he and his wife could visit us the next evening.

Earlier, my foot used to be suspended in mid-air, so movement had been very limited. But now, with this new shoe, I felt suffocated. Every fifteen minutes, I would ask someone to help me open the Velcro strap and my sister would stick it back again. I was disheartened and wondered how I would manage once I was back home in India. Negative thoughts started flooding my mind, but I consciously tried to switch back to a positive way of thinking. The mood swings were challenging. The stress of leaving the supportive environment of the hospital, the thought of travelling all the way to India and questions of how I am going to cope weighed heavily on my mind. I was really looking forward to re-uniting with my family, but there were so many unwanted thoughts crowding my mind. A vague, vacuous feeling in the pit of my stomach made me feel uneasy and irritable.

But nothing could keep me bogged down for too long. Fortunately, nurses would come into my room and click pictures with me, kiss me and dance to the Hare Rama Hare Krishna song. Some of them even knew a bit of the cultural history of this song as, in the past, on their request, I had looked up information on the Internet and read to them a brief account of the story of Lord Krishna as well as the history of the Golden Temple in Amritsar. Whenever they found some free time, they would come into my room eager to hear more of the story. For me too, it was a kind of learning experience.

When the night-shift nurses left for the day, I would think of the difficulties I was going to face in the future, but I would try to prepare myself mentally to accept the challenges that lay ahead of me. I knew the difficult condition I was in would be a part of my life for a long time and I couldn't escape or run from it, so I would have to find solutions to all my issues from now on.

Before my sister left for the hotel, I had asked her to call up

Alain to brief him that we were hopefully leaving for India on 5 May. She dialled and I spoke to him. When I gave him the news about our departure, he was happy but sad as well because he wanted me to recover fully and only then go back. He also wanted his family to meet me. He said he would come see me on 4 May for sure, after his duty for the day was done. After my family left, I kept fiddling with the shoe. The nurse on duty came and filled two more big injections for the night and kept them in the refrigerator.

I requested the nurse whether I could remove the shoe for some time as it was making me very uncomfortable and my back was aching due to the weight of the shoe. She said it was okay to remove it for a while, but I must try to wear it most of the time. After she gave an injection in my stomach, I slept, but at midnight, she came and woke me up to remind me to wear the shoe. She kept two pillows under my leg to make me feel comfortable. And yet, I felt a lot of discomfort. I couldn't sleep the whole night and thought I would go crazy wearing the mask on my face, gloves on my hands and the shoe on my leg which then had to be placed in the stand. Just the thought of wearing all this for more than a year seemed like a nightmare. And on top of that, there were bandages, cream applications and many other causes of discomfort.

To distract myself, I started watching a movie, but I couldn't focus on it because of the pain in my back, which felt stretched and pulled taut with the weight of the shoe. But the stubborn girl that I am, I knew I had to get used to it, so I didn't remove it until the morning.

❧

3 MAY 2016

I was unable to lift my foot and was dead tired, feeling as if I'd worked out the entire night. The exhaustion was either because of the shoe or the exertion of the last few days, but I didn't tell anyone. The first thing on my mind that morning was the discontinuation of my

IV and removal of my stitches. At 0900 hrs, the nurse administered another injection and said she'd check with a doctor. Finally Dr Peeters came and said it could be removed now. The nurse took blood samples to check how long it took before blood started clotting; this is a standard check carried out before the removal of an IV drip. Satisfied, the nurse who was to remove the drip asked me to follow her instructions. I asked her, 'How long have you been working here?'

She said, 'It's been twenty-six years.'

'Will it be painful?' I asked.

'Not if you follow my instructions,' she replied, and made me lie down flat on the back. She said she would ask me to hold my breath and at the count of three, she would remove it. I was asked not to speak, cough, or try to get up for at least thirty minutes. Once she undid the tapes, I held my breath, waiting for the count of three, but at the count of two itself, she pulled it out. I didn't even realise it! She applied pressure on the area for ten to fifteen minutes, and then placed some cotton there and taped it. She came back thirty minutes later to confirm that there was no bleeding.

The IV line was probably sixteen-centimetre-long; it was a wire-like tube inserted from the neck over the collarbone deep in the intravenous central line and pushed until the tip reached the larger vein near the heart. When I asked her how it was inserted, she explained, 'We follow this vein that goes down from the collarbone.' What expertise and confidence a person requires to do this; God bless them, I thought. I felt so relieved.

I asked Carine if I could wash my hair. She immediately got a tub full of warm water, a brand new shampoo and some dry washcloths. She asked me to lean sideways on the left side, while sitting on the bed, kept the empty tub on the table and asked me to look into it, face down. She poured some water on my hair, gently applied shampoo, washed my scalp and poured warm water finally to wash off the shampoo. The colour of the water in the tub was brownish, like what is shown in detergent soap advertisements, where they clean a dirty, stained shirt and it comes out sparkling clean.

What a relief it was washing my head and cleaning the little hair that I had after forty-three days! I looked very different afterwards. Since my clothes had got a little wet in the process, Carine got me a brand new dress with a cartoon print. I loved her for that! By then, my sister and Rupesh had arrived. Then Dr Hans came in. She held my hand and spoke to me for some time, asking me to take proper care and to rest well. 'You must follow our instructions. Nidhi, you are a strong lady. It was a pleasure treating you. Keep in touch. You will do wonders in life,' she said with a smile.

She informed me she was off duty for the next two days, so I wouldn't meet her on the day of departure. She said, 'today I came only for you, to say goodbye to you. We will miss your smile... we will miss you, Nidhi.'

I hugged her and cried. I didn't know how to express my emotions. I kissed her hand and said, 'thank you for giving me a new life.'

She replied, 'It's your rebirth, don't forget that. And it will be more beautiful than before.'

I had always seen her smiling cheerfully, but today she seemed emotional. She said, 'It's great that we did the best for you and are really very happy with the results, but it is sad that we may not see you again.'

I promised her that I would come back soon, walking, to make them feel proud of the work they had done on me. She smiled, waving at me as she left. I couldn't control my tears. All the feel-good factor post IV removal vanished and I was overcome by emotion. I was touched by her generosity. I saw tears in her eyes when she left; even the nurses started crying. I promised myself I'd see them soon again, as they had put in their heart and soul for me; they were such remarkable people.

The nurses then exchanged phone numbers and email addresses with me. I told them I wasn't good with apps but would stay in touch.

The Indian ambassador, Mr Puri, gave a call and said, 'I heard that you would be flying soon. Unfortunately, I won't be able to join you (at the airport) as I have to go for an urgent meeting that day. But my wife will be there with Sumita to see you off.'

He, however, added that he would come to see me at the hospital

Nidhi Chaphekar

today. I felt great that a man of his stature had thought of this wonderful gesture. All of us are tied up with so many things in our daily lives, but going an extra mile can make a real difference to someone's life.

I told Rupesh and the nurse that I wanted to see how they used to enter the balcony of my ICCU room and the entrance through which I had been brought into the hospital on a stretcher. They agreed to show it to me after lunch.

✦

Our friend Rohit was to visit me today. He had told us yesterday that he would join us for lunch, that he'd bring lunch for everyone. I was hungry and eagerly waiting for him to arrive. He changed his clothes and walked into the room at 1300 hrs. The moment he saw me, he stood still for a while, and then said, 'thank God, you are back. You had shocked the daylights out of us.'

I asked him to sit beside me. He told me he had come to see me thrice, and the second and third time, I had been very critical. He would go to the window area, look at me and pray to God for my well-being and then go back.

Then Rohit asked me, 'But why did you take this flight? I heard it was not your flight anyway!' He was overcome by emotion.

'But look, I am fine now,' I tried to make him feel better. Then I asked him, 'Did I look scary when you entered the room a while ago?'

He smiled. 'Well, it was difficult to recognise you but your smile left no doubt about your identity!'

I was hungry and asked him to help me onto a WCHL so that we could go have lunch, and he wheeled me to the visiting room. He had brought chicken for Rupesh and cottage cheese for Jolly di, Roopa and me. He had also got some desi parathas. It was delicious food. He said the kids had helped him make it. As we ate, Rohit told me that on the day of the blast, he had been in the United States for his younger son Karan's karate camp. The finals were held four days later, and he won a bronze.

'Karan would have won the gold, but we were both so depressed and tense because of the situation you were in, that he couldn't give his best. He dedicated his medal to you and he has made a video about it and posted it on YouTube.' He showed me the video. I was really moved.

Rohit had got a lot of dry snacks for us, but we asked him to carry them back as we would hopefully be getting discharged from the hospital on 5 May. 'I'm glad to hear that,' he said, 'but never mind, in case you can't have these snacks, please distribute them.'

At 1700 hrs, we enjoyed some tea together. He also told me about how his friends in the United States had held prayers and lit candles in churches for me—a huge number of well-wishers had looked out for me.

He showed me videos of the prayers performed for my well-being by his father's followers (he was a spiritual guru) and of his relatives who conducted prayers for me in their houses. I thanked everyone with all my heart. After Rohit left, I was lost in thought about how so many people came together to save one life. Each one of them, in their own unique way, had prayed for my life to be saved. I wondered what so many others had been doing while I was in deep slumber; they would have had sleepless nights. God bless each one of them.

A little later, I was taken to the back of the hospital from where visitors would enter the ICCU window gallery. This was the first time I was taken out on the WCHL without any equipment, like a free bird. They showed me the stairs they would take. There was a button and a camera; when you pressed the button and spoke, your voice could be heard by the receptionist. Then you had to identify yourself through the camera and the receptionist would open the door. From there you could climb up and reach the window of the particular room you wished to visit. A little ahead, they pointed out, was my room. I noticed the big tree and beside it, the lamppost I used to see from my room. The memory of that lamppost horrifies me even today. The ominous shapes in the shadow of the tree and the lamppost would appear in my nightmares. I then saw the helipad and the route by which I'd been brought in initially on a stretcher. After that I went to the garden. I loved the green, leafy path there. On my way back, I saw the lady who used to clean my room go past in her red car. She stopped to give me flying kisses and waved at me. I waved back.

Later, Mr Puri and his wife joined us in the visiting room. He was so happy for me and spent some time talking to us. He said, 'You are unbelievable. You stood by the statement made by your husband.'

I smiled with pride. He said, 'this is what life is, but, Nidhi, you are really very lucky to come back to enjoy it, and I would say everyone, especially the doctors, worked hard to get you back. So never look back, always give your best. From where you have come back and after what you have seen and experienced, there's not even a strain on your face, which gives us all the strength to deal with our ordeals.'

Mr Puri is a wonderful man, always full of energy and life, a sincere human being. After a while, he and his wife presented a box of sweets for my kids. 'Be in touch,' they said while leaving, 'the kids would love to see you back.' I thanked him and told him he was one of the most humble human beings I had ever met. Everyone was quiet after they left. I was never someone who could take the pain of farewells. I still can't.

While I was sitting there, Nurse Laurence came up to me, wearing her civil dress, and hugged me. She said, 'I won't be able see you off as I'm on vacation from tomorrow.' She kissed my hands and I returned the gesture. She shared her number with me so that we could stay in touch. She added with a smile, 'We all wish you Hare Rama Hare Krishna. We are happy for you and will miss you.'

My heart was thundering away because of all the emotion I felt. I requested to be taken to my room.

Later, Jigar Joshi and his wife Nitika visited us with a big, five-layer tiffin box. They came one by one and sat by my side in the room. They were both very happy to meet me and shared their experience of that fated day. Jigar said he had got a call from the Jet Airways manager base at Brussels airport asking him to check if a Nidhi Chaphekar, one of the crew, had arrived at any of the hospitals in Antwerp, as they had heard that many casualties were taken to nearby cities after the third blast at Maalbeek metro station. When Rupesh confirmed that I was in Sint-Augustinus Hospital, they came by twice but because my surgeries were in progress, and also for security reasons, they weren't allowed to see me. The next morning, when they rang to check on my status, they were told that I had already been airlifted to the burns centre hospital in Charleroi.

I thanked both of them for taking such pains to find me and for coming all the way from Antwerp to meet me. Nitika had got delicious food, which we all enjoyed. Jigar recalled how we were once on a flight to Newark, where an elderly guest was quite aggravated. The two of us, along with the crew, had handled the situation.

Later, they dropped my family off at the hotel and went their way. Here in the hospital, I lay in bed, feeling low. So many people were helping my family. I wore the shoe once again and as I was very tired after talking so much the entire day, I slept like a log for an hour. I got up when Christopher came with the injection. I dozed for just a couple of hours, but the rest of the night was restless like the previous one.

❦

4 MAY 2016

I noticed that my leg was more swollen than before. I told the nurse about it; she said it was probably because of the shoe. I couldn't even move the tip of my toe. I prayed to God—*Be with me, please don't do anything that would delay my travel.*

Carine came in with breakfast and said she wouldn't be able to see me the next day as it was her day off, but she would still try to come. Fredric too said the same. Carine fed me and told me to 'Be good and come back to meet us.' She tied a thread around my hand to ward off the evil eye and said, 'this will take care of you. Never remove it.'

It was the birthday of one of the nurses, so she brought a cake and we cut it in my room. She fed me fruit. I cried. The nurses put on the Hare Rama Hare Krishna song and started dancing, which changed my tears to smiles. Imagine how you would feel dancing to the tune of Hare Rama Hare Krishna on your birthday! One of them said, 'We will all listen to this together in your absence to remember you.'

Then it was time to do the bandages. I was looking forward to the removal of my stitches. The nurse called Dr Saidane. He said, 'Cut them, and no physiotherapy for the legs for forty-eight hours. Don't put any pressure on the legs.'

'Will there be pain?' I asked the nurse.

'A little,' she said.

While continuing to talk to me, she cut all the stitches. I observed the process of cutting the thread and pulling it out. As it was on the sole of my left foot, I couldn't see what it looked like. So I asked her to click a picture and show it to me. The nurse warned me not to leave it bare till it healed completely. 'Be very careful because it's still deep,' she had cautioned me.

After washing and cleaning the wounds, they were bandaged. By then my husband and sister arrived. Jolly di started packing everything that was lying around in my room. She gave the nurse a bag containing my clothes for the next morning. Then she asked the nurse to explain everything about my medicines. They had already made a printed chart for this purpose and handed over the medicine doses for twenty-four hours after discharge. The nurse gave my sister the injections I take in the stomach every night. They gave a backup injection too, just to be safe. They also gave five diapers and a padded sheet for the journey. My sister packed everything in a travel bag, putting the medicines in pouches. My room now looked empty. I asked the nurse why she had given us diapers. She said, 'the doctor instructed us to. According to Dr Peeters, it would not be possible for you to go to the aircraft toilet. It would be a lot of trouble even if you took the help of people, so the best way is to use a diaper.'

I fell silent. Each day seemed to bring surprises my way.

Jolly di and Rupesh had to leave early today; they needed to dispose of all the stuff lying in the hotel room. 'Everyone who visited brought so many things,' she explained. 'We used to tell them, please, we already have so much, but they would think we are just being hesitant.' And so she had called Sumita di to help her as one entire side of the room was filled with packed food (dry snacks, biscuits, and so on).

I was feeling very low today. At 1700 hrs, Alain called to say that he would leave in some time and would be here around 1900 hrs. When he reached, the nurse informed me—'A police officer has come to see you.' I told her to bring him in as I was too tired to go to the visiting room. Alain was asked to change into antibacterial clothes.

He was really happy to see me and exclaimed, 'Nidhi, O Nidhi, so finally you are going back!' He had got me gifts. He gave me a big box set of three scented candles and said, 'Whenever you light these, you will remember me.' Then he gave me a pair of black Ray Ban sunglasses and said, 'My little sister, your eyes are very deep and expressive. Now people will want to see them more. I don't want that at any point you feel emotional or weak, so do wear these when you go out tomorrow.' I refused several times but he kept on insisting, so I accepted his gift. He promised me that he would come to see me in Mumbai once I was absolutely fine, so I could take him sightseeing. We sat chatting for a while. Then he said he had to leave as he had brought his daughter along but unfortunately, she wasn't allowed to come in. I felt so bad to hear that. At least I could have gone out to the visiting room had I been informed earlier. But it was too late for that now. He clicked pictures. I thanked him for his love and wonderful gesture.

After Alain left, I lay in bed thinking how different we all look on the outside, how we all come from different cultures and backgrounds, but love remains the same everywhere.

After some time, I spoke to Christopher and his team and asked them to take all the chocolates from the refrigerator. They told me, 'It used to always be exciting to open the refrigerator as you had a lot of stuff for us, but now nothing will be there.' I was quiet.

My right leg had grown completely numb and heavy by then, and I could feel my heart thumping hard as well. I prayed, *God, please be kind to me*. I tried to move my leg but couldn't lift it at all. I thought of raising the shoe but found it impossible to bend that far as my leg had gone stiff. Christopher removed the shoe and lightly massaged my toe and upper calf. He checked my blood pressure. It was a little low. He asked me not to worry about it. After consulting the doctors on the phone, he gave me an injection.

I was unable to sleep. To divert my attention I put on the Hare Rama Hare Krishna chant and kept chanting Jai Mata Di. But my mind was disturbed. The upper portion of my leg was so stiff. I called Christopher again. He moved my leg a bit, but I couldn't feel a thing. He raised the leg, folded it, and turned it to the side. But there was no sensation at all. He said, 'If it remains like this, we will call the doctor.' An hour passed and still the situation showed no change. At 0200 hrs, he contacted the doctor.

It was the same feeling I had had initially on the day of the blast. I felt frightened but kept telling myself that all would be fine. The doctor arrived within half an hour. I briefed her that today I had worn the shoe for more than eight hours and hadn't done physiotherapy, which I normally did twice a day. She pressed the tips of my toes, lifted my leg, folded it, and turned me around. She gave me an injection. She said, 'I think it's because of the shoe you were wearing and possibly because you haven't done the physiotherapy. But you need rest. It could also be because the IV has been removed recently and the body is not strong enough to take it.'

I got scared. My first thought was — *Nidhi, this may now delay your trip. But don't think about it. Just take it easy.* She told me to try and move my leg a bit, but I failed. She kept four pillows under my leg and elevated it to a forty-five-degree angle, but I was still not able to move my toe. It was swollen and very stiff. Finally, she said, 'Just sleep, we will see what is to be done early in the morning.' I don't know when I drifted off to sleep.

❧

5 MAY 2016

I got up at 0730 hrs and brushed my teeth. Carine was not on duty and I missed her. My breakfast was placed on the table beside my bed. I asked the other nurse to apply butter on the toast. I missed Carine's lemon tea.

After breakfast, some of the nurses came to my room. They had got a bunch of flowers and wished me a happy journey. I was finding it hard to say goodbye but I had to, as their shift was coming to an end. The nurses opened my bandages, washed the area completely and redid them in a different style. They even made me wear a white compression band (that began at my ankles and came up to my calves) and told me not to remove them till I reached the other hospital in Mumbai. The nurses sponged my body with Betadine as it was going to be a long journey. I wore my own clothes after forty-four days! I looked in the mirror they got for me to show me how healthy and good I looked. Then the nurse washed and packed my silicone mask in the bag. She said. 'We will put the diaper on when you are just about to leave.'

By this time Jolly di and Rupesh arrived. My sister said, 'Baby, you're looking very cute.' Rupesh kissed my forehead and Jolly di held my hand as though saying, 'Well done.'

I received a call at around 1030 hrs from Fredric and Carine to say that they would not be able to make it as their kids were home because of a national holiday and they couldn't get them along. They apologised and wished me all the best for the journey. Then Dr Hans called and said, 'We will see you again. Don't forget your promise!' My physiotherapist came and said, 'Wish you a great recovery, but don't forget us.'

I was struggling with my thoughts. At 1100 hrs, I was asked to wear a diaper as it was time to leave. Madan bhai and Sumita di arrived. Sumita di had taken a day off only to come and say goodbye. Then I got a call from one of the journalists, Kurt, who worked for *Het Laatste Nieuws*. He said they were waiting outside the hospital to take my interview. He had apparently tried many times to get in touch, but all this while they had been denied permission.

They learnt that I was leaving today, so they were allowed to come and see me.

I told him, 'Well, so long as you can understand that I am an employee of a company and without their consent, it would not be possible. But yes, I can share a few words with you if you want to know about my hospitalisation.'

I gave him a brief telephonic interview for ten minutes. I told him, 'the love I received from the people in your country and from the hospital staff is incredible. The staff here are exceptional. The doctors here are no less than gods for me. The concern shown in my case is commendable. I love Belgium, especially people working for Grand Hospital... I never felt I was in a hospital undergoing treatment.'

He was happy to hear me lavishing praise on the staff. He told me he and his team would be waiting outside, in case there was a chance to click some photographs of me. The family wanted to take me to the visiting room but the nurses suggested I stay there in my room till the ambulance arrived as it was going to be a very long journey. So Sumita di got the tiffin inside and fed me. She said, 'I always loved feeding you, but I hope when you come next, you will eat on your own.'

It was already noon by now, but the ambulance had not yet come. Roopa had coordinated with the insurance company to send across an ambulance and a doctor, but when she called them to check, she was in for an unpleasant surprise—because of some miscommunication, they had not booked it for this Thursday. She began calling everyone possible. Being a public holiday, no one was working, and it was proving to be impossible to make alternative arrangements. She called up Dr Peeters to check if they could book a big car and asked whether I could travel with my foot stretched out on the front seat. But Dr Peeters refused. Everything came to a standstill. Because of the public holiday, no extra ambulances were available in the hospital or nearby. Then she asked him if the only ambulance standing in the hospital premises could be provided, but he told her it was reserved for hospital emergencies. He reminded her sternly, 'I had told you that Nidhi can only travel if a doctor accompanies her. Even if the ambulance is provided, how are we going to arrange for a doctor to accompany her?'

The doctors who had come from India for this purpose had arrived in Paris the day before and were to accompany me from Paris to Mumbai. Even if they left now, it would take them more than three hours and then there'd be no way of catching the flight today.

Then I spoke to Dr Peeters myself and assured him that I was fine and could go without a doctor. He replied, 'Your lungs are an issue and even your legs. We noticed you suffered yesterday. This may lead to many problems.' Yet we persisted with our request.

Finally he said, 'Okay, call your doctor halfway to accompany you. Secondly, you will sign an indemnity bond that you are doing this at your own risk and the hospital is not responsible for this.' We requested him again whether he could please ask the authorities to release this hospital's ambulance for us. He gave in and said he wanted two people to accompany me in the ambulance.

It was already 1315 hrs by then. Amidst all this panic, I asked them to let me do my last 'pee pee' in the hospital as we had a long way to travel. After freshening up, when I reached the visiting room, I saw Sumita di preparing a plate for pooja. She said, 'I had told Rupesh when he first arrived that *dilwale dulaniya lekar jayenge*, and today is the day the bride is going home, so I have to perform the rituals!'

She covered my head with a red dupatta, and put sindoor on my forehead. When she lit the diya, I was scared that the fire alarm would go off. (In the back of my mind was the constant thought that things were not going the way they were supposed to today.) I told her to extinguish it quickly. She said a prayer for me and then at last, we were taken to the covered garage-like area where the ambulance was parked. When they were placing me on the stretcher, the reporters came running from outside, taking photos and asking questions. I simply said, 'I love all of you. You people are great!' I waved to the nurses who came out to see me off. I waved to Sumita di and Madan bhai. As promised, I wore the sunglasses gifted by Alain.

Nidhi Chaphekar

Roopa sat with me, along with a helper. I was wearing sunglasses, so no one saw my tears. But I saw theirs. I saw my family following us in a car. Along with my family, Vishwanathan had come all the way from Amsterdam to see me off. Roopa was reporting every ten minutes to Dr Peeters. She was in touch with Sami, a ground personnel staff member from Paris who was driving Dr Kharam, as they had to meet us midway. The road was under repair, so there was a lot of traffic and our ambulance slowed down to a speed of ten kilometres per hour.

Roopa was tense and said, 'Why does everything have to happen today!'

I told her, 'Chill, if we managed so much, we will manage to reach on time.'

She told me we were already late, and we were running out of time. Our words went back and forth like that for nearly forty-five minutes. She was losing patience and asked the driver if there was any other shorter route, but he said no.

Dr Kharam called and told us that they had already taken a U-turn and were waiting at a gas station to the right side. It took us nearly thirty more minutes to get there because of the traffic. I saw Dr Kharam running towards the ambulance when it stopped at the gas station. Roopa got down and Dr Kharam joined me. She had been asked by Dr Peeters to inform him after joining us in the ambulance. After she briefed him, Dr Peeters spoke to me too.

He explained to me that things were not going to be easy, but I must keep up the same strength I had shown in the hospital.

He said, 'So finally you are leaving us...'

I said, 'No, I will come back soon to thank you, but walking, and not in an ambulance or WCHL.'

He added, 'I wanted to share one thing with you. We thought that it was not possible to give you a second life but we were successful in doing so. Please do take care of it as there may not be a third chance for you. We will all miss you.'

'I will miss you too, ' I replied.

After I disconnected the call, I wept. Dr Kharam comforted me.

'Don't do this,' she said. 'this will make you feel low. Think of the fact that you are going back home!'

I was tired of being in the same position on the stretcher for such a long time and wanted to sit up for a while, but she didn't allow me. On reaching the airport at 1715 hrs and and on being brought out of the ambulance on the stretcher, I saw a full set of Paris–Mumbai operating crew, along with the captains, standing in a line. They knew that I would be flying today with them and coincidentally we had reached the airport at the same time. When they saw the ambulance arrive, they waited, knowing I would be inside. They welcomed me with applause until I was put on a WCHL. I told them, 'I love you all... see you on board.'

Paris Airport Manager Paters and Duty Manager Shalaka were waiting for me. They presented me with a bouquet and a greeting card. They had arranged a WCHL that could keep my legs at a raised level as directed by the doctors. I could see that many people around us were wondering who I was and why I was getting so much attention.

It was time to say a special 'thank you' to Roopa who had been with us right from 1 April as support for my family. A special thanks was due to Vishwanathan too. My luggage was taken care of and I waved goodbye to Roopa and Vishwanathan until they were out of sight. Shalaka and Paters took us to Immigration. I was stopped by the immigration officer as I had no visa and my passport too was damaged. So Paters explained to him in French that I was actually a crew member and a victim of the terror attack. He showed the general declaration copy bearing the names of the crew who were to operate the flight on 22 March 2016. The HR department at Jet Airways had sent a letter stating the same. Even our Indian embassy had drafted a letter by Ajay Aggarwal to be handed over at Immigration in case of any problem.

From there I was taken to the aircraft. I was given seat 6A, which had a curtain. I requested the helpers to hold me under the shoulders, by the thighs and not lower than that, and then to lift me at the count of three. My husband and three other men lifted me and placed me on the seat. I had not peed for six hours now, and it felt as if my bladder was going to burst. I asked the doctor whether before takeoff, with the help of the crew and my husband, I could use the washroom. But she didn't allow me and asked me to relieve myself in the diaper. My sister drew the curtain of my seat. I tried really hard, but in vain. Then she made sounds just as one would if one were asking a small child to do it. Five minutes later, I did it. But there was so much that it flowed out of the diaper and wet my pajamas and the seat. With Rupesh's help, my sister changed my pajamas and managed to put a dry sheet on the wet seat. I was feeling so ashamed wondering what the crew would think of me. But there was nothing I could do.

Then it was time for takeoff. I said bye to the ground staff, Shalaka, Paters, Sami and the rest of the team. My sister sat one seat ahead, in 5A. The two doctors were accommodated in 5D and 4D, so that they could see me at all times. Rupesh was in 6D, the seat exactly opposite mine. Even for takeoff, my footrest was kept at a ninety-degree angle as I was not allowed to suspend my legs downwards. I was wearing the shoe now. During takeoff, I felt as if air was being pumped into my wounds and my feet were becoming heavier.

The crew served drinks after takeoff, but I was asked by the doctors to be a good girl, eat and go to sleep. A special meal was brought for me, consisting of dal, rice, small wheat rotis and cottage cheese. I felt some heaviness while breathing. Meanwhile, Capt. Raamy made an announcement on board: 'It is a very special flight for us because we are taking back our crew member, a survivor, a warrior, Ms Nidhi Chaphekar, who was injured in the bomb blast that took place at Brussels airport on 22 March 2016. She is recovering well by the grace of God. We are lucky to take her back. We salute her strength and resilience to fight against all odds. On behalf of the entire family of Jet Airways, we wish her a quick recovery.'

I felt very important. It was a wonderful moment. Some people started coming to my seat to get a glimpse of me. Premier guests, especially, began asking—*Is she the one seated there?* I waved at them and thanked them for their respect. After dinner, Dr Anita (the aviation specialist doctor called from Delhi) gave me the nightly injection in my stomach, just as they had done in the hospital. I was asked to sleep. The doctor was not ready to draw the curtain because they wanted to keep a watch on me. I was very uncomfortable because of the heaviness in my leg. I put two pillows under my right leg to raise it a bit. I could feel everyone's eyes on me, including my family's. I decided to try to sleep and closed my eyes.

❧

6 MAY 2016

I woke up at exactly 0600 hrs. The crew were taking rounds in the cabin. They knew I liked Indian masala tea and within no time, Jayant, one of my crew, got some for me. He expressed how happy they all were after meeting me. He said, 'there was not even a single day when we didn't discuss you, whether in the briefings or at the airport or in the flight or during the layovers, and everybody was so sure that you would be fine soon and come out of it.'

By now my foot was numb and heavy as a log, so I took his help to remove my shoe. I pushed the shoe underneath my seat as there was no other place to keep it. I tried to massage my foot a bit and the doctors asked me if I was okay. I told them I was good.

In the meantime, my sister got two glasses, one empty and the other full of water to brush my teeth. They asked me to have breakfast but I refused, knowing that then I would need to visit the washroom, which I knew was not possible. Jolly di asked me to pee so that she could change my diaper, since we did not know how much time it would take us to reach the hospital after all the clearance formalities on landing. I used my second diaper then and my sister placed towels on the sides of the seat as a precautionary measure.

Rupesh comforted me, 'Don't worry, I will clean you,' but I was so hesitant.

Dr Anita came and spoke to me. She said, 'Nidhi, I want you to know something about yourself. You are a wonderful person and in all my aviation history and experience, I have not met such a cheerful person. You never gave us a feeling that you are a patient.' She added that she was glad to have accompanied me. I thanked her.

Soon it was time to land. I looked from my window and could see the buildings coming into sight. I was so excited! When we passed by Vashi bridge, I knew it would take less than 120 seconds now. Being trained crew, sometimes we used to count the seconds, so when in exactly 110 seconds it touched down, I clapped. The plane was parked in the bay. The 2L exit door was right behind my seat. The moment the door was opened, a team of ground personnel, supervisors, Ms Pom, Meet and Assist Manager Maya, and my captain from Flight no. 9W 228 of 22 March 2016 from Brussels to Newark, Capt. Sangeeta, and many others entered, along with the WCHL staff. Maya shook my hand, placed a small Ganesha idol on my palm, smiled and said, 'Welcome back.'

They were in a hurry to take me out. I repeated the earlier instruction to the helpers who were to lift me—'Do not touch my legs. Lift me up from the shoulders and thighs. On the count of three, lift me.'

Standard procedure requires the Premier class to disembark first, followed by Economy. Instead, I saw Premier guests giving me a thumbs-up. I was put on the WCHL on the count of three. From door 1R, which is the first door on the right side of the aircraft, the ambulift was attached and I was taken in the ambulift along with Rupesh and Ms Pom. My sister and the doctors had to clear Immigration. Thankfully, Customs sanctioned special permission to clear me and Rupesh via the VVIP gate, but in all the hurry, my shoe was left behind under the seat and no one realised this until I reached home three days later.

The moment the ambulift touched the ground and the door was opened, I saw a huge crowd, including the loader, waving, clapping and holding up a banner with the words 'Welcome Back Nidhi' on it. From the ambulift I was transferred again onto the stretcher, and finally into the ambulance. Just as the doors were closing, I heard my name being called loudly and I raised my head to say thank you. At that precise moment, someone took my photo and this picture was posted on social media. Ms Pom and Rupesh sat with me in the ambulance and we were taken straight to Water Stone Hotel, where my family members were waiting. We had decided to stay in this hotel as it was simply not possible for me to go home and escape the media.

But reporters had already got the news and were waiting for me at the airport exit's VIP gate and my ambulance was chased all the way! Many reporters were standing at the hotel gate, but no one was allowed inside. The moment I reached, I could hear thundering applause outside. When the ambulance doors opened, I craned my neck and saw the people who had gathered calling out loud—'Nidhi, welcome back!'

As soon as my stretcher was lifted and placed on the ground, my mom, my daughter and son, my nephew, sister, brothers-in-law, all came close to me. I hugged all of them one by one and told them to shift me to the WCHL. Again the helpers were given the same instructions, but this time, my family members lifted me at the count of three. I saw tears in everyone's eyes. But I was bold. I knew this feeling of helplessness was temporary. The leg height of this WCHL was not adjustable, so I had no option but to leave my leg suspended downwards. I was a bit apprehensive but I didn't tell anyone. All my fear vanished, though, when I saw another banner unfurl—it said 'Welcome Nidhi'; everyone had written special words for me on it. The hotel team too had tears in their eyes. I stayed strong.

I was given a room on the ground floor so I could spend half an hour with my family, after which they would take me to Breach Candy Hospital. Once in the room, it was a reunion with my family. I hugged my children first. Vriddhi was not ready to leave me and when Vardaan hugged me, he was howling. I saw him crying so much for the first time. I was told that after they got the news of the blast, he had not cried at all.

He asked me, 'Where did you go? Why did you leave us? We will never let you go again.'

Then my mom hugged me; she too was crying. Seeing her, I couldn't control my own tears. My eldest sister, Goldy, and her husband, Satish, had come down from Delhi. Her eldest son, Sameer, had come from Doha. All of them showered their love on me. I had never seen my brothers-in-law with tears in their eyes, but this day was an exception. My brother-in-law, Nilesh, who was capturing the moment with his camera, and his wife Madhuri, came and hugged me. My mother-in-law is a very soft-hearted person, and she was too scared to hug me in that condition. She stood with her hands folded tight, trying to pluck up the courage to come close to me. She was among the last to hug me. Amarjeet jiju, who had been with me in the hospital for nearly three weeks, welcomed me back and hugged me with love. Everyone met Rupesh and congratulated him for his dedication, determination and patience. My mom told him that he has been a real hero.

By that time, Jolly di arrived from the airport, and everyone started thanking her because she had been by my side throughout for a month in the hospital and had told my family that she would bring me back with her. My mom told me, 'Don't worry, things take time but they change. Time never remains the same, just don't lose heart.'

My kids' school, NIS, had sent a huge, handmade welcome card for me with a bouquet. Actually, the kids had taken permission from the school to go late as I was arriving that day. After about half an hour, when I was asked to proceed to the hospital, everyone wanted to accompany me, but Rupesh and Amarjeet jiju decided that they would come with me for now and would later decide when and who was required to come to the hospital. When I was taken out of my room in the wheelchair, I met a few managers from my company. They said, 'It was family time first and now it's our turn to welcome and hug you.' Dr Aparna from Jet, Lama, the admin staff, and Rupesh accompanied me to the hospital. Right behind my ambulance were Amarjeet jiju and Ms Pom, and behind them were reporters in their press vans.

Inside the ambulance, on my way to the hospital, myriad thoughts crossed my mind. I had survived a bomb blast, been in a medically induced coma, undergone several surgeries, am helplessly dependent on others for my basic needs and now, I have finally reached home. It could only be called a miracle — the result of God's grace. But my story doesn't end here. It was only the beginning—of intense struggles with the body and mind, and of a brand new chapter in my book of life...

Nidhi Chaphekar

Part II

'Not all storms come to disrupt your life;
some come to clear your path.'
–ANONYMOUS

6 MAY 2016 (CONT.)

The moment we reached Breach Candy Hospital, the stretcher I was on was removed from the ambulance. Even though my face was mostly covered, a reporter managed to take a picture of me and this photo was published in a leading tabloid, *Mumbai Mirror*.

I was taken to room no. 406. The doctors informed me that they would repeat all my tests. I was quite tired, as I had been moved from stretcher to wheelchair more than six times that morning, and there was more to go.

On the first day itself, they started with the prescribed line of tests. First came the CT scans of my legs, eye orbit, and then chest X-rays. Then ECG, sonography, blood test, and finally my eyes and ears were tested. I was again taken down to another floor on the WCHL to get the tests done. Later in the afternoon, my general physician (GP), Dr Jamshed D. Sunavala, visited me, followed by Dr Darius Soonawala, the orthopaedic, and Dr Anil Tibrewala, the plastic surgeon. One by one, they all assessed my condition. In the evening, Dr Jahangir, the eye specialist, visited me. All of them said they would wait for the reports and then decide the course of treatment.

The only problem I was facing was that it was not possible for the nurses to lift me up and they had to call the ward boys. Every time I felt the urge to pee, I had to tell them to place me on the chair and that I'd remove my pants later. It was a little embarrassing for the ward boys, and, of course, for me as well. I needed two people to lift me by the arms and at least one to hold me by the butt and another one to support me from my thighs. But I had no choice. Now it was Goldy di's turn to be in the hospital with me.

🍂

7 MAY 2016

At 0615 hrs, a nurse woke me up to sponge me. They had to finish this by 0730 hrs, she said. After 0800 hrs, any of the doctors could visit. Dr Tibrewala and Dr Soonawala arrived, took my history, examined my wounds, and by now they had read my case and knew how many grafts I had had and when the last surgery had been done. They went through my latest scans as well.

Dr Darius Soonawala pronounced, 'For two to three months, we cannot touch the foot. Forget about surgery. We will take a call later about when to do a bone graft. As of now, your skin is very tender and full of wounds, so it is not advisable to do anything.'

According to the doctors, it was the most specialised kind of surgery to perform; moreover, with so many wounds and grafts it was not at all advisable at this time. It could be really risky. But the bandages had to be done every day. Dr Tibrewala told me, 'You can even take a bath, but be careful about your wounds. And the washroom you use has to be absolutely clean. You cannot put your legs down on the floor. They should be kept on a stool at a height from the floor as we don't want any germs to enter the wound. That can result in other complications like an infection in the bones.'

He added that I could go home as no surgery would take place soon. But I needed to engage a nurse so that proper care could be taken; the wounds too had to be dressed carefully. At this point of time, I had a few fractures on my left foot and many on my right foot. Some wounds were like bullet holes. Others were broad and some were open and deep. I could see them even on the back of my legs, all along the feet as well.

I told the doctor, 'If you give me permission to dress and clean the wounds myself, I will do the needful.'

At first he was taken aback by my proposal. Then he thought I was joking. But when he saw how serious I was, he replied, 'You move with such great difficulty, how would it be possible for you to dress them? Your hands and legs are swollen; it's difficult to fold your legs and reaching up to the wounds would not be possible. One would need a super-flexible body for that. Your wounds are so deep that in some places, the bones are visible and if an infection occurs, it will damage your bones.'

But I promised him that I could do as good a job as the nurses did. He still countered my request. 'It would be painful for you and you may not be able to clean them properly.'

I insisted, 'Please give me a chance at least.'

Finally he agreed. 'Okay, tomorrow is a Sunday and you will get a discharge only on Monday with the consent of the other doctors. So I'll come in the morning around ten and have a look at how you dress the wounds.'

He instructed the nurse to wait for him as today's dressing had already been done. Being a Saturday, my mom, mother-in-law, husband and kids visited me. They were astonished to see the security at the door. No one was allowed in without a pass. My family was given ten passes with everyone's names written on them. The kids were the most surprised. They kept talking to me all day. In the evening, we ordered umpteen snacks from the canteen and relished all of them. The nurses were surprised and said, 'It seems a party is on!' I wanted to make every moment special for my family as they had suffered a lot.

The next morning, at 0715 hrs, the nurse woke me up and said, 'Are you ready to take a bath in some time?'

I said, 'I am fine with that.'

Getting into the washroom was going to be a task. I requested them to get a WCHL without the hand rails, as yesterday we had the toughest time because I literally needed to be carried and couldn't simply be shifted. We called two ward boys and they first shifted me from the bed to the WCHL. Then they pushed the WCHL towards the washroom. The most important thing was to take care of my legs. Deliberately, I did not remove my bandages in the room, so that even if by mistake anyone touched me or I end up banging my leg on the door or wall, it would hurt me less. One ward boy moved ahead of me into the washroom to pull the WCHL and the other one pushed it. The washroom was spacious enough for my WCHL to be wheeled in, thank God. I told them to level the WCHL with the pot so that I could freshen up and take a bath as well. It was a challenge to move me onto the pot because the pot was next to the wall at the back and there was no space for them to stand behind me there. So they had to lift me from the side, which was very difficult. We had to call two more nurses. After struggling for about fifteen minutes, I was finally able to sit on the pot. I asked everyone to move out, but one of the nurses stayed back just for my safety. My legs were placed on a stool. I was given a special liquid disinfectant soap to shower with. My bandages were then removed. I loved taking a bath, even though my skin was peeling. I did not feel like coming out of the washroom—I was taking a shower after fifty days! I felt like rubbing my skin, but that was not allowed, of course.

Coming out of the washroom afterwards was not as difficult, but it was still a task as the washroom floor was now completely wet. I had asked for a bathrobe so that I don't feel embarrassed in front of the ward boys. We had to wait for Dr Tibrewala. He arrived soon and asked me if I was okay to start with the dressing. I took an antibacterial sheet placed on the lower part of the bed and wore surgical gloves. Then I took pieces of gauze and applied Betadine solution on them. From the inside to the outside of the wound, I cleaned and scrubbed each one, changing the bits of gauze as required. It was so painful in certain areas; tears welled up in my eyes, but I didn't cry. After that, I applied the Betadine cream, then the Bactigras dressing, covered it with the gauze and then bandaged the wounds. The most difficult part was to dress the wounds in my right leg as they were on the back of the leg too. It was tough but not impossible.

When I was done, the doctor clapped and patted me and said, 'You are a real sherni! Punjab da puttar!' He added that from now onwards he would call me Gabbar Singh. I laughed out loud! Dr Tibrewala had been patient as the entire process had taken me a lot of time. He told my family members that he was fine with me dressing my wounds myself. I smiled and thanked him for his confidence in me and promised that I won't let him down at any point.

My family decided I would first stay at Jolly di's place. There were many reasons for this. Jolly di has a bigger house, so my mom and Goldy di could easily be accommodated. I would get a separate room; and without Jolly di's permission, no one could enter that room, so I would be safe from infections. There is no elevator in the building I stay in and my house is on the fourth floor. It would be very difficult for anyone to make me climb four floors. She also said she would be a bit strict with me as far as timings were concerned and would be able to keep an eye on me at all times in her house. The doctors had warned that it was very important for me to rest and be given proper, timely care. The slightest negligence could lead to a big blunder.

Rupesh was to go and buy a suitable WCHL for my use. I had told him it should be small in size and have a movable armrest. In the afternoon, Dr Darius Soonawala arrived and said, 'We will start with the physiotherapy, so call a good physiotherapist home. Make sure you tell him or her that you cannot put pressure on the legs.' He added that a little pressure could be applied on my left leg, though only while doing the exercises. But I shouldn't ever try to put my right leg down on the floor.

❧

I felt great this morning, as I was going home. My husband and brother-in-law had bought a walker and a WCHL. I was discharged by 1130 hrs and was put in the ambulance. As I neared my sister's building, I wondered if people would see me and express pity. But to my surprise, no one was there! I was so thankful to God because every time I'd been lifted by people to place me onto the wheelchair, I had felt embarrassed.

My nephew Akshit (who is also a pilot), was there to receive me. They shifted me from the stretcher to the WCHL and we went up to the sixth floor. My mom was ready and waiting at the door with a puja thali. She did the aarti and kissed my forehead. My sister welcomed me home. My room had been readied. My mom gave me a bundle of currency notes, and when I asked her about it, she simply said, 'It's a gift for your rebirth. Keep it with you.' I felt great, as if I had come back from a long war on the battlefield. Goldy di also presented me with an envelope full of money. I received lots of gifts from the rest of my family as well. We ate homemade food and then I slept for a while.

When it was time for Rupesh to go back home, I told him, 'Before you go, I'll go to the washroom, so that Goldy di and I get a hang of it right now with you around. At night it will be just the two of us—Goldy di and I—to manage all this.' He agreed and went to the drawing room.

I shifted from the bed to the WCHL almost on my own with little support from anyone. The WCHL stood about six to eight inches lower than the height of the bed. My sister took me to the toilet. I raised myself by letting my weight rest on my arms. I felt great, but when I returned to the room, I was not able to get back onto the bed. Goldy di then decided to lift me from the back with her hands under my shoulders.

Now to lift a sixty-kilogram adult is no joke. But she was very confident she could do it herself. However, while lifting and turning, she lost her balance and I almost fell on the floor. To my luck, I had put more than half my weight on the bed and was holding onto its edges. She screamed, though, and everyone got alarmed and rushed into my room. Rupesh and my brother-in-law lifted me up then. I felt a strain in my right leg, and everyone started crying. I told them, 'this is the first lesson I have learned – to be more independent, because the confidence you have in yourself, no one would have that. So from tomorrow onwards, I will drag myself onto the bed, and maybe for a few days I'll need a bit of help. But don't worry.'

My family wanted to hire a full-time helper for me. I insisted that if they did so, I would break down. They should let me manage things, as all this while I hadn't been allowed to do anything myself. I explained to them that the worst that could happen was another fracture. 'But don't let me stop trying. I know I can do it.' I assured them I would be careful. After a lot of debating and discussing, finally everybody agreed.

It was then that we realised that my special shoe was missing. We immediately called the airline manager for Lost and Found, informed my department head and also sent an email. It took them two days to locate it and have it delivered to us.

My sister was to sleep with me in the same room. She is a very deep sleeper, so her only worry was that given my nature, I might try things on my own. She extracted a promise from me to wake her if I needed anything at all. We laughed, hugged and kissed each other and slept comfortably that night.

❧

10 MAY 2016

It was the first day I took a bath without the help of the hospital staff. I asked Goldy di to fill a bucket with water and add some antibacterial solution, while Jolly di got fresh neem leaves, as neem has antibacterial properties. She added the water in which she had boiled the leaves to the bath water. Placing my legs on a stool, I sat on the pot and took a shower. What a wonderful feeling it was!

But now how would I get back onto the WCHL, I thought, as

the bathroom was completely wet. So we spread a towel on the WCHL, locked it as close to the pot as possible; I then held on to my walker and put pressure on it. My sister lifted me from behind. I raised myself enough to cover the short distance from the pot to the WCHL. To shift from the WCHL to the bed, I dragged myself up with my elbows and rolled my body on to the bed, assisted by my sister. It was perfect. I did not allow my legs to touch the bed.

The next challenge was to dress the wounds. I wore my surgical gloves and placed a fresh, clean dressing pad on the bed. I started cleaning the wounds with Betadine solution. Then I applied the Betadine cream. The nurses in Charleroi used to apply a white wax-like ointment with a soaked piece of gauze, which they gave me when I left. I applied that too and the dry gauze pieces, and lastly, the bandages. Oh my God, it took me more than an hour to dress all my wounds!

In the same way, I had to then apply cream all over my body for the scars, burnt skin, patches, grafts and removed skin. I only needed help to apply the cream on my back. I wore my compression gloves. The doctors treating me in India had given me compression stockings for my legs, and wearing these was another Herculean task. They were super tight as that would aid good blood circulation, reduce swelling and the chances of blood clot formation in my legs. I was advised to wear them for at least six months or until I became fully mobile. (I wore them for ten months.) Goldy di asked me to wear a thin polythene bag around my feet before putting on the stockings, so that it would then be easier for me to pull up the stockings. On top of all this, the dressings were causing a hindrance and to make it worse, the cream applied on my legs was sticking to the stockings. What an ordeal it all was! The whole process, right from taking a bath to getting fully dressed, took more than two hours. By the end of it, I was so exhausted!

Afterwards, I had some coconut water and breakfast. I was very hungry by then; I hadn't expected the cleaning and dressing to be so time-consuming. Today the kids were supposed to come directly from school to meet me. So I took an hour's nap. By 1130 hrs, my physiotherapist Sabah arrived.

She went through my scans, X-ray reports, took my full history, and said, 'Okay, so let's start.' We did some exercises for the legs and hands. She observed that the muscles were very weak in both my legs and hands, but the legs were worse.

❧

11 MAY 2016

My new cell phone had just been activated. My earlier phone had exploded in the blast on 22 March 2016. This new phone had been given to me as a bravery award from one of my friends. It came with a stylo, which was so thoughtful as I would not have been able to use the touchscreen with my gloves on. I was very excited to see a phone in my hand after such a long time!

Today I thought of having my breakfast first, before the two hours of bandaging and putting on stockings. If I were to be true to myself, I was enjoying my independence. The moment I finished dressing up, I thought of calling my father. That's when I realised that I had no saved phone numbers. And so, the day started with adding phone numbers in my phone, one by one. It was a very irritating process because the moment I was about to save a number, I would get a call from someone.

Everybody wanted to come and see me because the news of my arrival in India had reached them through either the newspapers or WhatsApp. My family decided to set down strict timings for visitors. In the mornings, I would be very busy with the dressing and after six in the evening, I had my physiotherapy sessions. So we decided on 1530 hrs to 1730 hrs as the visitors' time slot, and explained to each person painstakingly as to why such timings were necessary and why they shouldn't feel bad. I didn't realise how the day passed.

❧

Today was the first time colleagues from Jet Airways visited me at home. I also got my special shoe delivered through them. I was confused as to how they would react. At first sight, the tears would begin to flow. But I was in a very difficult situation because I was sitting on a WCHL and couldn't even stand, so how would I wipe their tears or give them a shoulder to lean on? Things were very difficult. As far as my family was concerned, I could understand, but when it came to friends and colleagues, it was a little difficult because you don't know how they feel about you. Either they feel sorry for you or pity you. The most difficult task for me was to narrate the entire story—how it happened, where I was, what exactly I experienced, who took me to the chair, when I reached the hospital, what all I saw, on and on. Somewhere within me, every time I narrated the story, I would be reminded of the ill-fated day all over again.

In the evening, my physiotherapist told me, 'Monday onwards, we will exercise with a weight added to each leg... it will help improve muscle strength.'

She also got a one kilogram dumbbell for me to hold during hand exercises. (I couldn't hold the dumbbell tight as my hands were not able to close around it fully.) I actually gave her a look when she said this because I had never been to a gym and neither had I ever done weight-training exercises. I used to think of it as a waste of time because if you do regular work at home, your physical exercise for the day is done. But this is actually not true. One should exercise daily, for a few minutes at least. She taught me how to sit and stand (leaning on the walker and putting my left foot down halfway towards the floor) with the help of a walker. I would cry out in pain. My arms didn't have the strength to take the full weight of my body. I felt I would fall.

❧

13 MAY 2016

It being a Friday, the kids were supposed to come and stay with me for two nights. I was very excited. I finished my morning routine by 1130 hrs. And then the phone calls started, as many people wanted to visit. A few just wouldn't listen to my protests and said they were coming to meet me after lunch. Messages started pouring in. So I did something to make communication easier. I updated my status on WhatsApp with the words: 'Himmat e mardaan, madad e khuda (when men show courage, God sends help). Please send me your number as I've lost all contacts. God bless you all for your wishes and prayers, blessings always count.'

Believe you me, one by one the messages began flowing. I didn't have enough time to feed in all the numbers! My sisters and mom would scold me, asking me to rest and sleep, threatening they would hide my phone. Whoever came to see me brought fruits or dry fruits, cakes or cookies, chocolates or sweets, sometimes with flowers.

Today I got three bouquets. The kids were having fun too. Before I knew it, it was 1800 hrs — time for another session of physiotherapy. I was weak and slow in my movements, but I knew that only exercise would improve my condition, however painful it may feel.

Jolly di would give me the best of nutritious food. She would feed me coconut water, shakes, fruits, sprouts, salads, soups, and juices. My mom would give me a glass of warm turmeric milk before bed. I would be so stuffed that I wouldn't even be able to lift myself from the bed or change sides at night!

❦

14 MAY 2016

Since it was a Saturday, most offices were closed. And there were too many people dropping by to meet me. No one was allowed to enter my room. So I had to go out and meet them. I sat on the WCHL for two hours at a stretch and my buttocks started aching.

I would raise my legs and keep them on top of the table with a cushion underneath for support because it was very difficult to remain sitting on the WHCL like that for so long. Also, my kids were at home and all their attention was directed towards me. They wanted to know what people talked to me about, why all of them came to meet me and what they felt about me. It was a very unusual situation. I could see the pain in their eyes. They would walk away from the room when they heard questions like—Do you want me to push your WCHL ahead? Shall I get you something? Who puts you on the WCHL? Who gives you a bath? How about your wounds? When would you be able to at least stand? How long would it take you to walk? You must be scared of flying now?

On and on it went. Most times, I would reply that I did things on my own. But somewhere down the line, I realised that I needed to set an example for everyone, especially my children. And today I got the chance to prove that nothing is impossible. I have always been a confident person, but this incident had made me more confident, and so I resolved, no matter what, from today onwards I would do everything on my own.

I started with pushing the WCHL on my own, taking the help of walls, cupboards and doors to move in and out of rooms. I had to take the help of all the furniture and objects in the house as my WCHL was very sleek and had tiny wheels. So there was no room for me to wheel it around. I was not allowed to go into the kitchen but I insisted on being allowed to just take something out of the refrigerator. I tried to go to the washroom, but I still couldn't manage to move the WCHL in and out as the space inside was not enough to allow easy movement.

When the physiotherapist came in the evening, I asked her casually, 'How many steps today?'

She was surprised and happy to see my eagerness, and replied, 'Just take one step.'

She had taught me earlier how to manage my weight on the walker. She told me to use my left leg to just push at the ground a bit, while on my right leg the shoe was always on and lifted, which would ensure I didn't have to bear any impact even if it touched the floor by mistake. Today my arms were shaking. I couldn't lift my body, but somehow we managed to take the first step. I think it is all in our mind. Once you get rid of your inhibitions, you become a winner. I also told Sabah that we need to start working on my right eye. She asked me to perform certain eye exercises every two hours.

❧

We got some bad news too today. Goldy di's guru, Sardar Hardev Singh ji (the spiritual guru of the Sant Nirankari Mission), passed away in a car accident in Montreal. Goldy di cried the entire night. She had gone to Babaji's house in Delhi to seek his blessings for me while I was in the hospital. We all consoled her. Satish jiju went to Delhi the very next day because he came to know that Babaji's final rites would be performed there. I asked Goldy di to go too, but she was in two minds. Eventually, she decided to stay back with me.

❧

15 MAY 2016

I started shifting from the WCHL to the sofa and from there, back to the WCHL. It was very challenging, but I made it look as if it were easy. I started believing more in myself and gained from my mental strength. It is said that courage, in simple words, is an act of bravery. It is about your will power plus the powerful word— 'belief'. Every effort and intention of ours needs courage. This new desire for independence in me was my way of regaining my self-confidence, so that no one, be it my family members or outsiders, should pity me.

As it was a Sunday, there were so many relatives who came to see me from far-off places. Seeing me smiling and giggling, each one of them said the same thing—'We thought we'd have to give you a shoulder to cry on or boost your morale, but it is very surprising that you are boosting our morale instead!'

'We have learnt a lot from your behaviour.'

'You don't even look sick. You are behaving better than a normal, healthy, fit person would.'

'Nidhi, you are a real hero, you are a superwoman! You are our idol and an icon we all should look up to.'

My sister-in-law Inu's father too said, 'We salute your courage and resilience,' and he actually saluted me.

After everyone left, I sat pondering—if my behaviour alone could make such a great impression on people, then I could do more to spread the message of hope and faith and maybe I could even change the way many people think. If you ask me, my nature is to be positive at all times. God has given me a tough path to walk on, but with that He has given me strength and courage. It all depends on how we want to walk our paths, slow or fast.

I was really happy today because earlier, I had heard such words of encouragement and appreciation only from my family members. I always felt they were saying these things just to lift my spirits, to soothe my heart, but when many from the outside world also had only praise for me, and not because I was close to or known to them, I realised it was all about my positive thinking and my acceptance of what had happened... my basic outlook towards life had never changed. As they say, failure and tragedy happen to us in life. When they do, there are only two ways to react—either choose to brood and fall into self-destruction, or use the challenge to find your inner strength.

When my physiotherapist arrived, I took one step and asked her, 'Do you want me to take more?'

But she said, 'Let's rise step by step. How come today you did all the exercises without taking any break?'

Earlier, I would take a ten-second break after every two exercises. I realised that my mind was happy and I was thinking of the inspiring words everybody said to me, and that just showed that it's all in our mind really. I had taken charge of my situation, I knew. It was a beautiful day indeed.

❧

Nidhi Chaphekar

I was expecting my friend Rohit to visit. I called up the physiotherapist and requested her to come early. By now a few journalists had visited my Andheri house to find out when they could interview me. They had asked my family to give them the address of my sister's place where I was staying, so that they could publish an article. I asked Rupesh to tell them that we would inform all of them shortly.

Rohit arrived armed with a lot of gifts. Later, by 1950 hrs, Rupesh joined us, followed by my sister-in-law, brother-in-law and some of my sister's friends. All of them had been invited for a celebration. Rohit had brought a bottle of wine and after announcing that 'this is for Nidhi's victory,' he asked me to open it. Sitting on my WCHL, I uncorked the bottle of red wine to a huge round of applause.

Being a devotee of Lord Krishna, Rohit also gifted me an idol of the God.

What a memorable evening it turned out to be, with everybody sharing my joy and praising my positive attitude. Jolly di and Amarjeet jiju shared their experience with the others, explaining that not even once had I cried about what had happened to me. Even the doctors and nurses used to tell them that I was one patient who was always smiling and talking, that I had endless positivity in me. Some nurses and even the doctors had said that in their experience, they had never seen a patient like me. I was not informed of all this directly, of course, as they always thought, *let the world tell her this*. I would feel great whenever my family shared these things.

※

17 MAY 2016

I had to get up early today, at 0730 hrs, because a lab professional was coming home to take my blood sample at 0800 hrs. And my God, I was stunned looking at how many small bottles of blood he filled! I told myself, I'll eat extra well today in order to compensate for this loss and regain by tomorrow all the blood I've given away, ha ha! Then I had to go for a sonography, an ECG and other tests.

In the sonography room, the bed was too high and they had to call four boys in to help. I felt a little helpless but promised myself that I would gain more strength in my arms to climb onto the bed on my own the next time. I had to do the sonography as I had not got my period for three months now. I was worried about it. The report was fine; in fact, I had been told by the doctors at Charleroi that it may take a year for my body system to get back to normal.

In the evening, I was astonished when I saw that my physiotherapist had brought more weights for my legs and arms. She played a very important role in my life. She was also a tough cookie. She understood my nature, loved my fighting spirit and therefore, always gave me challenging tasks. She had even got foam strips that acted as padding (under the weights) in order to ensure the weights don't hurt and worsen any of my wounds. Oh my God, I couldn't lift my legs more than six or seven times, but I had to do all the exercises, ten times each. It took me more than an hour to finish.

Then it was time to take a few steps. The moment she removed my weights, I took a deep breath. She asked me whether it was aching.

I replied with a saying in Hindi, '*Mard ko kabhi dard nahi hota!*' (A man never feels pain.)

She had a hearty laugh. 'But you are a woman,' came her response.

I said, 'I am a lady but I have the strength of a man, so two-in-one.'

❦

18 MAY 2018

I had to travel to Breach Candy Hospital again for my fortnightly follow-up. It was raining cats and dogs. Goldy di wanted to join, but I told her I would manage. Rupesh and I left after lunch at noon. I got a little wet but thanked God that I was fully covered, so the water did not touch my skin. One by one, I went through my appointments with the doctors. The first appointment was at 1330 hrs and the last one was at 1630 hrs.

Once everything was done, I told Rupesh to rush to the canteen as I was starving! I ordered a masala dosa, an uttappam and a sandwich with tea — all for myself! Rupesh thought I would share the food but when it arrived, I told him, 'All this is for me.' He was dumbfounded! He gave me an accusing smile, as if to say, *I have been with you since morning. I first drove from our house to your sister's house, and then from there I brought you to the hospital!*

By the time his order arrived, I had already finished my food, but I did finally end up sharing the masala dosa with him. It was 1745 hrs by the time we finished.

Once home, everyone was eager to know all the details. I told them about what the doctor had said — I had been given some medicine to increase my haemoglobin and some multi-vitamins. The physician would review my condition after fifteen days, but all the medicines were to be taken for one month at least.

The orthopaedic told me that my wounds were still healing, so we must wait.

The plastic surgeon and skin specialist saw the wounds and was happy as there was no infection, and they were healing well. He told me I was doing a superb job of dressing the wounds daily.

The eye specialist said my eyesight was good, and although the metal piece was still in the orbit of my eye, unless it posed any immediate danger, no surgery was required. Nothing could be done to rectify the size of the right eye. I needed to keep getting a check-up every three months.

And the ear surgeon had not been able to come to the hospital that day.

After narrating all this to my family, I had dinner and slept early, as I was exhausted and feeling sick after the long day and car drive.

❧

19 MAY 2016

My mom had to return to our hometown in Punjab. Mom and Goldy di declared that since they had been here with me for fifteen days now, they would call my niece Mansi — my third sister Meenu's daughter — to take care of me for a while, especially since her final year exams were winding up the next day.

She was super excited to hear from us. So her ticket to Mumbai was booked for 21 May. Mom and Goldy di were to return to Amritsar on the 22nd. I told Mansi to get four or five types of sweets with her. I simply love gorging on sweets and Punjab is famous for them.

I wanted to spend as much time as possible with Mom before she left. Today I took two steps and my mom was immediately concerned, 'Be a little slow, please! Don't run! I know you can, but be careful. The body can only take a little exertion, but you are giving it too much pressure...'

❦

20 MAY 2016

Both my sisters went shopping today. They got me two new sets of nightwear, and that made me feel so good. After months, I saw something new for me to wear. I wanted to try them on to see how they looked, but Mom and Goldy di were firm and said, 'Wear them tomorrow, or else again today you will twist and roll on the bed, which may affect your wounds.' I didn't listen to either of them and went ahead and tried out both nightsuits anyway. They suited me well.

❦

21 MAY 2016

Throughout the day, Mom kept looking at the clock because my niece was to land at around 1800 hrs. On the other hand, seeing my mom and sister pack their bags was disheartening. I made funny faces to hide the sadness in my heart. But my mom understood, of course. She held me close in a tight hug. We both cried. Whenever she came to visit me in Mumbai, I would see her off at the airport or walk her till the door of the aircraft, and sometimes accompany her into the aircraft if I was operating it. And whenever I felt like meeting her, I would take a flight to Amritsar and spend one or two days with her. But I knew that this time the gap would widen. I promised her that as always, I'd visit them during Diwali — and that I'd be walking on my own and not using the WCHL or the walker.

'that's my girl!' she beamed.

When the doorbell rang, I told her, 'Let me open the door today.'

I wheeled myself towards the door. They were all surprised to see me opening the door. Rupesh said, 'Wow, that's my baby!'

Mansi, my niece, stood there staring at me. She dropped the bags she was holding and hugged me tight. 'Maasi! It's so good to see you back!' she gushed.

We chatted till late night.

❧

22 MAY 2016

My mom had set the alarm for 0400 hrs as her flight was scheduled to depart at 0605 hrs. I too woke up with the alarm, but she asked me to sleep some more.

Until the time Mom and Goldy di settled in their seats on the plane, I was awake and on a call with them. My mom had taken many pictures of me to show my dad and the rest of the family back in Amritsar — many of my family members had not seen me yet. It was decided that one by one, they would all come and be with me until I recovered fully.

Mansi couldn't sleep the whole night. It was the first time that she had seen me dressing my wounds myself. She also got scared seeing the mask I wore to bed. She was finding it all akin to a nightmare, but she remained quiet.

❧

Mansi woke up with the question – 'Why didn't you keep a nurse?'

I told her, 'Well, it is only because it would help me analyse my situation better and identify where the swelling and pain has reduced by applying the same kind of pressure. And most of all, I pass my time well and gain more confidence by doing it myself.'

She persisted, 'But don't you feel scared?'

'No, not at all. The nurses who do it are also human beings, so why can't we do it ourselves? The only difference is that it is their profession and they have trained their mind. Yes, training is required. And I am fully trained, having watched them do it for thirty-five days.'

My mom had told Mansi to ensure I am kept hydrated by giving me lime water, juice or squash. So every hour, I was given a big glass of one of the drinks. Mom had instructed her to not allow me to do anything as otherwise, my fingertips could get dirty with dust and moisture. So I was being fed everything. I had not made or eaten any food with my own hands. I enjoyed the pampering!

But in these fifteen days after I'd come home, I had not yet learned how to go to the toilet or for a bath by using the WCHL without anyone's help. I had tried pushing my wheelchair to the washroom but got stuck, because the space inside was not enough to roll it back out or even turn it another way. So normally, I would be wheeled into the bathroom by someone who would help me shift onto the pot where I could sit and take a bath. It would only be to wash my back that I would call for help, as I couldn't yet use my hands very well. Once I was done, I would call them again to get the WCHL inside. I wanted to stop this practice. I wanted to be independent. So I kept trying. It was just like trying to drive your car slowly forward and sideways when it gets sandwiched between cars parked on either side. I had to try many times before I finally managed to get the WCHL in and out successfully.

❧

24 MAY 2016

I told Mansi, 'Let's try going to the washroom with the walker.'

With great difficulty, I sat on the pot without letting my right leg touch the floor. I was wearing the shoe on my left leg so that it wouldn't hurt much. I really needed to build back the strength in my arms, but how could I expect to regain it in a month's time? I realised I couldn't get up. I tried, but in vain. Later, I called Mansi and requested her to either push me from behind or pull me up. Because I couldn't put my right leg down, even that was not possible and for nearly ten minutes, we both were stuck.

Finally I had to shift onto the WCHL. The height of the WCHL was almost the same as that of the pot, so I could easily switch by just shifting my butt from one to the other. I was very disheartened; at least my arms should carry my weight, I thought.

In the evening, I narrated the whole incident to my physiotherapist. She said, 'Let's see how we can work on it.'

She asked me to put weight on my upper arms but I was not able to as I was tired. She assured me that I'd be able to do it in two weeks' time. But I'd have to keep trying because my muscles were very weak.

❧

25 MAY 2016

I woke up with an upset stomach. I didn't feel like waking Mansi. I decided to go to the washroom on my own. So I pulled up the WCHL parked next to my bed and with great difficulty, I managed to sit on it. I pulled myself forward holding on to the cupboard, pushed away from the bed and finally reached the door of the washroom. I somehow managed to get in, but wondered how to turn the WCHL. So I tried to hold on to the edge of the sink, the walls and with some slow skidding of the WCHL, I eventually turned it towards the pot. Going in had been okay, but now how do I come out, I wondered. Again, with a lot of effort, I sat on it in the same way, and pushing the brakes myself and then releasing them, I made it to the door. The room's floor was at a slight elevation, about an inch above the washroom's floor level, so I had to push and pull, and finally about half an hour later, I did it! It felt like I'd won a marathon!

When I rolled over from the WCHL onto the bed, Mansi woke up and was surprised to see me getting into bed. She asked what had happened. When I told her, she got very angry and shouted at me.

I said, 'Relax, all is good!' But she was still miffed with me.

❦

Today many colleagues came to see me. Looking at my strength, everybody saluted me! I really liked the compliments I got. Almost everyone asked, although with much hesitation, whether they could take a picture with me. I smiled and asked them why they wanted a picture. They assured me they wouldn't circulate it on any media platform, and that it was just for themselves.

Whenever anyone would come home to meet me, at first they wouldn't know how to react, whether to smile or to feel sad. But I would always keep smiling. Not even once did I break down. I never wanted to. I told myself, *be the way you are.*

❦

26 MAY 2016

It was the last day of school for my children. Tomorrow onwards they would have holidays. Last year, I had promised them that I would take them this year to the United States, but it was not to be. I told them that if they wanted to go spend some time at their uncle's place there, I would make arrangements, but they said they wanted to be with me and once I was fit again, we would all go together. I kissed them both and thought about how much they were sacrificing in their lives just to make me feel comfortable. I asked them to keep themselves busy with some activities, knowing that I would not be able to do much with them.

The kids told me, 'We are going to pack our bags and will stay with you at Maasi's house.'

I was happy but also a little worried because one never knows — sometimes, unknowingly, because of our actions or words, kids get the wrong impression. I decided to be extra cautious.

Rupesh would come every day to see me. He would have dinner with us and go back at night. I discussed my thoughts with him. He pacified me, 'they are grown up and have a clear picture of you and your strength. Never hide anything; just let things be natural and all will be well.'

I told him how my arms shivered when I took steps because I would put my entire weight on the arms and it was not possible to do so much in one go. He said simply, 'Go slow.'

I started putting a little weight on the left foot, but because of the fractures, it would give me unbearable pain every time it touched the ground. I was unable to make a tight fist, so my grip was not good either.

✤

27 MAY 2016

In the afternoon, the kids arrived at Jolly di's house with two suitcases full of their stuff.

A group of ladies from Jolly di's locality wanted to meet me and they all came over at around four in the evening and had tea with us. They spoke so highly of me!

One of them said that if she had been in this state, she would have been depressed.

Another said, 'Your smile never reflects anything of what you've gone through.'

Yet another said, 'Your confidence to deal with it is amazing. The courage you show with your thoughts is pure and positive. Your face may not look good to others, but your eyes shine and have such deep beauty, they bring glory to you.'

My daughter was listening to all this. When my physiotherapist came home that evening, she questioned her. 'Is there any improvement in my mom's condition?'

My physiotherapist said, 'Last time, she took two steps.'

'today she will take three,' said Vriddhi, with pride in her voice. And so today, I took three steps.

'taking a step' meant leaning on the walker, then putting the entire weight on my resting arms, twisting the walker forward and just resting my left foot on the floor to bear some weight. The touching and resting of the foot was counted as one step.

Vriddhi told me that today onwards, she would sleep with me at night. But the worrisome issue was that she has the habit of moving about a lot and inadvertently hitting others on the bed with her legs while sleeping.

So I told her, 'If you can keep in mind that you have to stay in one position and if you move, you can hurt me, you are more likely to stay put in one place.'

Nobody was ready to allow Vriddhi to sleep next to me at night, but I made her confident enough to believe in herself.

At night, she slept next to me and until morning, she slept in the same position. But she did get scared when she saw me sleeping with the silicone mask on. She said, 'Maa, I took deep breaths and prayed to God but did not disturb you. You looked quite scary.'

I decided that I would wear the mask only after she would be fast asleep, but I did not tell her anything. I knew that many questions were going to pop up—Why do you have to wear the mask? For how long do you have to wear it? How will it help you? I simply told her that it was only required for a few days to help my skin heal.

Three or four days went by with no one realising how the days passed. And during one of those days, I received another pair of gloves from Charleroi. With the children at home, there was plenty to talk about and do, and then every day from four to six in the evening, the house was filled with visitors. The kids were loving it because the guests would bring all sorts of goodies! Also, we ran out of vases and corners to put all the flowers that people brought.

By this time, I could take a few baby steps but after that, I would not be up till the morning — so exhausted I would be.

One thing I was thoroughly enjoying was the sight of my children getting motivated by how their mom could do what was considered impossible for her to do quickly. It was a valuable lesson for them that nothing is impossible in life.

The word 'no' does not exist in my dictionary. I love taking on challenges and never look back. I do not want any child to learn to say: 'I can't'; I would only want them to learn the power of 'I can'. Never to give up in life is my mantra, for things turn around when we show courage and a fighting spirit.

❧

31 MAY 2016

A day spent in the hospital for my fortnightly review, meeting all the doctors.

This time, Mansi wheeled me around the hospital. When I met Dr Darius Soonawala and Dr Anil Tibrewala, I asked them whether it would be okay if I tried to move around with the help of a walker, putting weight on both my legs to make it a little easy for me to walk.

My physiotherapist Sabah had told me that when a person has a foot fracture and they don't have the option of putting on a plaster, one of the ways to make the healing process faster is to put slight pressure on it. She had told me to ask the doctor if I could put a little weight on the right leg with the shoe on. Dr Darius Soonawala was horrified at my plans and said an outright no.

'But you are not allowed to put your leg down!' he exclaimed.

I told him, 'I need to stop these injections for blood thinning and I want to be independent.'

When I asked him the reason for him saying no to my idea, he said, 'the heel bone in your right foot is hollow and there are fractures, with some small bones missing. So your foot may not be able to take the weight you put on it and could collapse completely.

Any excess weight may further rupture your bones, and that would totally crush the bones.'

I had persisted. 'What then?'

'then we have to cut open your leg, do the required surgeries, maybe put in a rod, and perhaps even other parts of the body might require further surgeries,' he had replied. And that would lead to further complications.

But that means we do have a way to handle the worst, I thought to myself.

I requested him again, 'then let me try it... as we do seem to have a solution to the problem.'

I promised him I wouldn't put much weight on the right leg. I would bear most of the weight on my arms and the left leg would bear the rest.

He finally agreed, 'Okay, but be very, very careful.' He then proceeded to show how it is done and asked me to do it in the exact same manner, saying, 'It should be just a touch of your right leg.'

I was relieved. It was such a beautiful feeling of satisfaction, being able to do this on my own.

❦

One thing that was extremely difficult was getting into the car and getting out of it. The last time, Rupesh had got a car which was lower in height but this time, it was an SUV which was much higher. Constantly having to be pushed from the back, for me to put my weight on the walker was very frustrating. I decided that today, I would do what I hadn't been able to so far...

❦

We were back home by 1800 hrs, but there was no physiotherapy scheduled as I knew I would be exhausted after the hospital visit. I recollected what the doctors in Belgium had said about the special shoe given to me to wear on my right foot—'this shoe is for your protection, but in an emergency, if at all you have to put your weight on it, make sure you do it just a little bit...'

And so, I put on the shoe on my right foot, and on the other foot, I used a slipper with a three-inch hard foam padding to match the height of the shoe. Then keeping in mind the doctors' advice, I put half my body weight on the upper arms and a little on my left leg, with the toe of the right foot touching the ground just a bit. After a few attempts, I managed to take my first step. I was shivering from the severe pain. But *this* was my first proper step.

I had done it! I felt elated! I walked using the tactic he had taught me. Everybody pepped me up with their praise. We would celebrate even such small but momentous achievements.

❦

I JUNE 2016

A new month began. It was a new beginning for me as well. I had started going to the washroom by myself, using the walker, a few times a day.

Sabah got a gift for me today — a thera band (a wide elastic band available in varying strengths, used to build muscle strength) and said, 'Every day with exercise, this band will finally break and then I'll reward you.'

My immediate response was, 'How? Why would it break?'

'When you pull it every day, the elasticity will gradually decrease and as a result, in a month's time, it will break,' she explained.

Now that she had said it would last a month, I wanted to reach the goal faster. Given my nature, I wanted to take up the challenge and hold the band for longer stretches.

Initially, I just couldn't do it. It was so tough! But Sabah would push me like a teacher, urging me to keep increasing the count bit by bit, every day. Four days into this routine, I felt like I had exhausted all my strength! She told me it would be painful for a few more days, but strength would build up in my muscles eventually.

❦

5 JUNE 2016

My third sister, Meenu, arrived today. She has a tender heart. She almost stopped breathing when she saw me. It took some effort to convince her that I was doing fine. She loves me so much, she kissed me and cried like a baby.

My mom had sent with Meenu two bottles of homemade almond squash, a few varieties of sweets and some packets of Indian rusk (my favourite tea-time snack). I was thrilled seeing all the goodies. Rupesh teased me saying, 'You are in too much demand!'

In the evening, Sabah realised that my left leg was swollen because of the extra pressure and stress; she recommended two days of complete rest. Dr Darius Soonawala also got worried and asked me to apply cold compresses and to keep my leg elevated. Sabah got me an ankle band to wear (which I still use) so that the swelling would subside. I was a little worried because I had just about begun taking a few steps and here I was being advised complete rest again! I felt like I was back to square one.

I also wanted to reduce my dependence on painkillers. All in all, I was taking around eighteen tablets a day, including multivitamins. I was determined to reduce my medication.

❧

6 JUNE 2016

I discontinued two painkillers. When I had asked my physician whether I could drop the painkillers, he said, 'Discontinue one every week, and see how your body reacts and feels. If you feel fine, keep reducing the medication every week, but if your body can't take it, don't stress it. Stick to whatever medicines you're taking then.'

By the evening, my body started acting like a fresh wound. The next day, I got fever. But even then, I refused to resume the painkillers I'd stopped taking. Since my swollen feet required rest, I hadn't done physiotherapy. I had no energy to even sit up. My eyes were burning with the pain. I read up on the Internet to understand what was happening. It was clear that this was a withdrawal symptom. When you give up any drug you have been used to taking, you face such withdrawal symptoms, but with time, they go away. I had not told my family about it. If I had, they would surely have forced me to have it again. So now everyone was worried about my condition and asked me to contact the doctor. I told them that the doctor said it could be because of the weather change.

It took me a week to adjust and come back to normalcy. And as soon as I was okay, I decided this week, again, I would discontinue two painkillers.

❧

13 JUNE 2016

I discontinued two more tablets. I was a bit worried but thought to myself, *it is not something that's absolutely essential for me; they are just painkillers after all*. But oh my God, the next evening I couldn't do anything! My legs and shoulders experienced excruciating pain.

Sabah figured out that something seemed fishy. She asked, 'Is there something wrong with you? Are you not feeling okay? Something seems amiss here. Are you taking your medicines properly?'

❧

As my passport had been damaged in the bomb blast, I had applied for a new one. For this, I had to personally go to the passport office today at 1130 hrs for the renewal procedures. I had no energy, but I had no choice either. There was a special lane for those who have special needs, so I could get inside without any delay. Rupesh would wheel me to each counter. First, I had to complete my biometric test. But my fingers posed a bit of a problem; they were soft and unable to apply the required pressure because of which the system couldn't scan them easily. After clearing this step, it was time to have my photograph taken by their system's webcam. I was a little embarrassed as the picture showed all my marks and scars, and the defect in my eye made it look half its normal size. The officer on duty knew my story, so I requested him if I could give a recent passport size photograph that was taken just a few days before the blast. Thankfully, he accepted my request. Within thirty minutes, all the formalities had been completed. There were systems in place for people with special needs, and I appreciated that we could take the help of those facilities at least in such places.

❧

16 JUNE 2016

Mansi was to travel to Delhi for her first job interview tomorrow, and thereon back to Amritsar. She is a chirpy soul, and I never knew how time flew during her stay with us. I was sad she was leaving me but also happy she was going for her first job interview. She was always on her toes for me, enthusiastically ready to try out my ideas.

Today, she went shopping and bought a lot of stuff for herself and gifts for me too. I told her, 'I should be the one gifting you stuff!'

She quipped, 'I like being with you. Spending time with you is my reward, so just chill, Maasi.'

I felt so good. God bless her. I really had a great time with her.

The next morning, she left the house at 0430 hrs and I stayed awake with her mom, Meenu, until Mansi boarded the flight. Meenu was feeling a little low, though she was making an effort to not show it. But I could understand how she was feeling. It is only natural for a mother to feel emotional... such is the beauty of a mother-daughter bond. The whole house was quiet for some time. Once my kids woke up, the atmosphere became a bit lively, but it was still sombre. Sometimes we don't realise the value of what we have, but when the person who brightens up our days is not around, we realise their worth.

❧

Nidhi Chaphekar

I did my physiotherapy as usual but was quiet throughout the session. I was thinking of Mansi as right after my physiotherapy, she would be ready with a milkshake for me. But before that she would feed me nuts.

Today, for the first time, I took twenty steps! Like I said, I enjoy taking up challenges. And that's how while doing my stretching exercises, the thera band tore and hit my right hand. I was only too happy, of course, but Sabah was worried as the band had hit my hand's graft. I told her it's okay, that I was fine and there was nothing to worry.

❦

Mom called me to ask whether I needed anything apart from sweets and almond squash because the next day my brother, Rishi, my sister-in-law, Inu, and their children, Ayaan and Inayaa, were coming from Amritsar to spend a few days with me. I was super excited.

❦

17 JUNE 2016

In preparation for my appointments with the doctors again tomorrow, I got all my blood tests done at 0800 hrs.

Sabah gifted me a new stretching band, one with greater strength. I could do only half of what I had done with the previous band. She got me a big bar of chocolate for my earlier victory, though, and told me, 'this band will endure for around two months as it is of the second highest strength.'

'One month only, I'm telling you,' I announced.

'With you, it is possible!' she laughed.

She told me to check with the doctor whether we could put a little more weight on the right foot, maybe half the length of the foot. We would be careful. We would use the shoe and try to put weight on the toes and not on the heel, so that the calcaneum (heel) is not affected in any way. She even asked me to get an X-ray done of the left foot because she felt that since we'd been doing physiotherapy for thirty-five days, the fracture should have healed halfway through. I made a list of questions to be discussed with the doctors.

❦

18 JUNE 2016

In the morning, I got ready to go to the hospital with Rupesh and Meenu di. This time, I sat in the car without help, simply asking them to pull the walker when needed. I was very happy.

I told my physician I had reduced five painkillers from my daily dosage. He asked me, 'But why do you want to bear so much pain?' I told him it was a matter of four to five days, and then my body would adjust. I asked him for how many more days would I need to take the blood thinner.

He replied, 'till the time you don't put weight on both legs. You may get blood clots in the legs if you stop that medicine. So ideally, you can stop the blood thinners when you walk as much as a regular human being, when you take at least two hundred steps, maybe not at a stretch but about fifteen to twenty steps every half hour.'

He appreciated my will power and approved of the blood reports too. The only problem was—he found a stone in my kidney. But he assured me it was not unusual; a kidney stone sometimes occurred as an outcome of excessive medication. He told me to discontinue the two haemoglobin tablets as my levels had risen, and that I could drop all the painkillers one by one, once I felt comfortable without them. But he did warn me, 'One by one means you should wait for a week after stopping one tablet, and only then stop another tablet.' So I needed to phase them out and not put an end to all of them at one go. Calcium and multivitamins were a must though.

At 1500 hrs, I met with my orthopaedic, Dr Darius Soonawala. He said, 'the wounds on your right leg are not so deep, except for one. Now we can think of doing the surgery if required. We will do an L-shaped cut, take a bone from your pelvic area and fix it in your foot.'

He said he would call and speak to the skin specialist and the

Nidhi Chaphekar

plastic surgeon, Dr Anil Tibrewala, right away. But Dr Tibrewala was busy with a surgery and could not answer the call. So he decided to take a photograph of my leg and show it to him when he'd meet him later.

We had many questions for Dr Darius Soonawala. I asked whether I could start putting pressure, about twenty-five percent of my weight, on the toe of my right leg with the shoe.

'Let me see,' he said, and made me walk with the shoe and the walker. He observed that my style of walking was quite okay. He was clearly worried, but after some thought, he finally gave in to my request. 'Make sure your heel does not take any weight at all,' he warned, though.

Next, I asked him the procedure for bone grafting. He informed me that he would use a part of my pelvic bone to do the bone graft. And then I wanted to know—'Why use my bone? Don't we have a bone bank here?'

He explained, 'It is not necessary that the donor bone will be of the same density and strength. It is difficult to get an exact match. The bone may be able to take pressure, but may not match with your body. So it's best to use your own bone.'

'Why not use an artificial one?' I asked.

'there is no guarantee for how long an artificial bone will work. This is the case of your foot, and you are just forty. The life of an artificial bone is ten to fifteen years. So don't take a chance.'

I told him I was still in touch with the doctors in Belgium and they said that sometimes bones grow on their own. Dr Darius Soonawala, however, was not convinced and said, 'there's a very, very rare chance of that happening because even though some of the outer structure is present, it's totally hollow inside, so it's one of a kind. It's a very big bone loss and not a small gap that can be filled. Even if it has to, it would take years to grow. It is one of the most difficult bones to grow. And as the blood flow over there is not much, it would not be possible with the injuries and other complications you have. We also need to consider the age factor and many other things involved.'

I was very disappointed, because all this while I had been

thinking my bone would just grow back by itself. We then waited to meet the plastic surgeon, Dr Tibrewala, in the emergency room as instructed. He came in at 1600 hrs. He hugged me first and apologised for being late. Dr Tibrewala is always smiling and cheerful. Half our worries melted away just by talking to him. When he saw the condition of my wounds, he was very happy. 'You are doing a great job,' he declared. He told the nurses there about how I did my dressing on my own. Then I told him Dr Darius Soonawala had suggested that if required we could go for surgery but wanted his opinion first.

His immediate response was a 'no'. 'there is no place to cut! Your skin is not at all healthy. You just go home, chill, and come back after one month. In the meantime, I will discuss this with Dr Soonawala.'

He reasoned that Dr Darius Soonawala favoured the surgery as he feared my leg could get damaged further without it and he obviously wanted me to be fit soon.

I was a little confused. What to do, whose opinion to follow? These thoughts filled my head. We reached home in the evening. I told my family everything the doctors had said. Amarjeet jiju then decided to send a message to Dr Sudhir Warrier — a highly renowned orthopaedic, and a specialist for hands. He had, in fact, talked to us about my bone graft while I was in Belgium, and we had asked his opinion about whether we should do the bone graft in Belgium or wait. We had even sent him all my reports and scans at the time and he had told us, 'We have very good doctors in India. You can get her here and we will discuss.' Dr Warrier replied promptly saying he would see me tomorrow at 2100 hrs.

With the help of the walker, I tried to put pressure on the right foot. But I couldn't do it. I told Sabah that the doctor had allowed me to try putting some pressure on the right toes. She said, 'No exercise today, but let's walk with the help of the walker, putting weight on your left leg. The right leg would be more of a support and you have to put more weight on the arms.' Both Meenu and Jolly di were standing on either side, so that even if I fell, they could catch me, and Rupesh was right behind me. I took the first

Nidhi Chaphekar

ten steps with great difficulty. The pain in my leg was severe and spasmodic. But I told myself I was fine.

After finishing that challenging physiotherapy session, I waited for my brother, Rishi, and his family to arrive. Vriddhi had gone with Rupesh to receive them. The bell rang at about 2030 hrs and I wheeled myself to the door. As soon as my brother saw me, he hugged me. Both of us cried with joy; we had no words to say for a while. It was a very emotional moment. He told me I was his superhero. We were up late into the night, talking about the incident.

❧

19 JUNE 2016

Today was Fathers' Day and I thought the perfect gift for my father would be me reaching the milestone of using only the walker, and not the WCHL. Right since morning, I was really enthusiastic about achieving this feat. I called up my father to wish him and asked him what he wanted from me. He said, 'I want you to start walking on your own without any help.'

I could imagine what a father would feel on seeing his daughter, who used to always be on her toes, in a wheelchair now. I replied, 'I promise I will fulfil your wish in no time.'

So today, I walked like a normal person, although only for a few steps. And to fulfil my father's wish, I did not sit on the WCHL. My brother-in-law encouraged me by folding up the WCHL, saying, 'Let this be kept aside.'

❧

When Sabah came home, I told her about my decision. 'I need to go back home by the end of this month. I want to climb the stairs myself. So make me independent.'

❧

At home, my brother Rishi and his family kept me happily busy and entertained. His son, Ayaan, who was just three years old, had seen me a few times during our video calls. He had asked them many times, 'What has happened to Nidhi bua?'

They'd told him, 'She was not careful while playing with a big firecracker. So she got burnt.'

On seeing me up front, he was bewildered by my appearance and kept shooting questions at me — Why are you wearing gloves? What happened to your face and neck? How come your hair is so short? Why can't you walk like us? What happened to your legs? Why have you got bandages on your legs? He went on and on.

I then showed him my burnt hands and asked him, 'Can you see what could be the consequences if you don't play carefully?'

'Who was playing with you?' asked Mr Curious Cat.

'One boy,' I replied.

'Was he also injured?'

I nodded my head.

'What were you playing?'

I was quiet for a moment. Then I had to tell him that there was a box of firecrackers at the airport and we had lit it by mistake, thinking it was empty. So then he wanted to know where we got the matchstick from. When I said we got it from someone who was there at the time, at once he asked, 'Who was smoking?'

Finally, I diverted his mind to the new games we could play that night. Later, I narrated the whole story to my brother. He became emotional and cried a lot but was glad I was back home and that too with no regrets. I told him I was happy with the way I was recovering. He shared that it was not just him and his friends and our relatives, but the entire locality that was full of praise for my courage.

'I am proud to be your brother. You are a real fighter, a champion, and my mentor.'

I was over the moon. Never before had I heard so many good things about myself from my brother! Oh, you can't even imagine how wonderful I felt.

At the time, there were some fourteen people around me at home. How the days passed I did not realise. Mornings and afternoons were spent meeting the challenges Vriddhi set for me. Evenings were set aside for people coming over to meet me. They

Nidhi Chaphekar

would talk to me freely, expressing their feelings. Some would be a little worried. But I'd tell them if so far all had gone well, then in the future too things would progress smoothly.

I believed in myself. I'd tell them that we can cure half our problems by thinking and talking in an optimistic manner. I always say: do not ever get scared by thinking about your future. Just enjoy the moment. Don't spoil it by putting pressure on yourself. As a popular saying goes, 'Stop being afraid of what can go wrong. Start being excited about what can go right.'

At times, having so many people in the house felt like a bit of a burden. We had to give so much time to others. I used to get tired from all the exertion on my body. Earlier, before the incident, I'd never felt this way, but now I would tire easily, which only meant I needed to make my body as strong as it was earlier. I read up a lot on the mind-body connection and learnt that the body may become weak at times, but it's all in our mind. So I determined to prove something to myself. The ability to be as fit as a normal, healthy person rests entirely in our hands. I decided to take on a bit of kitchen work. I could start with simple things like standing and making tea or filling water in the bottles. My family was supportive, but they were very scared of me doing all this with one hand, holding on to the walker with the other hand, and wearing the shoe on my right leg. But they didn't say anything.

Vriddhi would always be after me – 'Don't do this; you are wearing gloves, so it would not give you a tight grip and you may spoil the gloves. Has the doctor told you to do it? No, so what is the need for you to work?' And on and on she would go.

I was getting tired of sitting around gossiping, I told them. Let me do some work. That's when they suggested that I should write a diary every day. Even my mom and sister suggested that I should write things down so I don't miss or forget details. And then it struck me – there had to be something special that I needed to tell to the world. *Maybe someone reading my story would find the inspiration to be positive in life.*

The more I thought about it, the more I felt inspired to pen my story, but I didn't know how to start.

I gathered a few pages and began writing. Slowly, I filled page after page, narrating my story and experiences until the time I reached the hospital. But from there onwards, I had to gather information date-wise. I had to coax my family members to tell me the details about what happened, when, with dates and timings. They were all curious and asked—'What's going on? You are behaving like an investigating officer!'

I started enjoying myself. I remembered a journalist who had once asked me on a phone call, 'How will the world come to know about your story?' And I had said that I would write about it.

I was on a mission, but I couldn't find time to write every day as someone or the other was always around. Sometimes, people came to spend the day with me thinking I must be feeling low. Anyhow, I was on the job off and on. And the most difficult part was to gather information from people besides family. Some of them knew approximate dates and timings.

In the evening, when Dr Warrier arrived and saw my wounds and the scan reports of my foot, he explained the grafting process. And he added, 'Once it is done, we don't touch it for at least six months. Your wounds have not healed yet. I don't think the decision to operate on you will be taken soon.'

He told us that both Dr Darius Soonawala and Dr Anil Tibrewala were renowned doctors, and since he knew them well, he would first have a word with them about their opinions. I told him Dr Darius Soonawala had given me permission to put pressure on my right foot as long as I was careful. Dr Warrier guided me on how to place both my feet flat on the ground and put a bit of pressure on them every day while sitting, at intervals of two to three hours. I asked him whether there was any risk of the foot breaking under pressure. He explained the situation with patience.

'You have not fully recovered yet—you have multiple fractures along with brittle bones and open wounds. When the foot is injured, there is loss of bone, there are open injuries and wounds, normally we avoid surgery and we just let it heal by itself. Keep on doing physiotherapy and pressure exercises that help the bone gaps to fill up naturally. This is a very slow and rare process. But in your case, it is not possible as the bone is hollow. And moreover, if at all it breaks, then we will operate. But no surgery for the next four months for sure.'

I was relieved. I relayed to him that I had been told this injury would decrease my mobility and that of my ankle's too, and although I may walk, I would suffer pain, arthritic stiffness and other complications for the my rest of my life.

He smiled, 'I heard you are really strong, so keep on believing in your strength.'

❧

20–24 JUNE 2016

At some point, it struck me that since my house was on the fourth floor of my building, there were around seventy-four steps to climb. I never wanted people to be carrying me all the way on a chair. When Sabah came, I told her that as I've decided to go back home by the end of this month, I don't want anybody to carry me to my house. I want to climb the stairs myself.

Starting with four steps, I was trained slowly to climb a full flight of stairs to the next floor and then climb down again with support. There was a railing fixed on the side of the wall to help old people climb; I held it like a monkey holds on to the branch of a tree! I did not put much weight on the right leg.

In the evening, I got a call from Mita Arora, Deputy General Manager (DGM), Cabin Crew Operations and Performance. She said, 'We want to have a reunion party for Amit and you, together with your family, and a few people from Jet Airways. Would it be comfortable for you?'

I immediately agreed and said that I look forward to meeting them. Sabah suggested I colour my hair as it would be the first time I would be going out. She wanted me to look healthy and great.

❧

25 JUNE 2016

Rishi was to go back to Amritsar and my sister Meenu asked if she too could leave with him. She assured me that if I found it difficult to manage on my own, she would come back.

I told her, 'I think you people have made me fully independent.' I thanked her and my brother.

When they left, I felt a little low, and wondered how I would go back home in a day or two and carry on the way I had lived earlier. I had been away from home for ninety-eight days now! Jolly di was not keen on sending me back, but I felt it was about time I go as it was too much for her to take care of me and the guests for so long. Let's see how I manage once I'm back home, I decided. Everyone was worried, except me. They said I should engage a full-time house help.

I said I would, but let me go home first.

🌿

26 JUNE 2016

In the evening, Amit called and asked to meet because he'd been requested to narrate the entire incident to the Jet security team, through the resource management and disaster management teams at 1600 hrs the next day. I told him to come home in the evening. I had not used the WCHL in the past seven days. I was walking with the help of the walker and felt great.

Today I planned to stop using the blood thinner and two other painkillers as well. I told Vriddhi to go back home and pack smart casuals for me to wear and to send them with the driver.

In the evening, Amit arrived with his mom; she was very quiet. I told her, 'Aunty, not to worry, your son is a tiger. He can come out of any situation.' She smiled. But I knew she was anxious.

Amit and I went over everything as it had happened, where I was thrown off because of the impact and where he went later, what he saw and how it had affected him. We were almost on the same page. He also told me about how he'd called the Mumbai office to inform them of the blast, but he couldn't find me. I listened to all his recorded calls of that day. My God! His voice had trembled with fear; he had cried on the phone call! When he'd called his fiancée to say he got injured in a bomb blast, initially, she had been unable to believe him. It took some time for her to realise the truth and the gravity of the situation. She stayed in touch with him continuously afterwards. None of us ever imagine, even in the wildest of our dreams, that our loved ones or we ourselves could ever be a part of such tremendously tragic situations. The mind is indeed a strange creature.

⚜

27 JUNE 2016

As soon as I woke up, I told my sister we would call a hairstylist home to colour my hair. And so I did! Later I got a call from Jet, requesting whether I could share my experience with the three teams—security, disaster management and crew resource management—at about 1730 hrs.

I wore a pair of pants and a shirt for the first time after the incident; till now, I'd only worn pajamas and T-shirts. I applied some lipstick, lined my eyes with an eye pencil and wore earrings. I looked so different! I sat in the car with my diary; it was decided that I would go early and my family would join me later. I had told them to come around 1900 hrs.

I reached the venue on time. The disaster management people from AVSEC (aviation security) and Mita Arora were already there as they had listened to Amit's narration first. The in-flight VP, Ms Pom, joined us later. They wrote down pointers for training purposes. I was asked to narrate the whole sequence of events—my narration went on for over an hour. I was told the new model of threats would be based on our story and they would use our examples to explain how to tackle such situations.

'You are a real hero,' one of them said. 'For us, you are the brand ambassador for Jet Airways.'

Later, we were joined by our family members for dinner. It was fun... a very nice and different experience. As the hotel was a little far away, the exertion made my foot swell up again. To be safe, I had to use the WCHL. My foot was aching a lot. After returning home, I decided that tomorrow I would return to my home.

❧

28 JUNE 2016

In the morning itself, I called up Sabah and told her not to come as I would be going home. And I made plans with my sister to do something special. It was Tuesday. First, we thought of shopping in the mall. But instead, we decided to watch a movie, *Udta Punjab*. It was my very first outing to a movie theatre in four months. I was so thrilled! But my sister was worried. 'In the evening, you have to climb four floors... how will you manage?'

I said, 'Let me first enjoy this moment. Later we'll see what needs to be done.'

During the movie, people were curious—seeing me wearing gloves, using a walker, with my sister and Rupesh by my side. The burn marks on my face had them wondering. I enjoyed my favourite caramel popcorn, had coffee, and came back home. Then it was time to pack my bags. I hadn't realised there was such a lot of stuff!

❧

It was raining heavily. I sat in the car at 2100 hrs and it took us more than an hour to reach home. Once we arrived, Rupesh said he'd call and ask his brother Nilesh to come downstairs.

'You go... I will wait here,' I assured him. When he left to park the car, I said 'Jai Mata Di' and walked towards the stairs with the walker. The ground was slippery, and the pattern of circles on the tiles made the surface uneven, so I had to be very careful. I folded my walker and placed it by the stairs. Using the side railing, without any fear or pause, I climbed all the seventy-four stairs in one go. I did not look back even once.

I had once read somewhere that you become what you feel for yourself. If you say there is no pain, you won't feel the pain. Thanks to my physiotherapy and training, I could manage the stairs on my own. Rupesh reached our floor later than I did, so you can imagine my speed! He was yelling all the while from behind me, but I was confident and I did it!

When I rang the bell, I was asked to wait. Vardaan and Vriddhi, along with my sister-in-law's kids, Sakshi and Snigdha, did an aarti (a small puja akin to a welcome ceremony) for me. The house had been decorated with balloons. A 'Welcome Home Mom' poster had been made by the kids. Even at such short notice, the kids had managed to do so much to welcome me. We cut a cake. I had tears in my eyes as I entered my house after a full hundred days!

It was so good to see my room after so long. I was elated. But I am very finicky about cleanliness and about everything being in its proper place. So when I saw many of my bags lying around on the floor, I announced at once, 'tomorrow I will be on my toes.'

Rupesh said he was so sure I would say something like that, but warned me and asked me to relax.

❧

29 JUNE 2016

I started work on the house with gusto and did not listen to anyone. I wore surgical gloves on top of my medical compression gloves and started by unpacking my stuff. My kids pitched in a lot; Vardaan helped put away the heavy stuff. Rupesh too had taken leave from work to lend a hand. I would guide them most of the time, and they would help by arranging things.

At this point, realising the value of a woman's presence in the house, I decided I'd make my kids more independent. They should know where to keep different household articles, something that's very important to run a home. We mothers believe it is our duty entirely, but I think all family members should know how to ensure a well-maintained house.

The whole day passed in just trying to get the house back in order. I had told Sabah not to come for two days, as I knew I would be very tired. For three days, I missed my physiotherapy. My foot was now swollen; I felt as if the sides were filled with air! It looked double the normal size, maybe because I had let my legs remain hanging for a long period of time. I was worried, but I knew it was due to exertion.

❧

30 JUNE 2016

I had asked Sabah to come in the evening. Despite the swollen foot, by sitting on the stool or on the bed, I had managed to re-arrange three cupboards. My arms ached. It felt as though my legs were missing. But I didn't want to be a burden on others or pass on the work to my sister-in-law, Madhuri, as she had done a lot for me and my kids in my absence.

When my mom found out what I'd been up to, she was furious.

She scolded me saying, 'You had promised me you would sit quietly. If you don't, then I am coming back or I'm sending your sister back!'

Jolly di (whose place I'd been staying at until now) came to know and ordered me to come back.

I told her, 'Give me a few days. It will be fine. It is because I have been resting all this while and my body is not used to it.'

My kids also told her to take me back as I wasn't listening to any of them.

Rupesh complained, 'She laughs when I stop her. I don't know what to do!'

Then I made everybody calm down by explaining my rationale to them. 'I am careful while doing things. I also know that my health is important. Both Vriddhi and Vardaan help me by doing some stuff. This is another way of teaching them the spirit of positivity we have within ourselves.'

My sister argued, 'What if you hurt your leg? What if your

wounds get infected? What will happen then? Wouldn't that lead you to becoming dependent?'

I told her, 'I know how much weight I am putting on it. It's just because I haven't had adequate rest. But my point is, why think negatively? Half the problems one faces, one can overcome by thinking positively.'

The argument went on for nearly an hour, but I promised them that all would be fine. By then Sabah arrived. She took one look at my swollen leg and asked, 'What did you do?'

'A little work,' I smiled.

She took a deep breath. 'Your leg has to be kept at an upward angle of at least forty-five degrees, and you have to apply cold compresses at least thrice a day. If you want to stop the physiotherapy for a few more days, I am fine with it.'

I told her it had become stiff because I hadn't exercised. I was not able to pull in my foot or stretch it. Anyhow, we finished an hour of therapy. Everyone was angry with me. Pictures of my leg kept in the suggested position were sent to Dr Darius Soonawala and he too asked me to take complete bed rest and apply cold compresses. I followed instructions, and applied cold compresses on my foot.

❦

I JULY 2016

In the morning, I saw that the swelling had reduced by twenty percent. I resolved to keep my leg in the prescribed angle at all times, and I'd make an exception only when it was not possible to do work without standing up. Many of my crew and fellow residents in our building wanted to see me, but I firmly told them that it would not be possible this week.

When reporters had learnt that I was back in India, there had been a rush for interviews. I informed my management team that my family members were still getting calls asking for interviews. Being an employee of the company, I had to take their permission before I gave any statement to the press. My family insisted that only I should speak to the media as they were not comfortable doing the same.

Ms Pom was very understanding and said, 'Give us some more time. I'll speak to Corporate Communications and get back to you soon.' I relayed this to all the media persons.

The day was thus spent attending phone calls. Later, I felt a bit sick. When I checked my temperature, I was shocked to see that it was 102 degrees Fahrenheit! Now I better shut up and just sit quietly, I thought. I took a paracetamol and did not tell anyone about the fever. I rested in the evening and slept early.

❧

2 JULY 2016

This morning I realised I had a urine infection. There was an acute burning sensation while peeing. I called up my gynaecologist, Dr Pandit. He asked me to run a few tests, which I did immediately. In the evening, my condition worsened. My reports were also bad. I wondered what was happening. Dr Pandit asked me to start antibiotics immediately and prescribed another medicine. He said it could be a result of the urine pipe that had been inserted for a long duration earlier, and the high dose of medicines I had been on. He asked me to drink as much water as I could.

I realised my diet too had changed. At my sister's place, I used to keep myself hydrated—I would drink about four to six litres of water, and include a lot of fresh salads and juices in my meals. Here, for the past few days, my dietary habits had been different. I realised this wasn't a good thing for me, and right away I got myself some coconut water and instructed the vendor to get me one tender coconut every day. I even set a reminder on my mobile phone to keep myself hydrated with a regular intake of water, juice, milk or any healthy drink I may feel like having at that hour. My kids took charge of my diet.

I couldn't lie down; everything was giving me trouble. My

body was aching, I frequently felt the urge to use the washroom, I had mild fever, and my foot was swollen. All this was happening probably because I had not taken proper care of my diet, or maybe it was due to the change in the weather. Anyway, all I knew was if I was taking matters into my own hands and trying to do something about my health, then I should be able to resolve it.

❧

3 JULY 2016

I was asked to do another test today. The results were worse than before and Rupesh was worried. I was not happy, but I understood that healing would take some time. So I focused on having my medicines on time, a nutritious diet and keeping myself hydrated.

❧

4–14 JULY 2016

I felt a little better. I was hesitant about talking to anyone, though. Whenever anyone asked me how I was doing, I would say I felt better than before. A routine set in over the next few days. My mornings were busy with changing my bandages and the afternoons were spent with the kids and doing a little cleaning. The evenings were for physiotherapy. How the day went by, I wouldn't realise. Two weeks passed by in this manner, and my mission of cleaning and putting things in place was also almost complete. That was a relief! My kids too were happy to help me. This way, they learned the importance of orderliness and tidiness in housekeeping.

Everything was going well, when suddenly one night, someone knocked on my room's door. I have two doors to my room. The knock was on the door that opens directly onto the stairs. I felt a little scared as that was our emergency door. No one usually came in through that door. I was suspicious and at first, didn't allow Rupesh to open the door. He somehow managed to convince me it was okay and he would be careful. I was filled with the same dread I used to feel in the hospital room when I would have those nightmares.

And what an anticlimax it turned out to be—a dog had entered the building and was trying to get into our house!

But my mind felt unsettled once again.

❧

15 JULY 2016

I decided to resume writing my book today. It was so difficult for me to get the order of things right in the narration. So I made a calendar of important dates—all the crucial days of the journey so far, every time something important had happened. I had already started writing at my sister's place when I'd had some time to spare. Now I decided to get back to it in right earnest, trying to gather more information this time.

My check-up was due on 18 June and my kids' school would reopen on the same day. The kids were so excited about getting their new books and uniforms, and to meet their friends after the long gap. But now I was worried about how I was going to manage cooking for them daily. They would be at school from 0730 in the morning till 1530 in the evening every day. Earlier, I would feed them breakfast and then send them to school with three tiffins for their three breaks. In my absence, Madhuri had been doing this job sincerely and she assured me now that she would continue to do so. But I didn't want her to be stressed because of me.

I went to the market with the kids to buy new tiffin boxes. People started recognising me on the way. And at every step I was asked—What happened? Have you met with an accident? Why are there burns on your neck and face? Why are you wearing gloves?

The thing is no one has time to read everything in the newspapers and we tend to forget things easily; all of us are super busy in today's world. I never wanted to share the whole experience with everyone I met. So I would simply say, 'Yes I met with an accident.'

But I felt good to know that even after such a drastic change in my appearance, they could all recognise me! Some recognised me by my voice, of course. The kids exclaimed, 'Oh, Mom, how come so many of them know you!'

I told them, 'this is the impact you create when you meet people for the first time, with the way you talk and behave. Remember, always be polite and respectful, even to those you don't know. Every word, every gesture counts. And I believe if I am here today in good health, it is because of their prayers. God has created us and we have to create our own image.'

Since the kids had been called to the school the next day to collect their bags, uniforms and books, they asked me whether I could join them. I explained that I would only be going for the parent-teacher meets, since activities such as picking up school articles, etc., could be managed by them too. This way, they would become more independent. Rupesh agreed with my rationale. I did feel bad, as it would be the very first time my kids would go to school alone, while all the other children would be accompanied by their parents. But I told myself — *Nidhi, there is always a first time. Let them learn, you will not be with them forever. See how they perform.*

❧

The days were fine but the nights were tormenting.

At night, my fear — of someone trying to come and shoot me or members of my family, of losing my loved ones — would return all over again. I would not allow Rupesh to sleep in peace. I would end up frightening him with my worries. But he would not lose his cool and would always soothe my nerves. He would lovingly massage my head and help me sleep.

❧

17 JULY 2016

The kids were very excited to begin the next term and to celebrate, we all watched a movie together and slept at 2200 hrs, as we had to wake up at 0630 hrs. But again at midnight, I felt the same panic and fear return. Rupesh opened the door and showed me that no one was there. Even a small whisper of the wind would fill me with fear. Rupesh, however, would patiently pacify me and somehow make me sleep.

❧

18 JULY 2016

I had fallen out of the habit of working so much, so Rupesh helped me in the morning as I prepared and served breakfast and readied the kids' tiffins and water bottles. One and a half hours zipped by! In another hour, Sabah would arrive. There was such a lot of work pending, though—doing the laundry, making the beds, making my tea. Determined, I finished it all in fifty minutes and was ready for my exercises. By the time I was done with my physiotherapy, I was dead tired and just wanted to sleep, but some chores remained to be done, such as drying and folding the laundry. I don't like to ask anyone to do my work. I always prefer doing it myself. But Rupesh did all of it for me. He would sacrifice his work and would leave for the factory only in the afternoon.

When I was staying with my sister, every evening, Rupesh would religiously come straight from his office to my sister's place, spend at least four hours with me, and then go back home. The next morning, he would wake up early to help the children get ready for school, and after they left, he would either go to his factory or visit me to take me to the doctors. It is not easy to drive in Mumbai's traffic. But Rupesh never missed a day. He is the only one who would listen to everyone and always stay calm. I believe, in such situations, it is the family that suffers the most as they are all constantly trying to make us feel comfortable. But most of us forget this. If only we could keep this fact in mind, the suffering would be less. Being aware of this kept me going.

In the evening, I had to visit the doctor. This time, Dr Darius Soonawala asked me to do a CT scan of my foot first. He wanted to compare it with the earlier scans, to see if there was any difference in the bone growth. But on seeing the results, we found nothing. He then told me that in his opinion, we could operate now, as a further delay may cause more complications. He asked me to decide on a date for the surgery during the coming weekend and inform him about it. However, he said that he would also consult Dr Tibrewala, the plastic surgeon, as without taking his opinion, he would not like to proceed. The latter, however, felt there was no place to put in the stitches.

'We have scars all over the skin... it is not healthy either. I feel if we touch it now, we may spoil the case totally,' opined Dr Tibrewala.

As I had stopped the blood-thining medicine, Dr Jamshed Sunavala, my GP, did my Doppler test to rule out any blood clots that may have formed in my limbs. By God's grace, the reports were clear. The surgeon's words put me in doubt again. I wondered whose opinion we should heed. Both were doing their best under the circumstances. But my mind was confused.

We again spoke to Dr Warrier about it. He said, 'Okay, fine, what we'll do is show it to two or three more renowned doctors from different hospitals, just for an alternate opinion.'

❧

The days were passing very quickly. I hardly found time for myself. I had always thought that once I go home, I would be bored, but to my surprise, I actually had no time to even think! Morning routines followed by physiotherapy, then a little work, a shower, bandages, and finally lunch. Later, someone or the other would visit and stay till the evening and if time permitted, I would write a few pages in my diary. Then the kids would return from school and hours would pass listening to their stories — about their new activities and projects. We would have dinner and soon after, we would be in our beds.

My eyes, however, would be fixed on the window pane or on the door. Rupesh asked me, 'What are you scared of really?'

His question put me in deep thought and I gave him a look of concern. He hugged me and said gently, 'God is with you. He wants us to do good, to be good, to think well and to speak good, and all that will reward us.' He kept on reassuring me and finally I felt placated by what he said.

I made up my mind to fight the scary thoughts in my head.
From now on, I would make sure I meditate every day to strengthen
my mind.

❧

22 JULY 2016

Rupesh's birthday. This time, after a gap of three years, I was at
home on his birthday. So I was happy I was there to celebrate it
with him but also a little annoyed with myself as I had not got
him any surprise gift. Nevertheless, I had plans to celebrate it in a
grand manner. I called up Jolly di and Amarjeet jiju.

Inu and her children, Madhuri and her family, my mother-
in-law, and of course my children were all at home. As soon as
Rupesh left for work, we started decorating the house with balloons,
streamers, banners and flowers. My job was to fill air in the balloons.
Vardaan got a cake. Vriddhi made a beautiful card. We ordered
Rupesh's favourite Chinese food and chicken tikkas for him and
some vegetarian food too. When he entered the house in the evening,
the lights had been switched off, and the moment he switched them
on, we yelled, 'Surprise!' He was stunned! We all had a great evening
together and enjoyed the celebration.

❧

24 JULY 2016

Following our discussion with Dr Warrier, he had arranged a
meeting with two other renowned foot specialists. At the hospital
today, I waited an hour for my turn to meet the doctors. I wanted
to gauge whether it was necessary for the surgery to be done, and
if so, then when would be the right time to do so. I was seeking
votes for yes or no, as there was still a lot of confusion in my mind
over whether my foot could be operated upon at all.

The first doctor's advice was we should not open the foot as
there was no place to put stitches later. He said he could wait, but

his only worry was that I should not lose my balance. Also, the bone should not collapse. Then he observed my CT scan for a good ten minutes and came to the conclusion that not doing the surgery would also pose a huge risk.

'We can do this,' he said. 'We can do a one-centimetre cut, put in a cannula (a small tube) and through a syringe, I will first remove the tissues. Then using an injection, I will slowly insert the bone.' He also said that it is a huge risk to not do the surgery.

He told us this procedure was done for cancer patients. But when we mentioned the name of the plastic surgeon who was not in favour of operating, the doctor concluded that we should wait for some more time, that we should not take a risk.

I was supposed to meet another doctor at 1900 hrs in the same hospital. The moment I entered his cabin, I had a very satisfying feeling. I don't know how it works, but I have a strong gut instinct. When this doctor examined me and saw my X-ray and the CT scans, he said that due to bone and muscle loss, even if we did the bone graft, I could end up walking with a limp for the rest of my life. We briefed him in detail about the entire case so far, and I showed him my foot. The first thing he told me was that I should thank God and the doctors in Brussels who gave me back my foot as they had done a wonderful job.

Then he added, 'At the moment, you have thirty percent sensation. If we operate, you may get back more sensation, but it is also possible it would never come back and may get worse instead. And in this case, if your foot is reopened, the chances of infection are really high.'

He showed me a few case studies of the calcaneus bone, in which a person's calcaneus was fully or partially ruptured due to an accident or a fall. Out of a total of forty cases in which they had tried to operate and fix the bone, four cases required an amputation later due to the development of severe infections. Thirty-six percent of the cases failed and the patients lost sensation because of which even though the foot was still there, they couldn't place it down. In a few cases, the infection level became so high that it impaled the other organs. So, he explained that if I could feel my foot to some extent, and if I could even bear my weight, then I should just avoid surgery as the failure rate was more than sixty-five percent. He also said that sometimes, the body does not accept it and then the condition becomes worse.

He explained, 'Your foot has been restructured and we don't know the condition of the veins. There are small fractures to the structure of the bone shell, so it would not be easy to conduct the surgery.'

He checked the strength in my foot and leg, and was amazed. 'You are better than even a normal person!' he exclaimed. 'You are blessed to be walking despite the condition of your foot. Now if we try to operate, the brittle bone pieces would just break down as the whole area is affected and that would lead to multiple complications. When the heel is affected from the side, we normally do not operate because the infection rate is much higher and keep surgery as the last resort.'

I thanked him for his advice and took leave. I was smiling my best smile even as I thought about all he had said. I'm usually like that—even if I'm troubled, no one would ever know on the outside. While driving back home, Rupesh said, 'We are not going to operate it.'

I replied, 'Relax, God has helped us till here. He will help us further as well. Have belief in Him and in yourself, and know that nothing can go wrong.'

Everyone in my family was waiting to know what the doctors had said. After a lot of discussions, we concluded that out of four doctors, two had said we should not operate while the other two were in favour of doing it; so we would wait to know the last doctor's recommendation. But we thought it would be better to delay it for some time. There was a possibility that his opinion too would change over time, as there was too much confusion in our minds.

❧

Nidhi Chaphekar

26 JULY 2016

Ms Pom, along with a few people from the company management, came home to see me. This time she brought a really big cake, but I had no place to keep it in the fridge, which was already stuffed with three cakes! I had already cut more than thirty cakes at home! We enjoyed a different dessert every night.

I told Ms Pom about how people from the media were coming home and that it didn't look good turning them away every time. I asked her if she could arrange for official permission to speak with the media. She immediately assured me it would be sorted out in a week's time.

❦

27 JULY 2016

I got a call from the corporate communications manager at Jet asking whether I would be comfortable enough to speak in the presence of the media or the public. They wanted me to take a trial run. I agreed and they decided to come home on 29 July by 1030 hrs. I got calls from the HR department for other queries and was promised that all arrangements would be done by the end of the month.

Initially, I was glad they were going to ask me questions, but I wondered why they wanted to 'test' me. Were they going to tell me to change the answers if they didn't approve? Or would they ask me not to give too many specific details about my experiences? My mind was full of questions and doubts.

To relax, I meditated. One thing I was sure of was that I didn't want to use the walker on the day of my interview, as it would be four-and-a-half months since the incident. But as luck would have it, late that night when I went to the washroom, I failed to notice some water on the floor and stepped on it while using the walker. I skidded a bit and sprained my right foot. I applied a cold compress, yet my foot swelled up.

❦

Exactly at 1030 hrs, three gentlemen arrived and introduced themselves. One of them was from the company's corporate communications department and the other two were from an external PR agency. They told me they would go with a one-on-one interview and not a press conference. Since I'm not a professional, there was the risk that in the spur of the moment, I might say something contradicting earlier comments.

They explained at the start, 'We would like to record what you say and we may ask you some questions regarding events right from the day of the incident till today.'

It went on for an hour and forty minutes, without any break. Arun, from the agency, was satisfied with the way I spoke and asked me finally, 'Do you have any appointments next week with the doctors, or can we start making appointments with journalists?'

He said they would decide which channel or newspaper I would have interviews with, including the order in which they would be lined up. They would inform me before booking a date for the first interview, but it would take a week or so as they needed to prioritise the list and check for availability. They advised me not to speak with any foreign channel, but I told them we can't do that as this was international news and so it is very important for them as well to know everything as it happened. Moreover, I needed to thank the entire world for their prayers.

In the evening, I got a call from Arun. He wanted to compliment me. He said I could be a good speaker and should try my hand at motivational speaking. I felt wonderful on hearing this. I have always wanted to do something to help others. His ideas only made me more determined, more strong.

❧

31 JULY 2016

The doorbell rang in the wee hours of the morning... around 0400 hrs. We were surprised to welcome my nephew Rahul, who had come all the way from Doha. He was overjoyed to see my recovery and said, 'Maasi, you are a true hero, fighter, survivor and a role model for us!'

We spent the entire day talking and having fun with the kids. He also watched me doing my physiotherapy and asked many questions after that. Later, I came to know that the purpose of his visit was also to celebrate with us the three occasions that fell on 1 August—the day I joined Jet Airways, my brother's birthday and his own birthday. He added that there could not be anyone better than me to bless him on his birthday. I was touched.

❧

1 AUGUST 2016

It was midnight when we cut the cake. The kids were awake too, although they had to go to school the next morning. We video-called my brother, Rishi, who was fast asleep at the time, to wish him.

I was feeling great as I had completed twenty years with my organisation. I received many bouquets today. The evening party at home was thrown by my nephew. All of us had an unbelievable amount of fun. Rahul was to leave the next evening. How good times fly... we never realise. I loved spending two days simply enjoying being with everyone... something I had not been able to do for so long during my hectic tenure working as a flight attendant.

❧

3 AUGUST 2016

I got a call at about 1400 hrs, asking whether I could come to the PR agency's office tomorrow or the day after, that is, on 4 or 5 August, to do interviews. I was told I would have four interviews in a day, from noon to 1800 hrs. Each interview was allotted one hour, followed by a break of twenty to thirty minutes. I told them to schedule my interviews for 5 August and asked which ones had been given priority.

The man from the agency replied, 'We would go for *CNN-News18, BBC,* the *Times of India* and *Mumbai Mirror.* This way, you would be seen both internationally and nationally, and they broadcast it on the same day on their channels and the next day in the newspapers.'

I felt a little nervous thinking of what they would ask. Anyhow, I focused on choosing what I would wear. I selected one bright-coloured shirt and one light-coloured shirt, paired with black and white trousers respectively.

Just one day to go for my media interviews, I thought. While looking at myself in the mirror, I noticed that the size of my right eye was nearly equal to that of the left. The difference could hardly be noticed and this made me brim over with happiness.

❧

4 AUGUST 2016

In the morning, I called up my family to inform them I would be giving my first interview tomorrow. They were happy and firmly believed that my story should be known to all, not because something bad had happened to me but to spread the message of strength and positivity I had shown in bouncing back.

My mom, brother, sister, husband, and kids would often tell me, 'You handled it all with a smile and because of your attitude, you are coming out of it with pride. Your story should be an example for people who leave the battle halfway and wait for others to help them, and in the process, they give up the hope to survive and live well again.'

Mahatma Gandhi once said, 'My life is my message'. And that is the principle I follow. I want my energy and my courage to inspire others to live their best life. One should never give up the hope to live because everything is only a phase. Time never remains in the same place forever. If good times don't last forever, how can bad times? As the famous poet Shelley wrote, 'If winter comes, can spring be far behind?' Keep on pushing ahead.

5 AUGUST 2016

We started the interviews at 1230 hrs. My first interview was with *BBC* in English and Hindi. It went on for nearly forty minutes; this was followed by the second interview with Anuradha SenGupta for *CNN-News18*. It lasted exactly fifty minutes. She had come all the way from Delhi on a very rainy Mumbai day for the recording.

After a tea break, I had an interview with a journalist from the *Times of India*. She took more than an hour, following which the *Mumbai Mirror* interview began immediately, which went on for another hour.

I had four cups of tea and coffee that day; I had to talk so much! And because it was the first time, I had to repeat the same information several times, narrating the same story to everyone. I would think I'd missed something important, so I'd get confused and repeat the same bit of information multiple times. By the end of it all, my head was spinning! When we finally wrapped up at around 1800 hrs, I switched on my phone and saw a barrage of messages and missed calls from my family, all keen to know about the interviews.

I left after thanking everyone. On the way back, I got a call and message from the agency informing me that my first interview would be telecast on *BBC* at 1840 hrs. I was so eager to see it! So I called my kids and requested them to record it for me, and told my mom, sisters and brother to watch it too. I reached home at 2000 hrs. I didn't know how many had watched the interview, but calls were pouring in as if I had advertised it beforehand! I told everyone to watch *CNN-News18* at 2200 hrs which was going to telecast my interview during prime time—an unusual thing for an

Indian TV news channel to do—and to look out for the next day's print editions of the *Times of India* and *Mumbai Mirror*.

॥ॐ॥

After reaching home, I watched my *CNN-News 18* interview along with my family. I cried afterwards, overwhelmed by all I had gone through and all that I still felt. My family members and friends kept calling me, and those who couldn't get through the line sent text messages. All of them wanted to tell me how moved they were by the reality of it all. Many were in tears. I was on the phone till midnight.

॥ॐ॥

6 AUGUST 2016

The interviews were published in the *Times of India* and *Mumbai Mirror*. My management team members, friends, relatives, and even people who knew me in neighbouring localities reached out to me, saluting me for my courage and positivity and for giving them Gandhi ji's wonderful message—*An eye for an eye would leave the whole world blind.*

Revenge is not the answer, I firmly believe. Sow seeds of love, care, unity and peace, and let the coming generations reap the fruits of kindness, forgiveness, strength and progress.

॥ॐ॥

The repeat telecasts of my interviews had been slated for many days, and were gathering a lot of popularity and demand among viewers. I couldn't help but think—God has done so much for me, I must go to the nearest temple and bow in front of Him. I must thank Him for being so kind to us. In the evening, when I visited a nearby temple, many people recognised me.

I got so many compliments! I was surrounded by people on all sides. And while I stood there enjoying the moment, I thought to myself that my message had reached a few, but I now need to reach out to the whole world with it.

I received so many calls from the company management as well as Ms Pom and Mr Rahil Tuteja, the CPO, who were full of praise and said, they were getting a lot of calls from other media channels too. People were admiring my story and felt that I was a true champion for them. They also informed me that the repeat telecast of one of my interviews would be shown in all the airports around the world. I felt overwhelmed.

❧

Arun called later to tell me that Rajdeep Sardesai wanted to do an interview with me for *India Today*. But Mr Sardesai explained it would be different this time, as he would be in Delhi and would ask me questions via a satellite connection and I would be able to only hear him while he would be able to see me. I felt a bit scared. Arun assured me he would make sure Rajdeep spoke to me the next day for a pre-interview chat in order to help me feel more comfortable with the idea.

❧

7 AUGUST 2016

Around 1100 hrs, I got a call from my corporate communications manager, Mannu Hati, that Rajdeep Sardesai was on a conference call with him and would like to speak with me. I was speechless the moment he said hello! We spoke for about five minutes and he said, 'For any question you feel you don't want to answer, just say "no comments".'

The five minutes that he spoke to me was to make me comfortable with his voice and to brief me that in case I didn't hear clearly, I should not worry, I should simply ask him to repeat the question.

On 8 August, I was scheduled to do an interview with him.

❧

In between all this, an unusual thing started happening—some people would call to share the failures they had faced and ask me how they should deal with it. I would give them ideas to find different ways to come out of the situation. I firmly believe the effort has to be always and completely our own. Each one of us has that spark within us; we just have to ignite it. I would ask them to first strengthen their mind through meditation—if one's mind is strong, one can never sink. Thus, most of the days would be spent speaking on the phone.

I didn't wear my big shoe (the medically prescribed one) in any of my interviews, because I knew some people would see it and remark—'See, she can walk only because of the shoe she is wearing.' So I wore normal slippers to help myself gain confidence and believe that in spite of bone loss, without a cast, a person can still make an effort and the result can be graceful. Yes, I did take the help of the walker so as to not put much pressure on the legs, and to avoid further complications. It is always important to read your mind and body, analyse, give some time, and then take decisions.

❦

8 AUGUST 2016

By 1430 hrs, I reached the studio where my interview with Rajdeep Sardesai was slated to happen. I was made to sit in a room. In front of me was a camera, and behind the camera, a group of people from the channel's team was standing and watching. A microphone earpiece was fixed to my ear and the session started. It ended after an hour. Throughout the interview, people kept coming in and going out of the room. I was not satisfied with my answers because of the distractions. I came back home disheartened. The interview was to be telecast by 2040 hrs. When my family and friends watched it, they praised me generously and some said it was better than the first one.

I wanted to be more impactful and speak better every time. I would be especially mindful because it was the same story and the same message I would tell the world each time I spoke, but I wanted to use my words with care.

Some questions were so sudden. However, I never let any question go unanswered. Also, I never took questions in advance; it had to be spontaneous, in the moment. So sometimes, I wouldn't know how to answer certain questions or whether to answer them at all, but even then I managed to answer them all.

❦

9 AUGUST 2016

I got a call asking me whether I could do an interview for *Zee*. I agreed and the interview was scheduled for 10 August.

Then I called Jolly di and asked her to accompany me for some shopping. Rupesh and I, along with Jolly di, went to the mall. Being a weekday, it was empty. We reached the mall at 1400 hrs, visited just two stores, and I bought around six long-sleeved shirts for myself. But to my surprise, nearly everyone at the mall recognised me. They all cheered for me. They praised me for the love and faith I still have in me.

A few said that they had cried after seeing my interview but that it was very inspirational. Many of them took pictures with me. However, I wasn't used to such a lot of walking and standing for long periods of time. My legs started aching badly. I felt physically weak.

In the evening, I got several messages. Some were from friends. But a couple of messages in particular really inspired me. One was from Yogita, from the *Times of India*, saying, 'After reading your articles, we have received so many mails and messages to send you good wishes. A Homoeopathic doctor sent us an email after reading that you still have a metal piece in your eye orbit—she has said that there is a Homoeopathic medicine with which it can be dissolved. She has shared her telephone number and if you wish, you may contact her.' I was dazed to see the love shown to me by people. It only strengthened my belief that love is the most powerful force in this world.

Another such message was from Anuradha SenGupta of *CNN-News18*. She wrote: 'What struck me while recording the interview was how you didn't express rage or bitterness for what had happened to you. Instead, I heard gratitude for the fact that you had survived, vulnerability, and an open-mindedness to understanding why someone would do such harm to another human being. That was deeply moving. And I got a lot of feedback after the show was aired. Some senior media colleagues even tweeted that they thought this conversation showed what good TV could achieve. My work was easy, you were in fine flow and your answers helped explore deep and complex issues.'

She added, 'I have just discovered the joy of colouring books and sent you one to help you share the feeling. And to thank you for sharing your story with me.'

Some messages were screenshots of my interviews taken by friends and relatives to show they had seen me and wished to send me their blessings. It took me nearly three hours to read and reply to all the messages. One thing was clear to me—love is everywhere. I was full of admiration for people and the way they would absorb my ideas and appreciate and boost my confidence in turn. They were all pushing me to do better in life.

My life was becoming more beautiful by the day, although it was extremely busy as well. But I was not running away from anything. If you receive love and respect, you also need to give it back. That's why I make sure I always reply to everyone who reaches out to me.

The next day, there was another interview. It went well. Every day, I would end up meeting different people who would later send me messages telling me I was an inspiration to them.

❧

15 AUGUST 2016

Indian Independence Day. I felt very energetic. Just like our armed forces, I too felt like a soldier fighting spiritedly. And to my surprise,

Anil, a cabin crew colleague, came to visit, bringing with him nine teenagers from his locality. He said he wanted to show them how I too was like a soldier, not at the border but at home, braving all odds and showing in my own way that we get just one life, so we must live it to the fullest. He wanted them to learn from my example the important lesson that no matter how hard the past is, you can always begin afresh.

I served them lemon juice and chocolates, and we took photos. My kids too were impressed, I could see, by the respect shown to me by others.

In the evening, I got a call from Nishita Joshi to say she and her husband Jigar Joshi had come to Mumbai to meet their family and if possible, they would like to meet me too. The Joshis were the ones who had made frantic phone calls in Amsterdam when the blast took place to find out where I was. They had even gone twice to the hospital in Antwerp when they finally located my whereabouts in the evening, but both times, I was undergoing surgery and thus, they couldn't see me. They had come to Charleroi too.

We decided we would meet them tomorrow after my monthly appointment with my doctors. Nishita asked whether she could refer my case to her uncle who was a renowned surgeon in Mumbai. I agreed, of course. We planned to meet her uncle first at 1800 hrs and then meet our doctors at 1900 hrs.

❦

16 AUGUST 2016

When we met her uncle, he went through my files, scans and X-rays, and checked my foot. He asked me if I could walk and I walked a bit so he could see my condition for himself.

He smiled and said, 'With your confidence and energy, I can see that you have managed to walk slowly, which is remarkable... it is a miracle!' He added, 'Lady, don't ever let your foot be opened. Don't get any foot surgery done, otherwise you will ruin the foot.'

He believed that with the kind of attitude I had, one could heal oneself. He also assured me I would be fine in two to three years time.

'Keep on doing physiotherapy and don't ever stop stretching exercises,' he advised.

I was so encouraged by his words I felt like hugging him. Next, we went to Dr Soonawala and Dr Tibrewala. The former was busy with an emergency, so we had to wait a bit. When Dr Tibrewala saw me, he said, 'You are doing great. Be this chirpy person always! Just keep up the same spirit and do physiotherapy daily.' He was very happy with my progress.

Dr Soonawala told us I was doing an amazing job, but somehow he still feared that the foot would not last long without surgical intervention, and yet we couldn't have the surgery unless all of us were ready. He also said it would be a very complicated surgery, so he had to take the consent of the plastic surgeon as well. He would always notice even the most minute changes in my foot and would emphasise that I continue my stretching exercises.

Both the doctors never charged me any visiting fee. When asked, their answer was always—'We can do at least this much for you.'

Since the next day marked the Parsi New Year, I wished them both and then proceeded to Nishita's home as her family wanted to meet me. I met her parents, her son, sister-in-law and brother, and her husband, Jigar. They were full of praise about how well I spoke during my interviews. They said many of their friends often discussed me and added that even though I carry the marks, scars and difficulties of the tragedy, they have always seen me smiling and cheering others up. 'You are a courageous lady indeed,' said one of them.

I told them about my philosophy. What had happened was my past, so why should I spoil my present and future by worrying about what would happen. 'When we meet real tragedy in life, we can react in two ways—by losing hope and falling into the pit of destruction, or by using the challenges to find our inner strength. We all have it within us. Some like to find it, but some sit and brood over the past.' I told them how I believe we only get to live life once and I was lucky to be blessed with a second chance, so I should be enjoying every moment of it.

Nidhi Chaphekar

Afterwards, Nishita and Jigar took us to Malabar Hills Club. I was visiting a club after ages. Live music was playing and a couple was singing. I noticed that many people were staring at me; some recognised me and some looked confused, as if they weren't able to place where they had seen me. We occupied a centre table and ordered our food. The moment I finished eating, a young man came to our table and said, 'May I have the opportunity to take the ladies to the dance floor?' Nishita politely refused. Rupesh and Jigar informed him that I can't dance as I have injuries.

But the music was tempting me. I love dancing, and it had been six months since I'd danced. The doctor's words rang in my ears — *Your confidence can beat anyone...*

I stood up and said aloud, 'Excuse me, I would like to join you.'

Everyone was shocked! 'Nidhi, don't go, please sit!' they tried to dissuade me.

But I assured them I would be careful. I told the man, 'Don't push or pull me, let me be a slow dancer.'

The moment I reached the dance floor, it was as if my feet started dancing on their own! I danced for nearly the duration of an entire song! I thanked the young man. The moment I was back at my table, people started coming and congratulating me for the strength I had shown after the Brussels blast, and the spirit I nurtured. When the singer saw so many people around my table, he thought there was something wrong and approached us. Then he heard what the others were saying and recognised me from the photo he had seen on the Internet. He looked shocked as he shook hands with me and told me, 'We could never have expected a person who is due for a calcaneum surgery to be so active, to dance! Please allow me to introduce my wife to you as she is your fan and would be so glad to meet you.'

His wife asked me, 'From where do you get this strength?'

I said, 'See the people around you, appreciate your family, acknowledge the beauty of nature, the beauty of all the varied colours around us, the love and compassion of all who are in our life, the relations you have built, and be thankful to God that you are alive to cherish them. There is so much you have. Your strength will automatically rise. Never let your heart lose hope, and always listen to what it says.'

Standing near us was an old man, probably around ninety years of age, with a woman who seemed to be either his sister or his wife. He came to me, held my hand, and with tears in his eyes, kissed my forehead and said, 'I prayed to God for your well-being. You have gone through so much, but I am happy that you never lost the strength.'

I thanked him and said, 'I am fine today not only because of my strength but also because of a very important factor—prayer. Prayers always count.'

I felt so overwhelmed with all the love I received.

While leaving the club, an old couple came up to me and the gentleman said, 'I lost my sister in the Mumbai blast. But I am glad to see you back.' I was at a loss for words.

❧

17 AUGUST 2016

I got a call from Arun informing me that *Times Now*, ANI (*Asian News International*), and *BBC Radio* would like to interview me. He wanted to schedule the interviews for tomorrow. But as I would be celebrating Raksha Bandhan the next day, I said, 'Let's keep it for the 19th.'

The only worry this time was how I would sound on *BBC Radio* as till date I had never given a radio interview. Anyway, I didn't want to worry about it for now.

Time flew by. We had guests from my husband's family coming over to see me. So I planned to cook today. Everyone was against the idea, but I told them, 'Just wait and see the tricks I know!'

I wore three pairs of gloves. First, my medical ones, then the surgical ones, and then the rubber ones so that I don't harm my hands. I placed a stool in front of the gas stove and sat on it; then on a very low flame, I began cooking. I did get a lot of help of course from Madhuri, the kids and Rupesh. I had to remove the top two layers of gloves in an hour's time, as the perspiration was causing the medical gloves to become soggy.

I cooked paneer and dal makhani for the first time in six months. It was such a hit! Everyone appreciated it. I thanked God for giving me the courage to overcome challenges.

❦

19 AUGUST 2016

I had interviews lined up today. Starting at 1100 hrs, one by one we finished all the interviews by 1630 hrs. The radio interview was on Skype where I could only hear the interviewer and not see her. The question I found the most difficult to answer was when I was asked for my comments on the photo of the child injured in the Syrian bomb attack, sitting in an ambulance, whose picture had gone viral just as mine had. I had just read the headlines in the morning newspaper about the incident that had happened on 18 August. I did not go into the details of the story, but I commented on how unfair it was, on human grounds, to capture the image of a child who is so innocent and was not even aware of what had happened. Why publicise the child? The poor child must be traumatized and in shock, and to make it worse, we so-called human beings were being heartless about it! Rather than provide help or reassurance to the child in that situation, we were trying to capture his pain and confusion on camera! He had barely started the journey of life, but we were robbing him of his innocence simply because we have technology? Once he grows up, he would surely ask who gave the media the right to do this. He may reflect on how much pain he suffered, how he cried when he felt abandoned. He would always revisit that trauma in memory, the outrage and confusion, but would know that he would never seek vengeance. He would tell himself—it happened to me, but I believe it was the fault of adults; I was and I am innocent.

Is it only us adults who have access to media footage? What about kids, teenagers, who would ask you a hundred questions related to this child? What about the communal hatred we have generated? After looking at the picture, children would not keep quiet; we may not even be able to answer some of their questions. As a result, we would be misshaping their beliefs and they may conclude the whole community or world is like that. After all, a child comes into this world with no stress or worries, no preconceived prejudices.

I actually had tears streaming down my face as I answered the interviewer. I had very strong views on this matter—no one has the right to use our pictures as and when they want to, without our consent. We need to behave with civility. Often something new catches our eye, and we simply click and post a picture or a write-up online or circulate it, but do we think of the possible consequences before doing so? Do we realise there is an individual, a particular personality and image behind the picture? Nobody has the right to sell anyone's personality. We need to think and behave with compassion and forethought. I wanted to bring about this awareness among people, and mentally resolved to do something about it in the future.

The only quote I could remember at the time was one by Mahatma Gandhi—'If we are to teach real peace in this world, and if we are to carry on a real war against war, we shall have to begin with the children.'

❧

20 AUGUST 2016

I got a call from Kurt, a reporter at the Belgium newspaper *Het Laatste Nieuws*. Kurt had been in touch with the doctors at Charleroi for merely a month while I was there, and had been enquiring about how I was doing. He had tried to reach out to me, but I was not allowed to give any interview. Yet the photographer had managed to click pictures of me coming out of the hospital while they were transferring me into an ambulance the day I had to leave. I had said a few words to thank the doctors and the team at the hospital who had done such a remarkable job. I had spoken only for a few minutes, but this man had heard me speak. Later, he got in touch with Sumita di at the embassy and managed to get my number. He told me they would like to interview me, as on 22 September, it would be six months since the incident and they wanted to publish a big article about it. I invited him to join me with his team on 28 August for my birthday celebrations, but he said they could only arrive by 31 August and would stay with me for three days. They wished to capture glimpses of my everyday life, of my daily routine, how I coped with my condition. They required an invitation letter, so I sent them one.

❧

24 AUGUST 2016

My kids had a presentation at school today for which the parents had been invited. I had told them I would come. When I reached the school, their head teacher was amazed to see me. Many other teachers also came over to where I stood and spoke to me. Their words touched me deeply.

One of the teachers said, 'Your kids are very strong. The strength they showed when both of you were not here was amazing. Not even a single day were they absent. We thought it would be a challenge for us to handle them but really, we have to tell you, they were so understanding and bold all this while. We came to know from news reports that you were in a state of induced coma and severely injured. To our surprise, we saw your kids coming to school! All the classes were set to pray for you. We hugged your daughter. Your son was quiet. When we spoke to them, they said, "We are okay and we know our mom will be fine and will travel back soon. She is very brave. Nothing will happen to her. We know her." Hearing this, we had tears in our eyes. The kind of confidence they showed in you proves they think so highly of you, and we realised that we should also admire your strength.'

❧

I had an interview with *The Week* magazine. We started at 1400 hrs and were supposed to finish by 1600 hrs, but it was evening when we finally wrapped up. The editor who interviewed me, Mr Tiwari, said, 'It is a one-of-a-kind story. The image I had in my mind before coming here was different, but you proved me wrong. I am glad I came here because your story can inspire many people, especially those who have lost hope.'

I said I had read somewhere that 'the word *hope* itself stands for *Have Only Positive Expectations*'!

Mr Tiwari was a writer. He told me, 'I would recommend you to please write a book. It would be an inspiration for others to learn from you. From no angle do I find that you are sick or ill or have gone through so much!'

Every day I met different people and their words meant a lot to me. I would share everything with my mom and also with Ms Pom who is a true friend. They used to encourage me a lot. Rupesh and the kids were proud of me. My daughter would always keenly listen to what people said about me.

❧

26 AUGUST 2016

We sometimes blindly believe in others, but not in our own selves. Today, though not for the first time, I heard something that upset me. But whenever someone has said anything unkind to me, it has always made me stronger and believe in myself more than before.

Some of the elderly ladies from the nearby locality came to meet me today. After some time, one of the women said, 'You are like my daughter, so I am advising you to be more careful. Keep a watch on your husband. Now he may not have any interest left in you and might find you boring as he is young.'

Another one said, 'trust me, ask him to legally sign all the money and property in your name as he may later leave you, since you are no longer working and your medical condition is also not good. The kids are small, think about them.'

I was stern in my response. 'If your advice is over, can I take your leave?' My reaction was rude but it was required.

Their words were like a bug; the more you let a bug stay, the more it will gnaw at you. It's always better to believe in oneself. I didn't tell anyone about what the women had said, because I believe that those who love me would never leave me, and I closed that chapter.

❧

27 AUGUST 2016

At around 2330 hrs, when I was about to sleep, I saw a message from Ms Pom. When I read it, I couldn't believe my eyes. It informed me that on 25 August, the APAI (Air Passengers Association of India) had celebrated its silver jubilee and had recognised me with the bravery award in the Special Jury's category. I couldn't understand much and I searched the Internet for details. I found that the award had been announced and given by Textiles Minister Ms Smriti Irani and our CEO received it on my behalf. I felt really nice but then felt bad as well because it is a different feeling when you receive an award yourself.

Anyway, it was a wonderful start to my birthday. I woke up Rupesh and told him the news. He couldn't believe it either.

He said, 'Your company should have informed you about this.'

I messaged the corporate communications manager, Mr Mannu Hatti, and the CPO regarding this. Mr Hatti replied, 'We were also not informed, and we are surprised nobody informed you.'

It was a big thing and he too was unaware! My family and friends were so glad to hear about it. I felt on top of the world!

❧

28 AUGUST 2016

In the morning at 0930 hrs, my daughter said, 'Get ready quickly... we are going shopping for you. You need more clothes!'

I was very excited by the idea of shopping but it being a Sunday, I was in two minds. Rupesh, Vriddhi and Vardaan forced me by saying that Jolly di would come along too, so I should get dressed soon. By 1030 hrs, I was out of the house. On the way to the mall, they said they had to pick up Jolly di from her place. When we got there, she said she was not yet ready, so we should come over and have tea.

The moment we reached her floor, I saw decorations everywhere, and when I went in, I saw a priest sitting facing a Ganesha idol and photos of other deities. Everything was decorated with flowers. They had planned a surprise for me! They had organised a puja to pray for me, for a long, healthy and wealthy life. Jolly di had made the arrangements and everyone was aware of it but no one had told me. And 'shopping' was just a ruse to get me to her place. It had been exactly two months since I last visited her place.

The priest gave me a chair to sit on, but according to Hindu tradition, a puja is done sitting on the floor. As I was not allowed to sit down and had not even tried it until then, they were scared when I said, 'Let me try at least.'

Placing two cushions on the floor, I sat carefully, but after an hour I was unable to keep my leg straight. I massaged my leg, stood for ten minutes, and then once again sat down even while everyone was vociferously urging me not to do so. The priest said, 'Be comfortable. God never asks us to put ourselves through pain.'

But I said, 'He has given me the strength and courage to do it, so I will sit down.'

I hadn't felt so good in all the last few months as I did in that moment. In some time, I saw my mother-in-law, Madhuri, Nilesh and their kids entering the house. They smiled at me. All of them had known about it, but they had kept it a secret in order to surprise me. The ceremony went on from noon to 1430 hrs, after which we had lunch followed by tea. We left Jolly di's place at 1730 hrs. Everything

Nidhi Chaphekar

was done so beautifully that even today I feel the grace of it.

In the evening, the kids made me cut a cake. We ordered pizza and relished it.

Days were passing by so quickly, at times I felt dazed. I thanked God for keeping me alive to see such a beautiful world and to be with my family, the most wonderful people.

I believe in the maxim—Don't cry over the past; it is gone. Don't stress about the future; it hasn't arrived. Live in the present, appreciate this day, pray and be grateful to God and He makes life more beautiful.

❧

29 AUGUST 2016

In the morning, I got a call from *France 2* (a French national television channel)—they wanted to make a small documentary on me. I asked them to see me the next day. To my surprise, they wanted to shoot everything at home—including how I did my physiotherapy and managed my daily routine. I agreed. I asked my physiotherapist to come late in the evening tomorrow.

❧

30 AUGUST 2016

At 1100 hrs, the *France 2* team arrived and we spoke for a while over tea. Navodita from their team had been in touch with me via messages. After meeting her and her teammates Thomas and Nicolas in person, I felt nice. We started shooting at noon.

First, they interviewed me, asking more or less the same questions everyone asked. Then they opened their laptop and asked me to recollect events and describe my location from the video footage they showed me. I saw a few pictures I had never seen before. I had tears in my eyes when I told them I was right next to the bird sculpture and had just turned to my left when the bomb exploded. No matter how many times I narrated the story, my eyes would always tear up as vivid images flashed in front of me.

One of them said to me, 'We thought you must be feeling low, but on the camera you spoke marvellously... you spread such positivity!'

I shared my views with them. 'What I saw will die with me, as there are no words to describe the trauma we went through. But to prevent this from happening in the future, we all need to introduce love and peace among people once again. We know it is there, but we are not valuing it. And to do this, it is very important to let my voice reach out to the world.'

I had also asked them if they could convey my gratitude to the royal family through their channel as I really wanted to thank them personally. Nicolas said he would put me in touch with the office of the king.

Soon it was time for my physiotherapy session, after which the kids came home. The *France 2* team was more than happy to meet them.

Nicolas and Thomas were from Brussels and were really touched when I spoke highly about their people, when I talked fondly about the medical team and staff in both the hospitals there who had helped us immensely. They said they were really sorry for whatever happened to me, 'but [it's great to see] you still having so much of love for the people. You give out a very different message.'

I told them, 'there's a saying that life is ten percent what happens to us and ninety percent how we react to it.'

❧

Kurt, from *Het Laatste Nieuws*, had landed from Belgium in the morning and was trying to get in touch with me. I was tired, but I can never break anyone's heart. So I said, 'Sure, come any time.'

We wound up the interview with Navodita and her team at 1630 hrs and had some snacks. Ten minutes after they left, Kurt and his cameraman Joost arrived.

Kurt held in his hand a big page folded about eight times or more, almost like a small notebook. I had tea with them. Kurt explained they would like to be with me for the next three days.

He said, 'Do what you do in your daily routine and we will only interrupt you if we need to.'

They would interview me in the morning, and for now, they would put together a little summary, just to understand the present scenario. Kurt started with a few questions and jotted down only one or two words every now and then on the folded paper in his hand. When I asked him, 'How would you understand these notes?' he smiled and said, 'I have been doing this for years now.'

We went on and on for nearly two hours. Then I told him, 'I think this much should be enough for the day.'

'Your story is so interesting and amazing... and I got so involved in it that I just did not realise the time!' Kurt paused, and then added, 'Coming to India from so far away has been more than what I expected.'

When they left, I noticed the kids were waiting for me. They complained I never gave them my time these days.

I explained to them, 'Whenever I can, I make it a point to be with you. That's why on Saturdays and Sundays I make sure I am with you all the time. But this is also very important because being a survivor of such an incident, facing the after-effects of it while still in recovery, the most important lesson we learn in life is to have courage to overcome our fears. One who is not courageous enough to take risks will accomplish nothing in life. People face defeat in life many times, but maybe my message to the world can bring a change in their lives. You all make me strong, so now it's my duty to make others strong too. At least I can try. Maybe they need someone.'

The kids hugged me. 'Mom, you are doing a great job,' said Vardaan.

'We are proud of you,' beamed Vriddhi.

❦

31 AUGUST 2016

At exactly 1100 hrs, Kurt and Joost arrived. I spoke till 1330 hrs and I think I covered all the topics and events I could remember.

'thank God I came in early. I want to publish your story on 22 September, and I think it would take me at least two weeks to write the whole story,' announced Kurt after I finished.

He wanted to visit Jolly di's place too, where I had spent the first two months after returning from Belgium. So we headed to Andheri West and reached her house at around 1400 hrs. We had some snacks there and he spent time talking to Amarjeet jiju and Jolly di. When he saw the room I had occupied and understood how I managed to get into the washroom, his eyes filled with tears.

While having tea, I received a call from Breach Candy Hospital, asking if I would be available to see Dr Milind Kirtane today as someone had cancelled an appointment. A Padma Shri awardee, he is considered to be one of the best ENT surgeons in Asia. I had been unable to get an appointment with him earlier, and once when I did manage it, he had been ill for nearly ten days and so I couldn't meet him. I immediately agreed to reach the hospital by 1800 hrs.

It was already 1530 hrs. I told my sister we had to leave immediately. Joost required our family photograph; Jolly di asked him to visit again tomorrow evening. Kurt said he had obtained enough content for his story and he didn't need anything further.

I wanted to buy some fruits for home, so on our way back, I got down at the market. And there I saw my kids coming back from school. They got out of their car to meet us. Joost took the opportunity to click a few photographs and said now there was no need for him to come back tomorrow for the family pictures. I then asked, 'Which of these fruits do you not get in Belgium?'

One of them pointed at a stack of custard apples. So I asked the fruit seller to pack a few kilos each for both of them. I selected the unripe ones to be packed and took a ripe one from the fruit seller, scooped out the pods and showed them how to eat it. It was yummy, and they loved it! (When they got back to Belgium, Kurt sent me a picture of his son enjoying the fruit.)

❧

When I met Dr Kirtane, he examined me and said, 'You have a hole in the left eardrum and we need to operate.'

He explained that when doctors know the details of such an occurrence, they give it about three to four months, but in my case five and a half months had already passed by in this condition, so it would not be possible to get back the original shape and form of the ear. Once they operate, it would be fine in three months though, he assured me. I was never one to wait. But he told me the junior doctor, Dr Dhruv, would tell me about available dates for surgery by tomorrow evening. He felt sorry for not being able to do anything about the tinnitus — the buzzing sounds in my ear with which I have to live.

❧

1 SEPTEMBER 2016

I had planned to meet my father on 18 or 19 September. I was excited and busy counting the days left. But when I called Dr Dhruv in the evening, he gave me two dates — 14 September and 21 September — and informed me that after this month, he only had dates available after Diwali. That would be after 4 November. When I asked him about the recovery time, he said it would take three months for me to fully heal post-surgery. And how long before I could fly, I asked him. Six weeks, he said. I told him that I would get back to him tomorrow with a confirmation. It was a difficult situation for me because I had always celebrated Diwali with my parents, but I knew that if I waited, there could be chances of an infection setting in. So, I decided to cancel the trip and planned to get the surgery done on 14 September. I always make my decisions myself even though I discuss them with everyone. I take everyone's opinion and then choose to do whatever I feel is correct.

❧

Ganesh Chaturthi, an eleven-day festival celebrated with great pomp and energy, especially in Maharashtra, was to begin the next day. Many families buy a new Ganesha idol for worship during this period. I went to buy sweets and garlands for Ganesha, as every year we visit seven houses to offer prayers and partake of the Lord's blessings. It is a beautiful time to be in this city. A few people recognised me in the market and I received warm enquiries.

'Wow, a new look!'

Some said, 'Looking at your strength—hats off to you, ma'am! Even after so much suffering, you are doing all this.'

I said, 'Ganesha helped me in rising once again in life, so there should be something I should do to thank Him, isn't it? I have always done this in previous years, so why not this time too?'

When people praise me and say such nice things, it gives me the stamina to stay positive in life.

❧

4 SEPTEMBER 2016

The day I was waiting for. I wore a salwar suit for the first time since the incident. I felt my short hair did not go well with my attire but I was happy nonetheless. We left for the darshan. In about ninety minutes, we reached the first house. It was on the outskirts of Mumbai, in the heart of Vasai. Many of our distant relatives and their family friends were seeing me for the first time after the incident.

'You have got a second life. God has been very kind to you. It would be great if you would do the aarti on our behalf,' said Rupesh's cousin Raju. Performing the aarti in such an atmosphere gave me an inexplicable, charged-up feeling.

The puja went on for about thirty minutes. I loved visiting one house after another. Wherever I went, I was met with looks of surprise and so many questions and good wishes.

By the time we returned home in the evening, I was so tired I slept like a log. But my lesson for the day was this: Most of us think that people judge you on the basis of your looks but we must understand that we also have the ability to change the way people think with our own behaviour and confidence. Never stop yourself from participating in activities around you, and enjoy living life to the fullest. Life never rewinds time for you.

❦

7 SEPTEMBER 2016

Sidhi from the *Guardian* came to interview me. She brought a recorder along. She had sent me a very beautiful letter while I was recovering. I spoke for nearly three hours without a break. I showed her my watch, bangles, chain and ring and such, and narrated what had happened to them. At 1430 hrs, Atin, the photographer, arrived. We were waiting for him to take a few pictures, but I was asked to recall some more of the story. Atin also said it would be better to wait as they needed some pictures with my kids. The kids got home at 1615 hrs and Atin continued shooting live as I spent some time with them. Before we knew it, it was 1830 hrs and it suddenly struck me that I had been invited to attend a dinner at a doctor friend's house, so I quickly requested Atin and Sidhi to wind up.

Although I was tired and sleepy, I had made a commitment and so I got ready. At dinner, where they had called many more friends, they announced it was to celebrate the victory of a girl who had shown bravery at every stage of her journey, who was battling against all odds and was still smiling and blooming like a flower.

They said to me, 'One of the main topics we discuss when we see patients suffering or giving up hope is you. You are our benchmark.'

I felt so touched. I didn't know how to thank God for such an appreciative gesture. Hearing praise from different people across the world truly gave me the immense satisfaction of knowing that my existence counted for many, that with a can-do outlook towards life, I was directing others to value all the good in their lives.

❧

8 SEPTEMBER 2016

I prepared aloo parathas for the kids. It was another first for me! They were so thrilled. I too would find so much happiness in these small but significant activities.

❧

The doorbell rang at 0800 hrs. It was the lab pathologist who was to administer my tests. He took six bottles with him and said he would come back at 1430 hrs to take a second sample, so I needed to have lunch before 1230 hrs. I finished lunch at 1230 hrs sharp so there wouldn't be any difference in the values reflected in the test report. All these tests had to be shown to the doctor to get his approval for the surgery. I would get the reports the day after tomorrow. I felt sure all would be fine, but still needed official confirmation to go ahead with my surgery.

❧

9 SEPTEMBER 2016

In the evening, my mother-in-law and some of her friends paid a visit. When they saw me working in the house, they were aghast. One of them asked me whether I was allowed to work like this. I said, 'Aunty, doctors don't know your capability, so as a precautionary measure, they advise you to be safe. But yes, I know I have to take care of my hands. So I stay away from steam and direct heat as far as possible. I cook things on a low flame only if I have to. Imagine how difficult it would have been if I lived alone? We should try our best, and when we try with all our heart, we will never be let down.'

Some of them wanted to know whether the doctor had asked

me to practise hand exercises, such as opening and closing the fist, as my hands could become stiff due to the grafts.

I said, 'Yes, but if I do household work on a regular basis, I may not need to do these exercises after some time. Most of us strictly follow what the doctor says, but the doctor never stops us from trying to do other work... it is we who ban ourselves from trying it out. But if we find work that may help follow the doctor's instructions, it would give us more satisfaction too.'

Isn't it true? As Stevie Wonder once said, 'We all have ability. The difference is how we use it.'

❦

Another remarkable conversation happened today. I went to the Durga Maa temple. The pandit (priest) recognised me and the moment I said namaste, he asked, '*Kya ho gaya*?' (What happened?)

I was limping a bit and was wearing the terra band on my foot (which I was asked to wear for a few years). I was using the walker as well for safety. I narrated briefly all that had happened. He had tears in his eyes and said the religious beliefs of the perpetrators were to blame. I requested Panditji not to blame the religion but the individuals. We humans have created so many conflicts among ourselves. He was dissatisfied with what I said. So I told him no one is born a terrorist. It is because we have created differences among ourselves—we have put up barriers of religion and caste, and fail to understand that we are all humans. No religion teaches anyone hatred or revenge, but we fail to understand what we are truly here for.

I explained further. 'Okay, suppose I am a person who has no money, no value for religion, no good relations with anyone, is frustrated with life, has no value in society, can be emotionally carried away, and wants to take revenge because I am depressed. This means my mind is not stable... it is weak. And to vent my anger, I join a group. They give me so much money and training, and then brainwash me in the name of religion. They encourage me to become a martyr to get their rights and finally turn me into

Unbroken　　　221

a terrorist. I now want to sacrifice my life to take other lives as per the order of the group I work for and false teachings that I have been taught to blindly believe in. And I commit this disaster, but I don't realise that the people I've killed are ordinary human beings who just want to live. It is because my mind is in such a weakened state that I would be provoked to take such a drastic and rather inhuman step. This is the prime reason why we should do things to strengthen our minds so that before we accept any religion, we should learn to acknowledge that we are humans first, an individual, a kind soul. Now tell me who is to be blamed?'

He replied, 'I am surprised that in spite of suffering so much, you are still a person who finds love in every human being!'

I said, 'We only create differences among us. The Dalai Lama once said, "The very purpose of religion is to control yourself, not to criticize others; rather, that, we must criticize ourselves. How much am I doing about my anger? About my attachment, about my hatred, about my pride, my jealousy? These are the things which we must check in daily life." It's we who must generate love and make it bloom forever. What happened to me was fate... it was bound to happen, but see how God has been so kind and given me the courage to live.'

Panditji was glad to hear my thoughts. I told him, 'You are a man of God. You should never generate differences among people. Share love.' I felt it was not panditji's fault to think so. Such a thought could have risen in any human being's mind.

People around us came closer now. One of them said to me, 'We were following your news every day and we were also praying for you. You have proved that prayers never go waste. They have the power to heal a person.'

I thanked everyone around me; I was touched by their sentiments.

In the evening, I made chicken lollypops for the kids. This was of course done with the help of Rupesh, who prepared the marination according to my instructions.

My children cried tears of joy, as they saw it as a sign of their mom returning to normalcy. I felt so satisfied. It feels great when you are appreciated, encouraged and loved, that too by the little flowers of your family. And it feels even more special to have a husband who is the reason behind each and every success of mine.

❧

10 SEPTEMBER 2016

Sabah told me today, 'Now we will start using a stability disc and a stepper to increase the strength in your legs. It is good for restoring your body balance, which is very poor.' So we placed an order for both these things.

She said, 'By the time you come back from the hospital, both the pieces of equipment should be home.'

I told her, 'Your wish is my command. And now I am going to pack my walker and keep it aside. I have to understand I can walk without it.'

'But keep it, for safety,' was her advice.

I explained that I now need to learn balancing, and if I find the walker beside me, I will always be dependent on it. And so I put it away once and for all.

❧

12 SEPTEMBER 2016

I had an appointment with Dr Kirtane today. I collected all the reports required and went to the hospital with Rupesh at about 1000 hrs. When Dr Kirtane saw the reports, he said, 'the reports are fine, but Dr Dhruv will give you the date of the surgery and will be at the clinic in the evening.'

So I came back home at 1300 hrs and left again at 1630 hrs for the doctor's clinic.

When Dr Dhruv saw my reports, he asked me, 'Why didn't you go to the hospital to book yourself for tomorrow's admission?' I learnt that the hospital had informed him that his patient Nidhi had not come for admission. We made a dash to the hospital. When we got there at 1900 hrs, the receptionist gave me a form to fill and asked me to get it signed by the doctor... only then would I get admission for tomorrow's surgery. She added that it would be better if we come in the morning, as they were closing for the day.

I immediately called the doctor. He asked me whether I could make it to the clinic in an hour. Rupesh and I rushed again, filled the form and got it signed. When we got home, I was tired and had zero energy. In the morning, Mr Lama, from my company's administrative staff, went to the hospital, submitted the form, completed all the formalities and, finally, I was asked to get admitted in the evening.

❧

13 SEPTEMBER 2016

I was admitted to Breach Candy Hospital, Room No 407. Jolly di was to stay with me for two nights. I was served dinner at 2000 hrs and told, 'No water intake after 2200 hrs.'

As the surgery would take place at 0800 hrs, I was advised ten hours of fasting. I forgot to tell them that if I didn't hydrate myself, I would get a severe headache. Jolly di and I were up talking till 2300 hrs. Then we turned off the lights. But I couldn't sleep throughout the night.

❧

14 SEPTEMBER 2016

At 0630 hrs, the nurse came and said to me, 'Please take a bath with this liquid.'

It was a disinfectant meant to be used as a body wash before the surgery. I was ready by 0730 hrs. I was taken to the X-ray room for a chest X-ray. I told them I could walk but the nurse said, 'We don't want to take any risk before the surgery, so please sit on the WCHL,' and I was back in the room by 0800 hrs.

I was so thirsty. At 1015 hrs, the ward boy came with a stretcher and I was shifted onto it. I was then taken in the elevator into a narrow passage. I realised the general lack of space in our hospitals... and yet we manage to run the show so well! It was a long passage, at the end of which I was taken into a room where there were two other people waiting on stretchers. One of them had just come out of surgery and another was about to be taken in for surgery. A few nurses were standing nearby, and I told them I was feeling very cold. They covered me with a blanket that had a warm underlining sheet that worked as a heating pad.

For nearly forty minutes, I waited there. I saw Dr Kirtane and he said they were taking a breather of fifteen minutes while readying the operation theatre. Once the theatre was cleaned and the machines were shifted as required, I was taken in. I mentally saluted our doctors, who are always overburdened with work. An IV was attached to my left hand. The anesthesiologist said she would give me local anaesthesia and then sedate me.

My surgery finally started at noon. I was turned to my right side. My face was covered with a green sheet, leaving only my left eye and nose uncovered. After sedation, I felt my body become a bit heavy. Local anaesthesia was administered to my left ear. I could understand that some kind of incision was being made behind my ear. I was told that the surgery would take thirty to forty minutes.

There was a big screen up in front of the doctors that I could also watch, although initially I closed my eyes. Then, curious to know what was happening, I looked up at the screen and saw my ear had been opened up and some sharp tools were going in. My God, there were so many veins! I couldn't take my eyes off the screen. The doctor started drilling in the ear.

I felt the pain and said aloud, 'Doctor, it's hurting me!'

He called for another injection. I saw the needle going into my ear. He had to drill deep because there was some skin destruction inside the ear due to the metals that had scraped the area, and skin had grown there; it looked like a tiny pearl inside. While he was explaining all this to the other junior doctors, I suddenly felt very hot and breathless, maybe because of all that I was watching live. I told the doctor about it and he instructed the assisting staff to remove the body heating pad (an inflatable shield filled with hot air). But even then I was sweaty. I asked them to take off my blanket as well. Dr Dhruv came and took it off and even raised the sheet covering my legs. As I continued looking at the screen, I saw him doing it.

I said, 'thank you, Dr Dhruv.'

Everyone was surprised about how I knew it was Dr Dhruv. I told them, 'I can see and I am seeing my surgery too.'

'You are not supposed to see that!' admonished Dr Kirtane.

He immediately asked someone to switch off the screen. But I kept telling him that I was fine with it. I asked him whether they had had some pictures taken of the surgery in progress. I had specifically requested them to click a few pictures while they operated on me, so that I would be able to view these later with my family. Dr Kirtane said yes, they had.

The surgery took one hour and forty-five minutes. Afterwards, the anesthesiologist said that in her forty years of medical practice, I was the first patient, as far as she could remember, whose vitals had not fluctuated even by a single digit. Amazing!

Later, they said they would shift me onto another stretcher. But I told them I would do so myself. And I sat up and shifted to the other stretcher. Seeing me do that, Dr Kirtane asked, 'I want to click a selfie with you... is that okay?'

I said, 'It would be my pleasure.'

'But after ten minutes,' he said. He would clean his hands and be back, he told me.

My stretcher was parked outside the operation theatre. Nurses were coming over and asking whether I was feeling okay. I told them yes, I was okay but thirsty. According to them, water could be served only after three hours. That is, 1700 hrs. I was dismayed to hear that.

Dr Kirtane came back a little later, stood next to my stretcher and tried to click a selfie, but couldn't get a clear image. So I told him to let me sit upright and request Dr Dhruv to take the photo. He was not too sure about this idea of mine. 'You might feel giddy!' he warned.

'But let me try, you are there na.' I was resolute.

He finally gave his phone to Dr Dhruv instead, who clicked our picture. When we reached the room, I shifted myself to my bed. Both the ward boys were amazed. One of them told me, 'You are the first patient we have seen who has come out of the operation theatre smiling and talking! We have seen people with mild incisions crying and yelling.'

I told them, 'From my point of view, pain is temporary. It may last an hour, a day, a year, but eventually it subsides. But the impact of a smile changes the world and has an ever-lasting effect. I also realise it is the love and affection my near and dear ones have for me that has ensured I have not felt pain at all.'

They smiled and left. Later, the nurses came in and told me, 'All the people here are talking about you, praising your will power.' They said they had read about me, about my undying spirit, in the papers, but today they saw it in person.

I told them, 'Pain can only touch you if you allow it to.'

I was told my ear would bleed a bit, but I should not worry and I should only sleep on my right side for the next ten days, because of the stitches and the raw wound. As I had requested for an early discharge, Dr Kirtane sent a message saying that he felt I didn't need any hospitalisation and if I wished, I could go home by late evening. I was so excited to hear that!

One of the nurses said to me, 'You may be the first patient to go home on the same day of surgery. But let this IV drip get over first, then we will make you drink and eat by 1700 hrs.'

By this time my head was spinning because I had not eaten anything or even had water. I told another nurse about it, and she made me drink some water. Within ten minutes, I vomited. She gave me some medicine with water. I vomited again. I told her I have this acute gastric problem. My head was bursting with pain. My sister announced then, 'We will not take a discharge today.'

I told them it was only because of an empty stomach and that I would be fine after taking medicines. But by this time, Rupesh and Jolly di and the hospital staff were scared too. I was given another medicine and yet I vomited again. This kept happening for some time. At about 2000 hrs, I was still in this state when Dr Kirtane entered my room. He was concerned and said, 'this is not you!'

I told him, 'Doctor, don't get worried. This is the only thing I cannot take—a headache. And lately, its frequency has increased.'

He said he trusted me. He saw my bandage had blood all over because of the pressure and force with which I was vomiting and hitting my ear against the bed in the process. He said he would send Dr Dhruv in to redo the bandage for me. I was finally given painkiller injections too. But still my condition didn't subside. Rupesh couldn't even massage the sides of my forehead as he would have otherwise because of the surgery in my ear. Finally at midnight, I had a little dal and rice and slept on my right side as instructed. It was tough not being able to turn sides all night but I managed.

❦

15 SEPTEMBER 2016

We had decided to leave early in the morning so as to avoid traffic. I woke up at 0730 hrs feeling okay, but my head was still heavy. I freshened up and had breakfast. At 0800 hrs, Dr Dhruv came to my room. He saw my bandages and changed them. He advised me not to wash my hair for two weeks, to avoid heavy exercise and to be very careful while sleeping. He prescribed a few medicines to be taken for three months.

The discharge papers took nearly two hours to be processed and I was discharged at 1100 hrs. Relieved, we set off for home.

On the way back home, I saw many Ganesha idols on the road being carried for visarjan and thought to myself, *Lord Ganesha came to people's houses for eleven days and is going back to His home today. I too am going back to my home today...*

Once home, I realised things were going to be tough as I could hear with only one ear now. I narrated the whole story of my surgery to my kids, and they were full of questions. Was I not afraid, they wanted to know.

I said, 'It's all in your heart and mind. Try to get control over them, and you will achieve whatever you want.'

❦

16 SEPTEMBER 2016

The whole day passed in thanking everyone who had read my story in the *Guardian*. So many people called to congratulate me for my strength, love, positivity and courage, and for the message I shared with the world. My friends from London and Canada saw it online. They passed it on to their friends and the message was being spread there too. I was feeling over the moon, not because I had become famous, but because people were admiring my strength and, in the process, their own courage was getting a boost.

In the evening, I got a call from my nephew, Sahil, from Doha. He informed me a certain Mr Dhiraj Mishra, who had made a movie named *Chapekar Brothers*, had called him many times to ask for my number. I told him to go ahead and pass on my number. But I couldn't help wondering why this person had called up my nephew and what the film was about...

❦

17 SEPTEMBER 2016

In the morning, I got a call from Mr Mishra. He introduced himself as a film writer and said he had made a movie named *Chapekar Brothers*. I asked him openly, 'But how do I believe you?'

He said he would send me the link to the film's trailer first and then would speak to me again. After I watched the trailer, I urged him to call me back. He told me, 'this film is about the freedom fighters, and you being a Chaphekar, are also a fighter. So it would be a pleasure to meet you. Can you make it for the promo of the movie?'

The movie was to be released on 23 September. He said they hadn't been able to decide a promo date as they were busy trying to get in touch with me, and thought they could have the promo on either 21 September or 22 September.

I agreed but also told him I may not be able to see the entire movie as my left ear had just been operated. He said, 'Your presence would create an impact. It's completely up to you and as per your comfort.'

I wanted to know about the history of the Chapekar brothers, so I did a Google search. The day passed by once again talking to a lot of people, but I was feeling a bit awkward as well since I couldn't hear in my left ear. Sometimes, all the attention I got from people was frustrating for me, as I felt I had no time for myself and my kids, but on the other hand, I would think about how perhaps this new life had been given to me for the very purpose of reaching out to people. Maybe my presence and my talks would help someone.

❧

18 SEPTEMBER 2016

As it was a Sunday, there was no physiotherapy session today. I felt relaxed; no need to get up early in the morning, no exercise. But I had guests coming to meet me all the way from Vasai, my husband's hometown. They were from one of the committees run by Vasai Samaj, a community of Marathas. They had tea with us. Seeing me talking cheerfully, one of them asked me in astonishment, 'From where do you get this energy?'

My reply was simple. 'Can I change my past? Can I rewind what happened to me? The tape of time is always in play mode, so it is up to us what to play on it. I can only make my present and future beautiful. For that I need to put away the bad memories so that there is place only for my good present and future to bloom. I take my life as it comes, with all its surprises. I strongly believe you become what you feel about yourself and that is the reason for my energy.'

One of them said, 'After meeting you, we feel that if someone needs to learn how to handle bad phases in life, they should learn from you.'

They wished to invite me to be the chief guest at their annual function on 27 November to share my experience and how I came out of it with all the community members who would attend. They got me a bouquet of flowers, sweets and a handwritten letter with a poem in Marathi, praising me. I told them I would love to attend and accepted their invitation.

After the guests left, Vriddhi asked, 'Mom, why does everyone praise you so much?'

I said, 'When you grow up, you will understand better.'

Vardaan asked, 'Is it because we have not seen you crying or complaining to people about whatever has happened to you?'

I smiled, 'Yes. We should not complain about what happened and why. Instead, we should find solutions to live with it happily, as life is for living, and we must enjoy life as much as we can. Life is about making an impact, not just making an income. As a saying goes, there are two most important days in your life. One is the day you are born, and the other is the day you find out why you were born.'

❧

19 SEPTEMBER 2016

Mr Mishra called today to say he would send me the invitation to the promo. It was to be held on 21 September at 1700 hrs. Soon, the producer of the film also called. I learnt that they would be felicitating me for my courage and bravery.

In the evening, when I told my family about it, everyone congratulated me heartily. They teased me, 'At least this time you won't wear the orange slippers!'

I had worn orange-coloured slippers during all my interviews so far—they had a comfortable padding and served the purpose of at least not resorting to wear the special huge shoe that was made for me; but they were bright and sometimes called for extra attention. So I took out my flats and tried walking in them. It felt very different. Since I was used to the padded ones, I was not able to take the pressure on my foot too well. I decided to ask Sabah about it during our physiotherapy session in the evening.

She felt I could go ahead but advised me to be careful and ensure that I walk for not more than fifteen to twenty minutes in those slippers.

To prepare myself and to overcome this challenge, I wore the slippers and walked about fifty steps, but I got tired. I said to myself, never mind; tomorrow I will try again.

❦

20 SEPTEMBER 2016

Today I had a doctor's appointment at 1800 hrs. I was feeling great as the bandages on my ear would be removed today. I had to meet Dr Tibrewala as well at 1700 hrs for my review. We left home at 1600 hrs.

Dr Tibrewala saw me and said, 'You look well. It's so good to see you without the walker. It's all because of your determination.' And before I could say anything in reply, he continued, 'Nidhi, there is a young girl who has arrived from Dubai. She is in her teens. She slipped and fell from the fourth floor. Her calcaneum is badly ruptured in both feet. They did her basic treatment there in Dubai, and now for further treatment she has arrived here. And on the basis of your case, I have told her to follow in your footsteps. We have not done a bone graft yet. I have told her your story. How you are managing everything and trying to walk normally. Look, it's not even six months and you are walking like a normal person! So, if she wishes to speak to you, I will give her your number.'

I readily agreed to talk to her. Then he examined me and said, 'Everything I see in you is better. I feel you have improved a lot… great work. Please continue with the physiotherapy.'

I told the doctor, 'After meeting you, I feel even more enthusiastic!'

From there we went to Dr Kirtane's clinic.

My turn came around 1900 hrs as Dr Dhruv was not available until then. The doctor opened up my bandage and removed the gel they had inserted in my ear after the surgery. He held an instrument to my forehead and asked, 'tell me, how much can you hear?'

I couldn't hear anything from my left ear. While removing my bandages, he had told the nurse to schedule an appointment for me after five to six weeks, but now when I said I couldn't hear anything, he seemed worried. He said it was strange and he tried again and again after putting a few drops, but I still couldn't hear anything in my left ear while my right ear was fine. He took a deep breath and I could guess from his expressions that he was really perplexed as to why I was unable to hear.

He asked me again, 'Not even a little?' I shook my head to say no.

So he asked his secretary to call me after two weeks. He inserted the gel back in my ear. I was smiling although he looked concerned. I told him, 'I have faith in God. And more than that, I have faith in you. Don't worry, everything will be fine.'

Rupesh was apprehensive too. While driving back home, he angrily asked me, 'Who told you to do the surgery? I had asked you to take another opinion!'

I told him, 'the doctor also said it could be because of the swelling inside.'

'But now the doctor is also anxious!' retorted Rupesh.

I reasoned with him. 'We cannot recall the decision to operate, so just chill.'

❧

21 SEPTEMBER 2016

The promotional event for *Chapekar Brothers* – a film featuring the story of three famous freedom fighters – had been scheduled for today. I was looking forward to it and decided to go traditional. I selected a red-and-black salwar suit. For the first time after the ear surgery, I planned to wear ear studs. I got dressed by 1600 hrs.

Rain was battering the streets of Mumbai. It was a strange

coincidence, but every time we had to go for an interview or a check-up, it rained heavily. I told Rupesh it was a blessing from God before the event. I carried my earrings and flat sandals down to the car, and when we reached the venue, I wore them.

Jolly di and Amarjeet jiju were waiting for us in the lobby. Jolly di was so pleased to see me dressed in Indian ethnic wear.

Mr Mishra introduced me to the film's team, including the producer and the main cast. There were photographers clicking away as we talked. I didn't know where to focus, what to do!

At 1800 hrs, they announced my name and presented me with a memento. One of the actors, Ramdev, said, 'I used to follow your story in the news every day.'

At home, I had over fifty trophies and more than a hundred certificates. The last trophy I had brought home was in 1996. This was the first in twenty years!

❧

22 SEPTEMBER 2016

It was exactly six months since the Brussels airport incident that had changed my life—22 March is a date I would never forget.

In the morning, I received two bouquets, one from a friend and another from Ms Pom and team. It was a gesture of appreciation for the attitude I had shown in overcoming my difficulties so cheerfully. The captains who had manned the flight on that day also called me at 1230 hrs. I told them, 'God bless you for your kind gesture.'

Rupesh recalled how everyone had searched for news about me from this hour onwards till 2130 hrs that fateful day. I recollected each and every horrible moment. I was in an emotional state of mind and shed tears afresh, but I felt happy and grateful that God had given me another chance to live. In Belgium, the Indian Ambassador Mr Puri, Shabir bhai, Sumita di, Madan bhai, and the policeman, Alain, read my interviews in two newspapers and called me to convey how proud they were of me. Alain also shared a photo in which he was standing holding the newspapers with his three daughters.

I was told I am a true messenger of hope for the world and my boldness and attitude towards life had brought me here. They felt the day was not far when people around the world would quote my example.

It feels nice to be in touch with people around the world. But on the other hand, I faced a severe time constraint in my daily routine as I found no time for myself. I would be flooded with calls from all over the world. And the thing was if I didn't reply, it didn't look nice. I would think to myself, people don't know whether I am tech-savvy or not, whether my speed of typing is good or not. So even though I appreciate and value all their love and concern, if I don't message back, they might think otherwise. So I would make the effort to send at least a brief message in reply. It was so difficult to type with my gloves on. I had to wet the fingertips of the gloves slightly so that I could type. And I couldn't use the stylus for more than a short while as that was causing my hands to ache.

❦

24 SEPTEMBER 2016

I had to attend the Open House event at the kids' school, as well as a parent-teacher meet. Rupesh was unwell, so I went by myself. It was the first time that many of the teachers and parents too would be meeting me. I reached at 0830 hrs. One by one, everyone, including parents whose kids were not even known to my kids, began recognising me and congratulating me on my fighting spirit and persistence. Many said, 'You have got a second life.'

I had to meet all the subject teachers individually. First, I went to meet Vardaan's Hindi teacher. The moment I entered the classroom, the teacher stood up and hugged me. She spoke good things about me and said, 'You are an example for my kids and family.'

Then I walked into the English teacher's room. She said, 'I am sorry, I don't recognise you.'

I said, 'I am Vardaan's mom.'

Immediately she stood up and shook hands with me. She spoke

highly about Vardaan and said, 'He had been really upset and had become quiet... he did not share his feelings. He's a braveheart and the most sensible child I've ever seen. I am so glad to see you back!'

Every teacher I met expressed similar feelings. They praised my kids for not missing school for even a day. They said it showed how brave I was and how brave I had raised my kids to be too. All of them told me Vardaan had check-point exams at the time of the incident and they were worried, but he had done brilliantly.

His art teacher added that Vardaan used to take care of Vriddhi like a responsible elder brother and that was a major change she had seen in him. They supported each other, in actions and not just words. Not even once had she seen them arguing. They behaved like mature adults. They were calm, positive, disciplined and most importantly, giving their best in every way. Listening to all this made me cry as I realised how much my kids had suffered. They had both understood the situation and behaved wisely. At times, I feel they grew up too soon. The experience I went through took away their childhood pleasures.

The curriculum head of the primary division, Ms Anjali said, 'Whenever you are free and feel like you can do it, we want you to speak to the kids in one of our assembly sessions, on "How to live life with the right attitude".'

I said it would be my pleasure to speak to the kids.

Many parents who were meeting me for the first time after the incident told me enthusiastically that they had not missed any of my interviews. A few said, 'If we were in your position, we would have died. How can someone deal with this experience?'

'Phases of life are temporary,' I told them. 'It will soon be part of the past and maybe erased from memory too.'

I felt really nice today, hearing such good things about me and my family. I thanked God for all that He was doing for me.

When I came home and narrated my experience, my kids exchanged knowing smiles. I hugged them and in my heart I felt sorry for taking away their cheeriness and that innocent, trusting attitude that only children can have so early in life. But I was glad that they had passed such a big hurdle with grace.

❦

25 SEPTEMBER 2016

The days were flying by. Today being a Sunday, the kids were busy with homework and presentations for the following week, so I relaxed by myself the whole day. But in the back of my mind, I kept thinking—*what next?* What should I try doing next?

The first thing that came to mind was that I should resume driving the car. Second, Diwali was round the corner and I wanted to clean the entire house. Earlier, because of my flight schedules at work, I would start Diwali cleaning a month in advance as I would do it over a span of twenty days or so. Now since I needed to be extra careful while doing all the house work, I decided to start doing things the coming week itself. I knew I could not work on the weekends as the kids wouldn't let me stand on a stool and clean the room, wall to ceiling. Nor would they allow me to lift anything. Rupesh would chide me if he saw me doing any such work. So I made up a schedule in my mind about all that I had to do starting tomorrow.

❦

26 SEPTEMBER 2016

In the morning, after my physiotherapy, I waited for Rupesh to leave. I worked nonstop for a few hours. I cleaned the walls and the beds first. The cupboards were left, but I knew that once I cleaned out the cupboards, everyone in the house would know about it.

For a month and a half now, I had a full-time housekeeper only to take care of my special needs. She would help me in my household work.

I was quite worried when I climbed onto a stool today. My housekeeper was with me but she couldn't reach the upper portion of the walls even with the help of the stool as she is short. The first thing I did was to put on three layers of gloves, so that the dust or water didn't touch the skin. I also covered my entire face such that only my eyes could be seen, to protect it from dust. Because it was my first day of hard manual work, when I finished cleaning one room by 1400 hrs, I was really tired. I took a shower and then slept soundly for two hours. When I woke up, my kids had come back home and I got busy with them.

❧

27 SEPTEMBER 2016

One of our airline cabin managers came home at 1300 hrs and we had a good chat. She told me, 'On every flight, you are a hot topic among the crew! They praise you a lot... you are still the crew members' favourite. They miss flying with you.'

Listening to her words, I wondered when I would resume flying.

She told me that she was at the airport when the incident took place. And when people heard my name being flashed in the news, they were speechless. Most of them began praying. Some said, 'Nothing can happen to her. She is a good soul.' She then added, 'I have learnt from you that if you give something good to the world, then over time, your karma will ensure you receive goodness yourself. As you are nice to everyone, God was kind to you.'

It felt wonderful to know about the lovely things that people had to say about me. But there had also been a not very pleasant thought that had been lurking in my mind for some time. I asked her about something I had heard from someone a few days ago—many also felt that I was taking advantage of the incident. She understood what I was trying to say.

'Yes,' she replied, 'there are a few who think that because of the incident you have become famous. That you got a lot of money by sharing your experience in talk shows. That the incident got a big push from the media, and you are actually perfectly fine but acting! They even think that you were aware that such an incident would happen and so you took this flight purposely to get fame. It was all planned!'

I was shocked to say the least. I wondered how people can even think like that. I understood that this could be the reason why many of my colleagues did not even bother to message me, forget calling! But I believe if you are true to yourself, you don't need to justify yourself to others because you have a clean conscience. I didn't want to dig deeper. I didn't want to give myself the chance to become a victim of their false notions. As a saying goes, 'Never waste your time trying to explain who you are to people who are committed to misunderstanding you.'

๏

29–30 SEPTEMBER 2016

Every day, from 1130 hrs onwards for a few hours, I would be busy cleaning. In the process, I discovered something wonderful. Until now, despite physiotherapy, my hands wouldn't close fully, and I wasn't able to make a fist. But now, I realised, I was able to do this easily! Also, earlier I couldn't balance myself while standing on one foot, but now even this was possible for a few seconds at least. I learnt that the more you try to lead a normal life, where you do regular things like walking around, maintaining a clean house, etc., the more flexible your body becomes. This gave my energy levels a major boost and I grew even more determined I could do everything if I persisted.

Next, it was time to try sitting on the floor and cleaning the lower level shelves in the cupboards. I was worried, what if something happened? How would I get up again from the floor? But if I didn't even try, how would I figure out whether I could do it or that there was still time before I could manage this task?

So I sat down slowly, holding the cupboard handle and bed for support. More than me, my housekeeper was anxious. She said, 'I wouldn't know what to do if something happens!'

I laughed and assured her nothing would happen.

After sitting on the floor for nearly an hour, my right foot became numb. So first I applied some cold compresses on my foot, just the way we do when we try to bring someone back to consciousness. And using the support of the edge of the bed, I knelt down on the ground and lifted my body. A little strain was okay, I told myself.

In the afternoon, my friend Pommy from London came to see me. She hugged me for a long time. She explained how she had gathered information from the management in her capacity as assistant manager at the London airport. With tears in her eyes, she asked, 'Why you?'

'We should think why such a thing could happen to anyone,' I mused.

'Agreed,' she continued, 'but you are such a good soul... you have a special place in everyone's hearts.'

I smiled, 'that's why I got my life back. See the good side of it!'

She asked me about the picture that had been taken and circulated. I told her I had not been aware of any photograph being taken at the time; I was dazed, troubled at the sight of people around me in distress and upset that I was unable to offer help to anyone. Helpless kids, women and men... everywhere I looked, people were crying, and I felt so bad because I didn't know what to tell them. Pommy and I spoke for nearly three hours. Later in the evening, we enjoyed some yummy panipuri at home. I was eating it after a gap of seven months! I loved it!

⁊

I OCTOBER 2016

So many festivals coming up this month... lots of shopping to do!

It was the beginning of a new month. I wanted to try something new. So I decided to drive the car by myself within the building compound. Everyone at home protested and tried to stop me at first, but Rupesh was in my favour. They were scared I would not be able to handle it because of the strain it would put on my legs. 'Let me drive alone,' I insisted adamantly.

And what confidence it gave me! I didn't allow anyone to sit beside me in the car. Of course, the main worry was whether I would be able to manoeuvre the car and not hit or injure anyone in the way! I am capable of driving with élan on the busy roads of any city in India. But things are a little different now and while driving around my residential compound, I realised I needed more flexibility in my feet. My feet could only stretch up to a certain angle. Just a matter of a few days of practice, I told myself.

❧

In the evening, I went to Parle market for the first time this year. I was distracted by the beautiful shoes on display in the shops. But I knew I couldn't buy any as I was not allowed to wear such shoes. It was tough for me but I fought back my emotions and told myself that once I recover completely, I would wear whatever I want to. Sometimes, you just have to let go of your desires, small and yet so significant. I felt like a kid. Just the way a child sulks when he or she insists on buying something in a shop and the mother simply refuses to. My head was the mother's voice and my heart was the child's cry.

❧

3 OCTOBER 2016

I went to a theatre to watch a movie with my husband, sister and brother-in-law. It felt so different to hear the dialogues only in one ear, and sometimes, the sounds kept echoing. When Rupesh asked me whether I could hear in both ears, I just gave him a look as if to say—*please let me enjoy the movie.*

In spite of so many hurdles and difficulties, I was genuinely enjoying my new life. Every day brought new excitement. All the challenges I had to overcome made up my progress card. I believe every person sees failures in life; they fall, but they have the ability to stand up again. And the determination to rise again shows courage; it means to never give up.

❧

4 OCTOBER 2016

I had to meet Dr Kirtane today. It was time for him to remove my bandage and the gel from the ear.

When the doctor carried out my hearing test again, I realised I could hear well. On my face I had a smile that stretched from ear to ear and in my heart, I only had gratitude for God and Dr Kirtane.

Dr Kirtane seemed equally jubilant. 'thank God you can hear!' he exclaimed.

He told me he had been worried ever since he found I couldn't hear in my operated ear. He kept wondering whether he should have got some more scans done before the surgery... to check if all my bones were in place and none had shifted because the impact of the bomb blast could have resulted in the dislocation of the small bones. If that had been the case, my hearing power would have reduced or completely gone. So I was lucky.

He told me to see him after three weeks, on 24 October, when he would check my hearing ability again. My biopsy report was also normal. Dr Kirtane then went on to ask me why I didn't seem stressed at all. I told him, 'If God has decided something for me, no one can do anything about it. If He has taken me out of the worst situation in life, why would He leave me hanging?'

'What confidence you have!' smiled Dr Kirtane.

I thanked God for being with me all the time. Not even once did I feel afraid of what would happen to me.

❧

Nidhi Chaphekar

11 OCTOBER 2016

Dussehra—a very important day for us. This is when Lord Rama is believed to have killed Ravana and brought an end to all evil. The entrances of our homes and offices are decorated with mango leaves and marigolds. Doing this made me feel very peaceful.

I also had to go to our factories to do a puja there. Every year on this day, we perform a puja in all the three factory units that Rupesh and his brother own, and we come back home after having lunch at a restaurant.

I decided that I would drive the car on the way back. The place was far from home, nearly an hour's drive. I wore the rubber gloves on top of my usual gloves for a firm grip. The kids were excited too. Initially, I was a little scared, especially while driving past buses or trucks, but after a few minutes, I got used to it and the old Nidhi was in form again. I believe it's all about what we think and how we think. One thing I am so grateful for is that my family, and especially Rupesh and the kids, have always shown complete confidence in me and supported me at every step of the way. This is very important because confidence isn't generated overnight; it's like a muscle you have to keep building.

❧

12 OCTOBER 2016

For a change, I felt like painting my nails. When I opened my box of nail polish bottles, I remembered that before I had left for that fateful flight, I had applied three colours for the first time to create a tricolour effect. Now when I picked up the green, orange and blue bottles, my hands shook at the memory. At the time of the blast, I had been wearing these very colours. I recollected what Nurse Laurence had told me at Grand Hospital in Charleroi.

She had said, 'the nail polish you were wearing, they were of different colours. We found bits of orange, blue, green, and all had merged due to the heat and had spots of brown and black. We had a hard time taking it off.'

They couldn't use force to clean my nails, so even after using an entire bottle of enamel remover, the edges of my nails still had a bit of leftover nail paint when I left Charleroi. I knew it was just a mental connection I was making; it was just a sudden reactive feeling that told me to stay away from those colours. I knew I needed to come out of that mindset. So I chose the green one again and painted my toenails with a double coat.

After a very long time, I had applied nail polish. It looked great! But the minute Rupesh saw it, he asked me to remove it as it reminded him of that traumatic time. I had to pacify him by saying it was just the result of the way we connect incidents with feelings.

I told him, 'What happened was bound to happen, but it was just by chance that I had applied this nail polish on the flight and I should use it again happily now.'

🦋

14 OCTOBER 2016

For Jolly di's birthday tomorrow, I wanted to surprise her. So I bought a cake and at 2300 hrs, we set out from home. When we reached her building, we learnt that her son, Akshit, who lived in Delhi, had arrived a few minutes ago. We called him up and asked him to open the door so we could enter the house quietly. At midnight, Akshit got Jolly di out of her room. She became so emotional when she saw all of us gathered there. She cut the cake, and we had a wonderful time. We returned home quite late.

I thought to myself, God has given me a reward after twenty years of sincere service — the chance to enjoy life like this with family and friends. It was as if God was telling me — *Whatever you missed, do it now.* I have always loved to give surprises to my loved ones, and earlier, because of my erratic working hours, it would not be possible for me to attend such events. But now not only was I not missing a single event, I was also being invited for more and more!

❧

15 OCTOBER 2016

To celebrate Jolly di's birthday, it was decided that we would all drive to Dara's Dhabha for dinner. It took us three hours to reach the place that was just a fifty-minute drive from home as the roads were jammed with heavy traffic. We sat on manji beds (charpoys) listening to a dhol being played live, but after some time, I asked them to stop playing, as the volume was causing pain in my left ear. I felt as though the insides of my ear were wobbling, as if someone were ringing bells inside. I didn't wish to spoil the mood of the gathering and pretended that everything was okay. We enjoyed the outing and I drove the car on the way back. It was so beautiful driving on the highway at that late hour.

I was enjoying each day of life in the best way. I felt truly very thankful to God.

❧

19 OCTOBER 2016

Karva Chauth. A day when married women fast all day to pray for a long, healthy and good life for their spouse. Women eat a hearty meal before sunrise, fast all day, and eat the next morsel with their spouse only after a puja is performed at moonrise. I woke up around 0430 hrs, had wholesome food, including fruits, nuts and some tea, then went back to sleep.

I had told my physiotherapist not to come today. The day passed well, but by late afternoon, due to the heat, I began feeling very thirsty. Everyone at home had warned me not to fast this year. My mom had instructed me that even if I did fast, I should keep myself hydrated and have fruits. But I had said, 'Let me try.' Ever since the incident, my body didn't allow me to stay hungry or even take long breaks between meals. I had to keep drinking water as well.

Unbroken

245

I had to get dressed in a traditional outfit. I had always worn a sari on this festival, but today, because of my visible burn marks, I felt uncomfortable and wondered if I should wear a salwar suit. At 1600 hrs, I made up my mind. So what if I have burns? I should wear a sari for my own happiness, I resolved. So I chose a brand new sari with a matching blouse and got dressed. I didn't feel as if anything bad had happened to me; in fact, I felt good. And when I set out for the temple, everybody complimented me and said I looked beautiful.

The lady in charge of the Mahila Mandal at the temple hugged me. She had always been very fond of me and considered me to be like her daughter.

She spoke aloud in front of everyone there about my courage and said, 'She is a true inspiration for all of us. A true form of shakti, of Durga Devi. It is Goddess Durga who has blessed her with a new life. Devi Maa is really kind.'

By the evening, my head was bursting with pain. Normally, moonrise occurs early every day, but only on this particular day it happens quite late and that's exactly what happened today too – the moon rose only at 2147 hrs. I performed the puja, had a few bites of food and went to sleep, too tired to stay up any longer.

The blast and its effect on me had made my body weak. But my mind was much stronger.

✿

20 OCTOBER 2016

Today was a learning experience for me. In the afternoon, I got a call from Ajit Sharma, a TEDx ambassador. I was not aware of what a TED Talk was. But he invited me for their annual programme in Jaipur to be held in December. I agreed to be there, but told him I needed permission from my company, and once they gave their approval, I would inform him.

When my kids got home from school, I told them about it and they were super excited. They explained to me what a TED Talk is and what a great opportunity it was. After listening to them, I felt

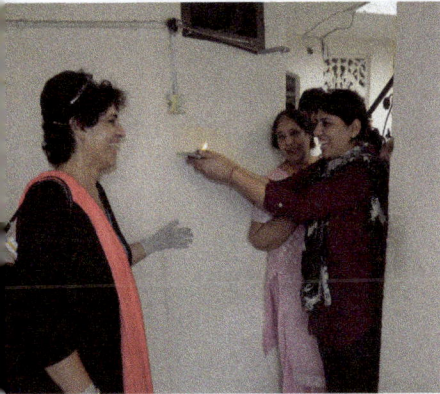

Being welcomed into my parents' house by my sister Meenu

With my family at TEDx Jaipur where I gave my first TED Talk

At the gurudwara in Amritsar, carrying the Shri *Guru Granth Sahib* on my head

A photo taken at the holy Golden Temple, Amritsar, after I managed to take a parikrama (circumambulation) — a distance of 2 kms, which was a big achievement for me.

Back in Brussels after nearly a year, recalling the horrific memories. Here, I am pointing at the hall (a parking area for fire engines) where my stretcher had been placed.

Narrating the chain of events that happened right after I heard the first blast. I am standing exactly where the bird statue used to be.

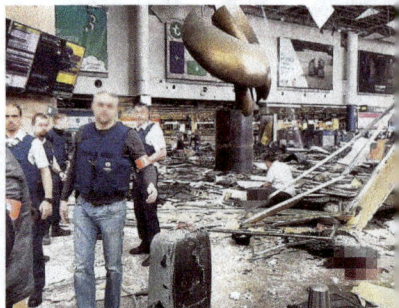

Scenes of complete destruction. These photos were taken on the day of the blast (photos sourced from the Internet).

Sitting on the same chair I had sat on—immediately after getting injured—one year after the incident to explain how it all had happened

The same place, a year ago, under completely unimaginable circumstances. These photos were taken by Ketevan Kardava and the one on the left went on to become the photo that everyone associates with the Brussels terror attack.

Meeting King Philippe and Queen Mathilde of Belgium

Being interviewed by journalists

Meeting the doctors and nurses at Grand Hospital

With Dr Liliane. She was the doctor who accompanied me when I was transported in a helicopter from Sint-Augustinus Hospital to Grand Hospital.

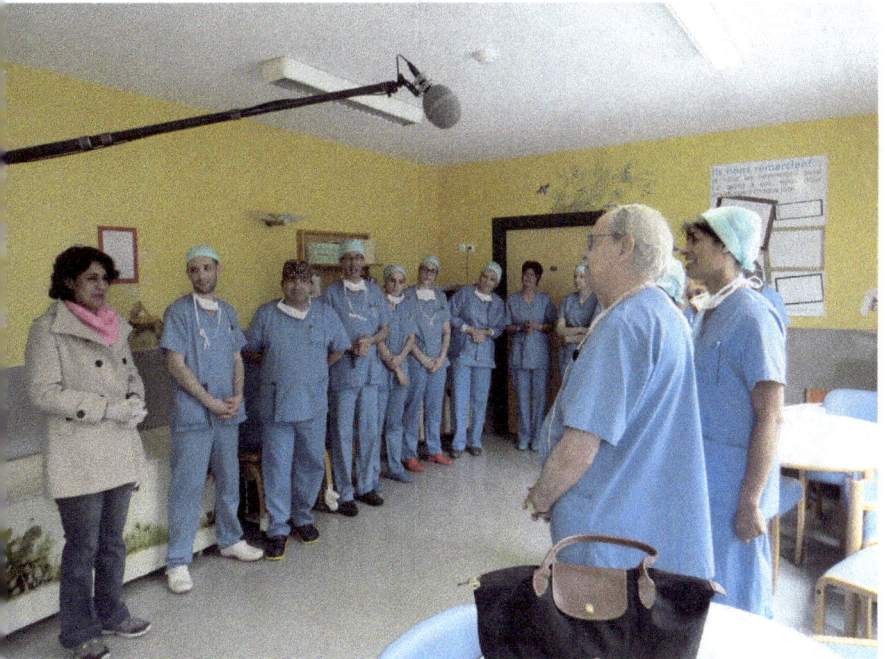

The documentary film crew had come along to record my meeting with these life savers

(L-R) Rupesh, Dr Hans, me and Dr Peeters

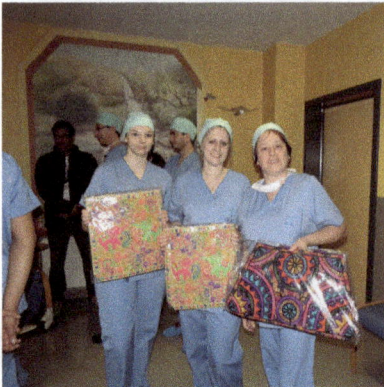

The lovely nurses, (R-L) Carine Joué, Aurélie Dumont and Aurélie Brancourt with the handmade bags I had gifted them

Rupesh and I at the Indian Embassy in Belgium

Wearing the 'token of remembrance' gifted to me by Alain. This was the jacket he wore on the day of the blast. It has his name 'Alain Zachary' emblazoned on the front.

My favourite Louis Vuitton purse, which I thought I'd lost in the blast, being returned to me by Inge Laurijssens — the wonderful police officer at Antwerp who found it and went the distance to give it back to me.

Paying my respects to those who lost their precious lives in the blast

A lunch party organised by the hospital staff especially for us

With Kurt, former editor at *Het Laatste Nieuws*, and his family

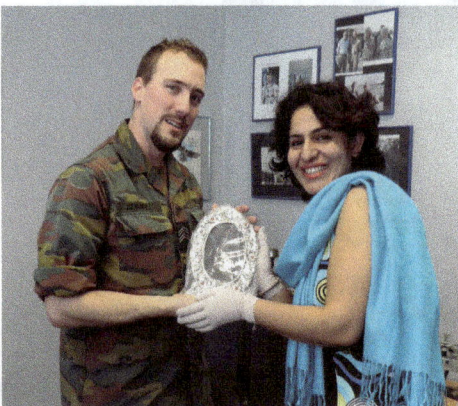

With Paul-Henry, the commando wh helped me immediately after the blas He is one of twenty-eight soldiers from 1 Star, the First Sergeant of the Battalion of Horse Hunters who wer posted at Zaventem airport at the tin of the blast.

Being interviewed by Ketevan Kardava

With Dr Beekeman, the senior-most doctor at Sint-Augustinus Hospital

With the doctors and staff of Sint-Augustinus Hospital in Antwerp, where I was first taken to for treatment

What a pleasant surprise it was t[o] be given a grand welcome by the Belgian Public Security at Federa[l] Police—a guard of honour salute[,] complete with a band playing or[n] horseback.

Being welcomed b[y] the D.G.A., D.A.S. of Belgium Public Security at Federal Police, Van Houtte Benoit

Signing a certificate that honoured me as the 'Godmother' of Direction Public Security of the Belgiu[m] Federal Police

With Alain, his lovely family and friends, and Shabir bhai

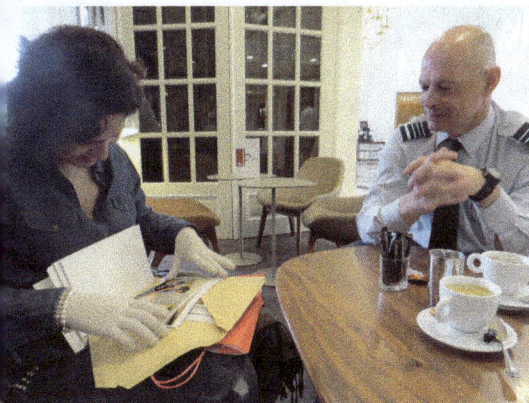

Col. Koen Hillewaert gifted me a special collection of photographs. I was overwhelmed by his gesture.

Stefanie Chassagne De Loof, the lady who can be seen sitting next to me in the photo that went viral

With Luc Lowel, the gentleman who helped take care of me and another victim when we were lying in the fire brigade hall, waiting for medical aid.

Doctors Who Treated Me In India

Dr Darius Soonawala, the orthopedic surgeon

Dr Anil Tibrewala, the plastic surgeon

Dr Sudhir Warrier, orthopedic surgeon and our family friend

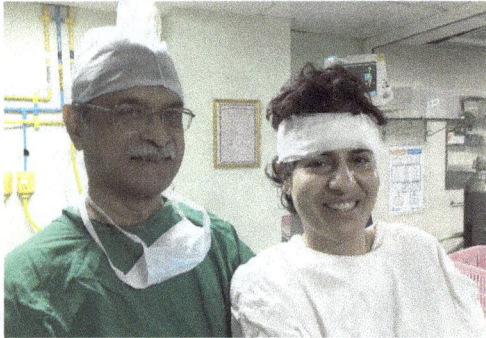

With Dr Milind Kirtane, the ENT specialist

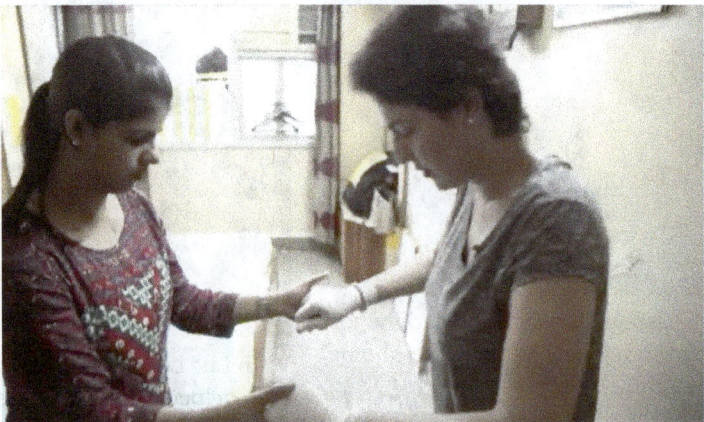

Training to improve my mobility with the help of Sabah, my physiotherapist in Mumbai

wonderful. But I was also nervous and my mind was filled with doubt. Usually when I listen to people giving speeches, I would be full of admiration for how well they spoke. I felt low now, thinking how I didn't have even ten percent of that kind of confidence or ability. I shared the news with my family and company management. They were all elated. They told me it was indeed a brilliant platform to put across my message to an international audience. I was thrilled!

❦

21 OCTOBER 2016

In the evening, my colleagues-turned-friends—Josimus, Rampal and Melvin—came to meet me. Josimus and Rampal were posted in Brussels when the incident occurred. It felt wonderful meeting them after such a long time. They had come to see me at the hospital in Charleroi but hadn't been allowed into the room then. We all had a heart-to-heart chat. They explained how tough it had been for them to find me. At the same time, they had to take care of three hundred odd passengers each. As there were no hotels available to accommodate the passengers, the national forces and the government of Belgium had made alternative arrangements. They showed me the picture of a hall where a thousand beds were laid out to let people stay. It was so endearing to know how the citizens of Brussels helped them with water and food, and it was sad to hear how difficult it had been for our team at Brussels to handle every challenging situation that arose.

They said they had cried as they waved at the last aircraft that took off after a few days from Brussels to Amsterdam, as a ferry flight to carry passengers from Amsterdam to India. Thousands of guests had to be sent to Amsterdam by road.

They had not slept for many nights in a row. Rampal told me he too had been at the departure hall at the time of the blast but was saved because of a pillar. What a horrific time it had been for everyone...

❦

A day of appointments with all my doctors. With the audiometry test scheduled today, I would find out about my hearing capacity too. I wanted to first test myself at home. I closed my eyes and paid attention to all the sounds I could hear. With complete concentration, I could hear the birds chirping outside, the sound of the ceiling fan, the honking of cars on the road, kids playing downstairs, and finally, even my breath.

In the afternoon, we left for all the check-ups. First we met Dr Tibrewala. The doctor saw my leg and said, 'Great! Keep doing what you are doing. We will only operate in an emergency. Your leg is still not ready for any surgery because of the wounds and scars. Even the skin is not healthy yet.' After a pause, he added, 'thanks to you, that girl who injured herself in Dubai is also doing well. She has not started walking yet, but she can stand now.'

I said, 'I am sure she will walk soon!'

Next we went to Dr Darius Soonawala's clinic. I told him, 'When I walk by putting weight on my heel, I feel pain in the centre, as if something is uneven in the heel itself.'

He said, 'It will be like that throughout your life or until we operate. Hopefully everything will be fine later.'

As far as the surgery was concerned, we had to wait until all the doctors involved gave their green signal. But I had a feeling that the bone would grow by itself!

Next was Dr Kirtane. I did the audiometry test and both my ears responded well. I had closed my eyes and fully focused on the sounds I could hear. The doctor was so happy to see the results. He told me he was glad to see me doing well and that he wanted to take me on a visit to an old-age home run by his friend. He felt my zest for life and outlook would give courage to the elderly and infirm people living alone in the home. I was moved and told him it would be my pleasure to go there with him. Later, I told him about the wobbling feeling in my left ear. He did a scan of my ear and found that the pearl-like growth he had removed was growing again. He said we would wait for it to grow more and see if it would detach on its own. Else, we may have to do the surgery once again to remove it. He told me to bear with it for some more time and gave me an appointment with him after a gap of six months.

❦

25 OCTOBER 2016

Vriddhi's birthday arrived and I had so many things to do to help her celebrate it in school.

I had kept her gift (an iPad) next to her bed. When she woke up and saw it, she was astonished. She came running to hug and kiss me and said, 'Why do you do so much for us?'

In the evening, when Vriddhi came home, I took her to the temple and offered sweets there. There is a tradition I follow: Whenever we celebrate any occasion in the family, I make sure people around me, including our building watchman, the drivers, housekeepers and workmen, are also part of the celebration. So we shared sweets with everyone.

❦

Madhuri and I made pizzas and Vriddhi cut a cake in the evening. It had truly been a fun-filled day. I thanked God for His kindness.

❦

27 OCTOBER 2016

Much of today, like the day before, was spent packing for my trip to Amritsar. I normally take one bag for each of us when we travel, but this time there were seven bags because I had bought so much to gift my near and dear ones! Everyone at home laughed at me as I packed. They teased me saying, 'Looks like you are shifting houses!'

Sabah strictly told my kids to make sure I did my stretching exercises every day; they were not to be missed even while travelling.

❦

28 OCTOBER 2016

Chhoti Diwali. On this day, people worship Goddess Laxmi who symbolises prosperity. We began the puja at 2015 hrs. I was witnessing this puja at my home after a very long time because most years, I would either be on flight duty or at my parents' house at this time of the year. I went to bed waiting eagerly for the next day to dawn... I would be meeting my father for the first time after the blast.

I slept early. I knew a Mumbai-Delhi-Amritsar flight route would be hectic. To make my journey comfortable, my colleagues had helped by sending emails to airport managers, operating crew and ground-handling staff (supervisors) to take special care of my needs. This would be my first domestic flight after returning from Brussels.

❧

29 OCTOBER 2016

My flight was scheduled for departure at 0955 hrs, but right since 0700 hrs, I started getting calls and messages from my colleagues asking me to inform them when I would be nearing the airport. We left home at 0820 hrs, as the airport is just five minutes away from our place. I called the supervisor to let him know I was on my way. They asked me to come to Gate No. 8.

At the airport, the ground staff received me. Other staff members encouraged and praised me. Two assistant in-flight base managers had also come to meet me. They insisted I take a WCHL as the walk within Terminal 2 would be very long.

I told them, 'You are with me, so it's okay. At some point if I feel I can't walk, I will call for it, but I don't want to assume I can't walk. I am sure I won't give you any problem.'

At the counter, they checked in my handbags as well because they wanted me to travel light. The moment I boarded the aircraft, my crew set cabin supervisor welcomed me with a big, warm smile. I felt so happy. All the crew members were new. They had not flown with me, but they came up to me and one of them said, 'In the morning, when we heard you are flying with us, we were overjoyed, because we have been wishing to meet you.'

The flight was delayed by fifty minutes. I was worried because I had only fifty minutes' time to make it for my connecting flight from Delhi to Amritsar. I prayed to God, *please help me out with this too.*

The flight was amazing. I felt pampered with the kind of love they showered on me. We landed at Delhi airport at 1300 hrs and the scheduled time of departure for the next flight was 1250 hrs. Our seats were in the last row. The moment the door of the aircraft opened, I thought they would announce — *Please meet the ground staff.* I had prepared the kids for the worst possible situation; they were anxious about missing the connecting flight. But somehow, I was sure we would make it. The announcements began for connecting flights to Lucknow, Varanasi, and so on. Eventually, there was a special announcement requesting guests travelling to Amritsar to meet the staff at the aerobridge.

When we stepped out of the aircraft, the commercial manager, Deepak, and a supervisor, Jasmine, were waiting to receive us. We were taken through the aerobridge stairs down to the tarmac, to take the coach to board the next aircraft. I thanked them and we boarded the plane. I apologised to the connecting crew. Since it was just an hour's flight, I had very little time to speak to them. But while deplaning, there was an announcement on the cabin system, asking us — me and my family — to remain seated. To my surprise, after all the other passengers deplaned, the crew got us a cake and drinks, and the captains came out and said, 'We are proud to have you with us!' I teared up when they presented us with a sketch of a lion they had made during the flight — it included everyone's good wishes. I hugged and thanked them all. I couldn't have wished for more!

As you land at the Amritsar airport, you can see the Santsar gurudwara from the runway itself. I bowed in respect at my first glimpse of it. A Shri *Guru Granth Sahib* paath (reading of the holy book of Sikhs) had been organised for me by my mother yesterday, but as it was the last day of school for the kids, I had been unable to travel. So the rituals for keeping the paath were performed by my brother and mother. The paath continues for two full days and nights, nonstop without a break, and the third day is the final ceremony. On all these days, it is read by the granthis.

My brother had come to receive us. My bags were the first to come out on the conveyor belt as they had been marked 'Priority'.

My hometown (a village near Amritsar) is hardly two kilometres away from the airport. We reached home in less than ten minutes. We had to park the car away from our house because the streets are narrow and with the Diwali rush, there were people everywhere. I could see so many people staring because everybody knew about me, but they seemed hesitant to speak to me. I went straight to my father's shop. I hugged him tight for a long time—I was hugging him after a whole year! He had tears in his eyes as he kissed my forehead and said, 'God listened to my prayers. I am satisfied now.'

After a pause, he pointed to my short hair and said, 'You look like an actress now!' I laughed. We chatted for a few minutes there before we went home. Meenu di did a puja to welcome me. Half an hour later, my aunt arrived. She hugged me and cried.

I told her, 'Don't make me sad. I am standing today because of your good wishes and prayers.'

I was visiting my parents' home after a year. Never had there been such a long gap between my visits.

In the evening, we had pangat, which is basically langar (a community kitchen that serves free meals to one and all) at our guruji's place—Shri Nirmal Swami Bhawan—which I have been visiting since the time I was born. My mom's eldest sister, who is more than eighty-six years old, also came to see me along with my sisters-in-law and a few cousins. They were delighted when they saw me walking. It was a beautiful reunion.

Guruji told me, 'It was because of your good deeds that you were saved. Your courage has set an example for all others.'

Along with my kids and other devotees, I served all the people who came for the langar. By the time everything was done, it was 2130 hrs. I was so tired, I just wanted to sleep. I drove back home, had dinner with my family and slept. The next morning, we had to be up early to go to the gurudwara for bhog, the final ceremony of the paath of Shri *Guru Granth Sahib*.

❧

30 OCTOBER 2016

A big day in the Hindu calendar. Diwali, the festival of lights, and my father's birthday as well. All of us were to pay our respects at the gurudwara where we had organised the paath.

We were asked to be there at 0730 hrs. I was the first one to wake up and be ready by 0630 hrs. I generally don't like to be late for anything, especially when we have been asked to be present at a particular time. At 0830 hrs, the final ceremony took place. As it was being conducted for me, they asked me to come forward and gave me their blessings. At the gurudwara, after the completion of the paath, if someone so wishes, they may keep the Shri *Guru Granth Sahib* on their head and enter the inner room where it is then placed on the holy bed of flowers. For Sikhs, the Shri *Guru Granth Sahib* is God.

For the first time in my life, I carried this holy book on my head (as I had expressed my desire to do so) and walked. I was worried about toppling and falling. With full concentration and courage, I completed the task. Ah what a feeling it was! I felt abundantly blessed.

Once back home, to celebrate my father's birthday, we decided to cut a cake in the morning itself. After a long time, we were all together and it felt wonderful. We had a lot of fun. This Diwali, we decided to be environment-friendly and not burn any firecrackers. Instead, we opted to have a late-night party with dance and music. In the evening, we did Laxmi puja and Vriddhi brightened up the house by lighting many candles. All of us sat listening to music and chatting with one another happily. A little later, we turned off the music too, as it was quite noisy.

While having dinner, at around 2230 hrs, we heard my cousin Vineet's voice calling out loudly and desperately to my brother—

'Rishi... Rishi!' We rushed out and what we saw was horrifying to say the least! A fire was blazing near the shop owned by our family, and even as we watched, it was moving dangerously close to the electric wires outside the shop. In small towns in India, there are some houses that are still kuccha (makeshift) where hay is stacked on top of the roof. Our shop is on the ground floor. The entrance to the shop had a sunshade covering made of thick fabric. This had already caught fire and the flames started spreading upwards to the roof as well. We were standing on the terrace of our house and watching this scene from the verandah. My brother rushed downstairs and called his friends. My mom tried to call the police and fire brigade.

I was anxious as the shop was full of electronic goods, and if the fire reached the shop, the consequences would be more than disastrous! My thoughts quickly shot to the big wooden bamboo stick lying on the roof of our house; I could use it to cut the wires before the fire spread further. Rupesh ran and got the bamboo stick for me. I told all the people standing on the ground outside to move aside and without wasting time, I started cutting the wires by pulling at them with one end of the stick. I thrust the stick into the wires and managed to disentangle them. Then I asked Rupesh, Mom and Meenu di to throw some sand that was lying on top of the hay, and spread it from one side to another so that the flames would mellow down. Then when people poured water on the sand, it put out the flames completely.

Later, everyone praised the presence of mind I showed. My mom and relatives talked about how someone who had been injured so badly earlier, in a bomb blast that too, would ordinarily have run away to save herself, but instead I had put my life in danger again to solve the crisis.

'this only shows,' one of my relatives said, 'you have in you the courage to face challenges at every step.'

Diwali could have ended on an unfortunate note. But the guiding hand of God ensured I had only gratitude in my mind before I lay down to sleep.

❦

31 OCTOBER 2016

My sister Goldy arrived from Delhi.

We went to pick her up from the railway station. When she saw me, she was so happy, she cried out of joy. She had been by my side, taking care of me for nearly twenty days after I had just arrived from Belgium. At that time, I had been totally dependent on her. We hugged each other tight. We sat talking late into the night. She was glad to see me walking like any normal person. She said, 'I saw you struggling like a bird who wants to fly when her wings are cut. But you always wanted to do things by yourself and were never dependent on us. This is the reason you are standing on your own feet today.' I felt happy and loved hearing that.

❧

1 NOVEMBER 2016

We celebrated Bhai Dooj. We dressed up and performed the traditional ceremony in the morning itself. My mom said, 'Because of you, we have been able to celebrate all the festivals together this year.'

Then we went to the bookshop in the city, from where my mom regularly orders books for the school she owns. The shop owner asked my mom, 'How is your daughter who had got injured?'

My mom looked at me, grinned from ear to ear and said, 'She is standing in front of you.'

He couldn't believe his eyes. He took a selfie with me for his kids. He said, 'they are big fans of yours and I am happy to have you with us.'

I was happy to see so many people inspired by my story. 'Please do write a book on your experiences,' he suggested to me. 'It would help so many, especially those who feel they are less capable than others.'

❧

4 NOVEMBER 2016

Back in Amritsar, my mother had organised a 'Maa ki aarti' puja at home. It was a three-hour puja and preparations were on. Mom had planned to distribute gifts to all the ladies who attended. For her, it was a sort of religious club; during my hospital stay, most of these ladies would collectively offer prayers for my wellbeing. At 1500 hrs sharp, the puja began. It went on for longer than expected, with a lot of singing and chanting, and finally concluded at 1940 hrs. Everyone had snacks, and gifts were distributed. As a token of love, some of them gave me cash too. Prasad was distributed. Later, when I narrated my story to them, many had tears in their eyes, and a few hugged me. Some said they could not even imagine what I had been through. When I showed them some pictures that had been taken while I was in hospital, they refused to believe it was me. Everyone said I am a miracle for my family. I felt great talking to them. Their encouragement spurred my own energy and will power.

❧

5 NOVEMBER 2016

I wanted to visit the Golden Temple but was apprehensive about whether I would be able to walk barefoot. I asked God to give me strength and not let me down in front of others. It is approximately a two-kilometre walk if you want to perform the 'parikrama', that is, a walk covering all four sides of the gurudwara.

I started the walk slowly. Rupesh and the kids watched me with worry, but I told them I had full faith. I was slow, and would take breaks, but no one got upset. Rather, they would sit with me in the shade, or just massage my foot a little. I had the biggest smile on my face when I finished the parikrama successfully. My mother gave me a proud thumbs-up sign. She hadn't walked; she had remained seated at the gurudwara's entrance. Later, she took us to another gurudwara called Shahida Sahib. She had taken a pledge that when I come back fully recovered, she would bring me to this gurudwara for its blessings. The paathi (the chief priest who reads the Shri *Guru Granth Sahib*) did an ardas (the prayer offered with folded hands) for me. I felt so energetic... as if a supreme force had entered my body. We returned home satisfied, and I felt as if my dream had come true. I thought about the number of people who had blessed me in the past. I believe I am truly the luckiest soul on earth.

❦

6 NOVEMBER 2016

It was a Sunday and our last day at home because we had a flight back to Mumbai the next day. The day passed quickly. There was packing to do and in the evening, my friends came over. They had arranged a surprise party in a mall to cheer me up. A few had thought I might still be in trauma, but looking at my high spirits, they too rejoiced.

One of them asked me, 'Did you never question why this had to happen to you?'

I smiled and replied, 'If I had not been there, someone else would have. Someone had to be there, so God chose me, thinking I may be stronger than the rest.'

She persisted, 'that means you have no regrets at all?'

'For me, the question was not why I was there, but why did the blast have to happen. What did those people get out of it? Why did they do it? How can we help each other? How do we prevent this from happening again in the future? God gave me my life back. I am hale and hearty, so why would I complain?'

My perspective changed their thinking too. I told them we regret what happened in the past but forget to enjoy our present, and we are determined to think of the future, which is not in our hands. Instead, we must enjoy the moment we have. It may not come back... because happiness and good times are not something we can postpone or set aside as a bank balance for the future.

They are blessings we need to conceive and spread today. The more love you spread, the more you will receive.

❦

7 NOVEMBER 2016

Saying goodbye to my parents has always been difficult, but this time I promised I would be back soon.

I met the airport staff in Amritsar. They told me when the news had reached them, they didn't know what to do. They recalled how my mother had to go to Mumbai to receive me when I came back from Brussels. She had looked extremely concerned and anxious to meet me, they said. The staff had found it tough to keep up their own strength. The manager told me none of them could even imagine the kind of trauma I had gone through. Seeing my confidence and body language now, they said nobody could tell the challenges I had overcome.

It was a short flight but every crew member came and spoke to me. They made me feel like a very important person on board. When we landed in Delhi, after the transit passengers had disembarked, the cabin manager took my hand and led me to the galley (food cabin). She thrust the passenger address system mic in my hand and said, 'Make the transit announcements.' I felt so thrilled!

When I finished making the required announcements, a crew member came up to ask the cabin manager, 'that was not your voice! Who made such a fantabulous announcement?'

I beamed.

She looked surprised. 'Now we know why in your *CNN-News18* interview you mentioned that people loved your announcements. It's so true! It felt like a recorded announcement!'

The cabin manager made special tea for me because she knew how much I love tea. When we were mid-flight again, a fellow passenger came up to me and said, 'I am a very big fan of yours!' I was taken aback.

When I got up to go to the washroom, a lady came and asked,

'Are you Nidhi Chaphekar?' When I nodded, she held my hand and congratulated me. I felt a little embarrassed; for me, all this attention was unexpected. Some others took pictures with me.

On landing, I saw a board held up for me by the staff. When I identified myself, the staff member said, 'We have got a WCHL for you. The arrival hall is too far away as the flight is parked at the last aerobridge.'

I said, 'I won't take it. Please let the elderly lady behind me who's wearing a belt for her back take it. It will make her comfortable.'

I made the lady sit on the WCHL and she blessed me.

All the ground supervisors were glad to see me. I got a call from Assistant Base Manager Deep too. They all came to meet me; I had carried boxes of sweets for all the departments.

❧

8 NOVEMBER 2016

Back in Mumbai. It was time to unpack everything and put them all back in place. I finished half of the unpacking by the afternoon and decided to do the rest tomorrow.

At about 1600 hrs, I got a call from Ms Lobo, who works with the Belgium consulate in India. She said that on 15 November, they would be celebrating King's Day in Mumbai at the Chhatrapati Shivaji Vastu Sangrahalaya, and that they would like to invite me for the event. I couldn't believe my ears! I agreed and gave her my email ID. When I spelt it out saying, 'It is tigressnidhi...', she started laughing and asked me, 'Did you create this email ID after the incident?'

I replied, 'No, it's my first email ID.'

'You truly are a tigress, an actual tigress!' she exclaimed.

❧

You must be wondering how I have been able to be so excited about each day that has come my way. Let me share my secret with you. Every day before going to bed, while meditating, I always thank

God for making my today better than yesterday, and that's how I look forward to the next day. When you look forward to something with positive energy, it will come to you as a lovely surprise.

❧

10 NOVEMBER 2016

Sabah advised me to see if I could start today's exercise with kicking my leg left and right, up and down, with a one-kilogram weight attached to it. I did it without pause—kicking on all four sides, ten times with each leg. But later, it felt as if my legs were no longer there! Sabah also suggested I start walking on the road now with proper shoes on. She told me, 'Just see how you feel. But be careful as the roads are uneven.'

I knew I must take her advice seriously, as my foot could only balance itself at a certain angle and our Indian roads are mostly rough and bumpy.

❧

11 NOVEMBER 2016

I wore sports shoes today. It felt a bit uncomfortable as my foot was still swollen. I wore Rupesh's shoes as mine didn't fit me because of the swelling. His shoes are a size bigger than mine. I walked for nearly one kilometre, but took three breaks because our roads are not exactly even and there isn't much walking space really. My foot began to ache afterwards, especially the heel. Rupesh asked me to sit in the car, but I refused. As I walked, he was either slowly driving behind me or ahead of me. It was a challenging but fun exercise for me.

❧

15 NOVEMBER 2016

Today was the King's Day celebration at the Chhatrapati Shivaji Vastu Sanghralaya. I was really excited. When Rupesh, Amit and I reached the venue in the evening, we were asked to wait outside, as only the host could enter the place first. At about 1920 hrs, we went in and met Pinkey Ahluwalia, the Belgian Vice Consul, and Consul General Peter Huyghebaert. They told us this was the very first time in the history of Belgium's Foreign Affairs department that such a grand event had been organised at this museum. In the consul general's speech, Amit and my names were also announced as survivors. Later, I met many consulate generals who were in attendance. Many appreciated me for my courage.

We enjoyed every moment of the evening. I did not get time to even use the washroom! I was surrounded by so many people eager to know more about my story. It was one of my most memorable experiences; my confidence soared. I could clearly see my goal in life now—I knew I had before me the task of inspiring people and touching their lives deeply. Life itself is an inspiration and we are all born with the innate ability to overcome challenges. Each of us has the power to change someone's life and we should not let it go to waste.

❦

17 NOVEMBER 2016

I noticed Pinkey and Amit had posted our pictures on Facebook, so I asked Amit to teach me how to write a comment in response. It was the first time I commented on Facebook. I felt nice reading all the responses.

❦

I had to go to the BSE (Bombay Stock Exchange) building today to attend a programme by the Artha Forum. What I liked most was the speech given by Shri Radhanath Swami. When I met him afterwards, I had tears in my eyes. This always happens with me—whenever I see a divine soul, the tears are unstoppable.

Shri Radhanath Swami said, 'Sometimes pain comes to give you the most precious moment of your life.' He believed my experience was proof of this. He gave the example of gold and said, 'You cannot find it until it goes into the blaze to let impurities out. Later, it becomes what we call pure gold. You too have the same pure identity.' I felt deeply touched. He invited me to visit his eco-friendly village, Govardhan.

Many in the audience at the venue came to know of my story and quite a few came up to take photos with me. Some asked me for my opinion on various aspects of life. I met some people who wanted me to be a speaker at their organisations and clubs. It was an enriching experience for me; exchanging views and thoughts improved my own overall outlook. I felt great that I too had something to share with all these people from different walks of life.

❧

23 NOVEMBER 2016

I was invited as a guest to the annual function of Dr Batra's Positive Health Heroes initiative. I met so many people who were paralysed, either from birth, or whose limbs had been amputated due to an accident, and living successful lives, facing all kinds of challenges head on till date. Interacting with them, I realised I had gone through nothing in comparison. And their minds and souls were stronger than mine. There was a man who had got a high-voltage electric shock and lost both his arms, but he was the best painter I had ever come across! I met Deepa Malik, a lady whose lower limbs were paralysed due to a medical problem that occurred after a few years of marriage but whose exemplary courage made her stand out in a crowd. She had worked hard and became the first Indian woman to win a silver medal in shot put at the Summer Paralympics 2016. I saw dance performances by a group of people who were either blind, hard of hearing or had both or one leg paralysed or amputated. It was mind-blowing! They performed so beautifully. I got goose bumps watching them dance. Tears streamed down my face seeing their spirit and energy that defeated their disabilities. I met each one of them and congratulated them.

The day renewed my belief that nothing is impossible in this world if you conquer your fears and hold on to your strengths.

❧

27 NOVEMBER 2016

I had to attend an event organised by Vasai Shakha, a community outreach group. This event was being organised after a gap of seventeen years. The organisers wanted every single person attending the event to hear about my experience and gain from the message I try to share with everyone.

On reaching the venue in the late afternoon, I was given a beautiful welcome. I was called up on stage. They offered some prayers and an introductory speech was given. Seeing the huge crowd of over two thousand people making so much noise, I thought that maybe they were not really interested and had been requested to fill up the seats at the venue. But I was proved wrong.

I spoke for about twenty-five minutes to an audience that maintained pin-drop silence. When I finished, they gave me a standing ovation—I felt overwhelmed. Many came up to hug and praise me.

The year of my rebirth was coming to a close. 2017 was only a month away.

❧

1 DECEMBER 2016

I was invited to share my experiences at the Rotary Club. When I reached the Trident Hotel, I saw a good number of people gathered there. I never prepare a speech beforehand; I speak from my heart. I was introduced to many students who had come there to listen to me. I spoke for about twenty-five minutes, and I could see many people recording what I said. When I asked them why they were doing so, they replied, 'For our family and friends who couldn't come but wanted to listen to you share your inspiring thoughts.'

❧

'Just as one candle lights another and can light thousands of other candles, so one heart illuminates another heart and can illuminate thousands of other hearts.'

—Leo Tolstoy

I believe I am that 'one candle'.

❧

2 DECEMBER 2016

Another exciting day. Sabah made me stand on the treadmill today for the first time in my life. She explained all its features and said, 'Walk at a pace of three kilometres per hour.'

Because I was required to maintain a uniform pace, after about ten minutes, I started feeling a little giddy and tired, and I stopped. Sabah felt great about having made me walk continuously.

'tomorrow onwards, we will do it regularly for a few months and we'll slowly increase the speed,' she announced.

Every day felt like a new experience being added to my life.

Meanwhile, I was informed that my TEDx talk had been postponed.

❧

3 DECEMBER 2016

My mom called to tell me about her friend's successful experience with aloe vera for treating scars and asked me to try it out myself.

I immediately arranged for some fresh aloe vera. I thought I should test the method first, so I applied some on my chest and let it dry for some time. I also used to consume a spoonful of the raw aloe gel as Mom had prescribed that when I had visited Amritsar.

When I peeled off the gel from my skin, I was happy to note that there were no rashes. I decided to apply it regularly. I had read somewhere that kiwi fruit too is really good for the skin as it helps the body produce collagen. So I began eating the fruit

Nidhi Chaphekar

every day. I would mix one spoon of kiwi fruit pulp with aloe vera gel and apply that on my body every morning. I would sit for at least half an hour like that, and to utilise the waiting time, I would meditate. For the past so many months, I had been drinking turmeric milk at night. This became my daily routine and I began seeing good results.

But now I had to switch my regimen again. Because from the time I had stopped wearing bandages, since there were no wounds to be dressed, my skin would become dry very quickly and give me a burning sensation even after applying the cream prescribed by the doctors. I would take fresh cream from milk and mix a little turmeric in it. I would apply this mixture every day in the morning and after a few minutes of rubbing it gently all over my body, I would take a shower. I would apply soap only on Sundays. This helped me a lot. But because I had to test the aloe vera, I had stopped the milk and cream method. Then I wondered — why not apply both?

So I began applying the milk-cream mixture in the morning and the fresh aloe vera mixture at night before going to bed. The truth is that every time I applied the mixture, I did it with the strong belief that it would work for me. The routine was sometimes tiring, but it was beneficial.

I did a lot of research on how to make the marks fade. I found out that even pure coconut oil can help. So I started getting light body massages on a regular basis using pure coconut oil. I believe nature has a remedy for most of our problems.

✣

7 DECEMBER 2016

I don't know why, but I felt like riding a bicycle today. I told my neighbour it had been twenty-two years since I last rode a cycle, and asked him if I could borrow his. He said, 'Go for it!'

With both Vardaan and Rupesh behind me on their cycles, I rode the cycle for four to five kilometres. Looking at me setting out, people were concerned and warned me against it. But I told them, 'One has to conquer all fears. I will be careful.'

❦

8 DECEMBER 2016

My wedding anniversary. For the first time in our seventeen years of married life, I did not have to apply for leave this year. To my surprise, Rupesh gifted me a new car!

He took me to the showroom and handed over the keys to me, and said, 'thank you for staying in our lives.'

I went on my first drive in the new car. We happily celebrated the day, and went out for dinner with family and some friends. Gratitude is all I have in my heart.

❦

9 DECEMBER 2016

I received a call from Nicolas from the news channel *France 2*. He said he was heading to Brussels to be with his family for Christmas and offered to personally deliver to the Belgian royal office any message I had for King Philippe. He asked me to write a letter and send it to his Delhi address. Then came the call from Ajit Sharma, the ambassador of TEDx India, Jaipur. He admitted that he was under the impression that I looked like someone who is still recovering and that I would be worried about facing such a big, live audience.

But after talking to me, he said, 'I have to make you speak to my wife and family, because no one can even guess what you went through. The smile you have, the thoughts you share are very rare to see in the world.'

I felt inspired and wanted to start something new, such as a relief fund for victims of similar attacks, or some venture that would promote education. I had read somewhere that destroying a nation doesn't really require the use of atomic bombs or missiles. It just requires lowering the quality of education. As it is rightly said, when you educate a woman, you educate a family, a generation, a nation. That is the power women's education holds. I shared my thoughts on this matter with many people, but no concrete ideas on what could be done came through. I wrote emails to those who I knew had the power to make a difference, including Prime Minister Narendra Modi, and even Malala Yousafzai. But some of these emails bounced back. Then I sent a handwritten letter to the ministry at Delhi. I had found all these addresses on the Internet. I stood firm in my belief that one day, change would come about. One day, my efforts would bear fruit.

❧

10 DECEMBER 2016

I was really happy at the effort Nicolas was making for my sake. I started writing, but like a poet, by the evening, I tore up each page. I did not know how to express myself and pour my heart out in words. On top of that, my handwriting is so untidy that it pains me at times. The entire day passed and I was unable to express my emotions in words.

❧

11 DECEMBER 2016

Finally, I managed to fill up three sheets of paper. As I wrote, I imagined it all happening to me. And today I couriered the letter to Nicolas and also sent him a message of gratitude for all his effort.

Later, I wondered why I wrote such a lengthy letter. Looking at it, nobody would read it; I should have typed it out and taken a printout. But then I decided to relax. After all, it was my expression as an individual and the hard work mattered, I told myself.

❧

14 DECEMBER 2016

I marked this day in my calendar as special because today my physiotherapist asked me to jump barefoot from a one-foot high stool. I was scared as I had not done anything like that after the incident. My legs shivered when I heard her command. But sometimes, we have to listen to our teacher more than our heart. And I did it. Just like that! I couldn't believe it! Not even a year had passed after I had been told by many doctors that I may not be able to walk or work or do other things like normal people. The height of the stool I jumped from was not much, but the confidence it gave me soared far above the skies. I repeated this exercise about ten times. Sabah slowly but steadily increased the pressure in my exercises.

❧

15 DECEMBER 2016

In the morning, I received a message from photojournalist Ketevan Kardava: the picture she had taken of me at the blast site, the one that went viral across the globe, had been listed among 'the 46 Most Powerful Photos of 2016' by the popular news portal BuzzFeed.

❧

20 DECEMBER 2016

Sidhi from the *Guardian* came home with a copy of its London edition that had my interview. She was eager to meet me again to share the impact of my interview. She told me, 'When I speak to you, I salute the way you think, your positivity and kindness, and I want to be like you.'

Sidhi and I are friends now. I cherish people like Sidhi and quite a few other journalists who have continued to be in touch with me. There were a few who had interviewed me, but once the interview was published, they never bothered to send me a link or reply to my messages. I have never charged a penny for any of my interviews as my only intention is to spread the message of love and hope as far as possible. But experiencing the selfish attitude of some people does make me wonder why they would behave so.

❦

23 DECEMBER 2016

The moment I switched on my phone in the morning, messages started flooding in. I learnt that my picture had been declared one of the most riveting photos of 2016 by the *New York Times*.

Then Ketevan shared the link to a video—'the Most Shocking Moments of 2016'—published by CNN International's Facebook page. It was a collection of the most iconic incidents of violence and destruction that defined the year internationally. And it had my picture from the scene of the terror attack.

I didn't know what to feel really. If my story had impacted the world, I wanted it to go to the root of all evil and touch those who were destroying humanity. I prayed to God that the impact created should make them feel ashamed of their past deeds and change their ways. I congratulated Ketevan and told her it was her brilliance and expertise that made her take these pictures and post them immediately, but I still felt that the media should have behaved more ethically.

2016 was nearing its end, and every day, leading newspapers around the world carried articles about my story. From 24 to 31 December, I received numerous WhatsApp photos and messages about various articles published worldwide. My picture was selected as one of the best photographs of 2016 by the *Guardian*.

It was chosen as one among the twelve most powerful images by Hugh Pinney from Getty Images for the *BBC*, as part of a collection of the most impressive images of the year that was about to end. Mine was selected for the month of March.

The same picture also made it to the *Washington Post* for the year 2016 depicted in photographs under the category of 'terrorism and its Victims'.

There were many more such acclaimed forums where my photograph was showcased.

I know photographs are often worth more than a million words. I would read all the coverage my photograph got, and while I was never upset over media coverage on what had happened to me, I felt more strongly than ever before that the media should instead be publishing positive stories and news that would make people look forward to the coming year with hope and happiness. I replied to all the messages I received, guaranteeing them that if they came out with stories that spread positivity and dwelt on the life-affirming actions taken, instead of depicting the depressing reality of destruction and loss, people would gain more from it and they would welcome the year ahead with open arms. I strongly go by this mantra — speak good and hear good, pray good and receive good, behave good and gain good. We do not realise the power we have within ourselves. It is all that lies within that finds its way back to us.

The best article was the one published by a Belgium newspaper, titled 'Heroes' — which featured the stories of all the people who helped us during our tough times. It also featured our hero Alain. Alain was so thankful to me but I told him, 'It was your karma and you had to be rewarded for it. This is just the beginning... the future will be great.'

❧

25 DECEMBER 2016

Christmas is a day my kids eagerly await every year, for on this day they get a lot of sweets and treats and, of course, when they were small, we (Rupesh and I) were their Santa. But now since they understand the concept of Santa better, they just make their requests through their prayers. We decorated the big Christmas tree in our house. We also went to a church and lit candles. This is another way to teach one and all to respect and celebrate all religions and their festivals equally.

❧

31 DECEMBER 2016

Since it was the last day of 2016, I decided to be home with Rupesh. We wanted to share some special time with each other. Otherwise, in all these years, my New Years had been celebrated at clubs, parties, and sometimes even on flights.

It was different this year. At midnight, I prayed to God to keep everyone smiling and to bring peace and harmony in this world. I asked God to generate that kind of power within me so that I can be a messenger of love, peace and humanity. I prayed that we should all sow the seeds of love and compassion, water them with faith in our relationships, and reap the beautiful fruits of peace and prosperity.

Every single night, I had started praying to God to grant a more beautiful day tomorrow. And every morning, before opening my eyes, I would join my hands in prayer asking God to make my days more fruitful and memorable. I had made a habit of doing this from the time Mom had told me, 'What you believe, you achieve. So before sunrise and before bedtime, you must pray for what you truly believe.'

❧

1 JANUARY 2017

I went to the temple and gurudwara for God's blessings. Something unpleasant happened there. While I was coming out of the temple, a lady came and asked me how I was doing. At the same time, another lady looked at my feet and gasped, 'Oh my God, the beauty of the feet has gone!'

I was fully covered and only my ankles and feet could be seen. The lady seemed to take pity on me as she continued to comment further, but I interrupted her, 'At least I should thank the Almighty that I have them!'

I have learnt that there will always be some people who behave insensitively or make fun of us, but we shouldn't worry. All that matters should be our feeling and our commitment to live well.

At the gurudwara, I met a few ladies I know. Some asked me, 'Why did you cut your hair?' I smiled and briefly narrated my experience to them. They realised it was me they had seen in the news stories everywhere. A few people gathered around me. Some asked how I was doing, some told me not to worry and assured me all would be fine. They advised me to continue having faith in God and told me what had happened was a part of the past and I should think of my future now.

But there were some women who started whispering to each other about how I used to look pretty earlier. They wondered aloud about how I would continue my job now, to which some others commented, 'It's all because of her karma.'

I looked at them and smiled. I didn't want to say anything that would sound rude; I wanted to stay positive. Yes, it was destined to happen to me, I reasoned, but maybe some of my good karma or my family's good wishes had got me back from the clutches of death.

I said to one of them, 'Aunty, this incident has proved that beauty lies in the eyes of the beholder. One day outer beauty will fade away, but my inner soul, my beautiful thoughts and deeds will remain strong.'

One of the ladies hugged me and said, 'Sorry if you felt bad.'

'Not at all,' I said. 'It is very important for me to spread this thought. Anyone who faces the worst of situations may feel defeated and weak, but together, we have to help make them strong again and come out of it. We need to make the person feel normal. We must do the best we can to motivate them with our words. Never pity or make the person feel sorry... because what has happened is the past. Nobody in this world, whether rich or poor, powerful or weak, can change the past. We can only make an effort to make the present wonderful and work on the future to make this world a more beautiful place.'

No matter how strong one considers oneself to be, it can take just a moment to break you down. I could have broken down too, but I believe there is some higher power that keeps me together.

To quote Walter Anderson: 'Bad things do happen; how I

respond to them defines my character and the quality of my life. I can choose to sit in perpetual sadness, immobilised by the gravity of my loss, or I can choose to rise from the pain and treasure the most precious gift I have—life itself.'

❧

7 JANUARY 2017

I had a review with Dr Darius Soonawala and Dr Tibrewala.

To be frank, it was difficult for me to express in words how I felt, especially in my right foot—sometimes it felt heavy, sometimes painful, sometimes imbalanced, or totally numb; at other times, I could feel a burning sensation or as though a bunch of needles were pricking through the sole of my feet—especially in the mornings. But I held on to the firm belief that the bone would grow back on its own and surgery would not be required. Dr Darius Soonawala would always support me in my decisions.

Dr Tibrewala, on the other hand, was not in favour of leaving things to chance. My foot was still swollen and the skin was very thin. On touching it, he said it was warm, and the natural healing was still taking place. The conflict was regarding how they would put in the stitches. From where would they open up the foot? So we decided to wait for some more time as I was progressing very well. He asked me to see him after three months, explaining that this kind of healing won't complete itself in just a few months.

❧

While scrolling through my inbox, I saw an email from *The Week*'s editor informing me that an article on me had been published by them. I had waited for so many months for this news! When I read the stories of the other people who had been featured in the same issue, I realised there were many valuable examples around us and each of them could teach us a great lesson. The story was titled 'Made of Metal'. I called to congratulate the editor on his hard work; he had met each one of the heroes in these stories and put together a write-up on them. It is true that great things are indeed achieved by hard work.

❧

I read the announcement in our housing society's circular about an upcoming sports event to celebrate Republic Day. I told my physiotherapist in the evening, 'Whenever I have been in town, I have been present for all the events and never lost any race.'

Sabah reassured me. 'Don't worry... together we will make it happen.'

We began doing new exercises every day, including jumping, fast climbing (of stairs), rigorous stretching, and such. The sports day was scheduled for 26 January. I was super excited! To my luck, or perhaps keeping my condition in mind, I found out that all the competitions lined up for the day involved fast walking. There were book-balancing and marble-and-spoon races as well as cricket.

❧

18 JANUARY 2017

I received an email from the Cabinet Deputy Head and Diplomatic Advisor to the King of Belgium, Mr Pierre Cartuyvels, asking if I had any plans to visit Belgium. I was thrilled—it was a very big deal for me! I replied thanking him and said I would inform them soon if I make any such plans.

I immediately messaged Nicolas, thanking him wholeheartedly for keeping his promise.

❧

26 JANUARY 2017

Republic Day. In the morning, I went downstairs with my family for the flag-hoisting ceremony. One by one, the kids' competitions started. When the women's events were announced, I too stood up.

Many people stared at me, I noticed, probably wondering how I would walk fast, that too on the uneven surface of the ground. But I smiled and said I wished to take part in all the three contests. First was the book-balancing race. Towards the end of the race, I picked up speed and walked fast with big strides and won the first prize. In the marble-and-spoon race, I had to concentrate on the uneven ground and also on the spoon and the marble balanced on the spoon held in my mouth, which dangled dangerously all the while, but I managed to bag the second prize! One of the residents exclaimed, 'No one would know you have a hollow heel bone. Most people would be so cautious about it if they had your medical condition, but the confidence you have is amazing!'

I played cricket as well but our team did not win. It was a nice, leafy ground surrounded by trees all around and that made me comfortable and relaxed, though I had covered my body completely to be extra careful about not injuring myself in any way.

It was a fun-filled day.

I was meeting many of the housing society residents after a long time. Some of them were curious to know if I was tired of sitting at home.

'Not at all,' I informed them. 'In fact, now I have time to do all that I didn't do for so many years. Watching life-affirming videos, reading a lot—which was a big surprise for my family, spending time with my kids, taking care of myself... The best thing is I meet so many people. Attending all the events I get invited to is so much fun. I have never been so busy before. The list of things to do is never-ending!'

Some sympathised with me about how difficult it was for a person who had worked for so many years to suddenly find herself idle with no job, poor health, and very few opportunities for activity. I laughed and told them, 'that's very true, but I see it this way. I worked hard day in and day out for more than twenty years, so God said—now take a break and enjoy all the lost moments with family, kids and friends. Earlier, I had to miss many occasions because of my busy schedule, but this year I have not missed even a single event.

We need to change our thoughts, that's all. It's all in the mind.'

⚜

30 JANUARY 2017

Today an elocution competition was to be held at the kids' school. The competition was for students of classes 6, 7, 8 and 9 combined. Vriddhi chose to speak in Hindi. There were three different topics she had to choose from. She chose to speak on 'A Personality Who Has Impacted Your Life'. She didn't tell me about the topic and said it would be a surprise. I was to know only on the day of the event. It was the first time she had written an entire speech on her own. The time limit was three minutes and any student who exceeded it would be disqualified. Earlier, I used to help her with writing and practising, keeping time when she would practise her speech, but this time she did not allow me to interfere. In the morning, I wished her good luck before she left for school. I was curious to know what she had written and how she would speak.

She came back from school with a glorious smile. She told me, 'Mom, out of all the grades combined, I stood first in the Hindi elocution today. Everyone, from the kids to the judges to all our teachers, cried.' I asked her why and she said, 'I spoke on you, Mom.'

I was astonished. I asked her, 'From where did you gather all the information?'

'From the Internet. And anyway, I know most of the details by heart now because every person who comes to meet you asks you about the incident, not realising we are around. I always see you speak to them with optimism. I admire the strength you have. I want to be like you, Mom.'

Her words were the biggest achievement a parent can ever have. I was moved to tears. She added, 'What you are doing is right. How you are handling the situation every day is actually an example of the art of living life well.'

For an eleven-year-old child to express this was surprising to me. I told her to narrate the whole speech and believe me, the way my little tigress roared today left me speechless! It was one of the biggest days of my life, and I wanted to celebrate the moment. The last line in her script was a Hindi quote:

'*Apne sahas aur himmat ko mat batao ki aap ki mushkile kitni badi hain, balki apni mushkilon ko batao ki aap ki himmat kitni buland hai!*' (Loosely translated, it means: Don't tell your valour and courage about how big your challenges are; instead, tell your difficulties how strong your courage is.) She told me she had taken these lines from the Internet.

She said she was proud to be my daughter.

It does not matter what others think of you, but it really makes you feel on top of the world when your child speaks so highly of you. I kissed her forehead and thanked God for always being with me.

Later in the day, I got a call from the Belgium national TV channel, *RTBF,* informing me that to mark the completion of a year since the incident on 22 March 2017, they wanted to make a small documentary on me. They wanted me to arrive on 17 March and stay with them till 23 March. I sent an email to my company management informing them about this and they gave the go-ahead. I thought about whether I was going in the right direction by doing this. This way I would meet everyone who had helped me. Also, since I was consulting with the doctors at Grand Hospital regarding my bone graft, I informed them about my trip and they asked me to visit them in person because simply by looking at the pictures I had sent them, they couldn't say much about my foot's condition. I wanted to be reassured about my decision to wait until the bone grows back on its own. So I sent an email to Dr Hans asking whether I could meet the team on 23 March.

❧

31 JANUARY 2017

I got a reply from Dr Hans asking for the dates of my visit so that the team would keep themselves free. Then I thought of sending an email to Mr Pierre Cartuyvels informing him tentatively, as requested, of my plans. I wrote to him that I would be visiting Brussels from 17 to 25 March.

❧

1 FEBRUARY 2017

I received a reply from the diplomatic advisor that King Philippe would receive me on Monday, 20 March 2017, at 1000 hrs, at the Royal Palace in Brussels. They asked me for my postal address, so they could send me the necessary access details and documents. When I read the mail, it was 2100 hrs. I didn't know whether it was okay to share this news with anyone until I had the official invite with me. I was overjoyed. In my hurry to respond, I missed mentioning the state and country in my postal address, then realised the error and sent another mail with the correct and complete address!

❧

6 FEBRUARY 2017

For the past few days, I had spent quite some time thinking about how to pen my thoughts for the TEDx talk. At first, I considered hiring a professional writer. But then I realised that the speech might end up being not as impactful as it would miss out on the emotions involved in my journey. It had to come naturally. To connect to the people in the audience, the words have to be from the heart because only a genuine sharing of your thoughts and yourself can leave a mark.

❧

10 FEBRUARY 2017

Vardaan's birthday. Last year, I had missed it because I had been in the United States, operating a flight. I had asked him a few days ago how he would like to celebrate the day and he had said, 'With you and the family.' I had asked him why he had such a simple wish, and he had replied, 'I've always loved celebrating my birthday on a very grand scale with all my friends. But this time, I want to celebrate it only with you and our family. I missed these moments earlier, but now I don't want to miss you anymore.'

We enjoyed the evening, cutting cake and having dinner at his favourite restaurant. I was visiting that restaurant after a year or more. The staff there were surprised to see my new look and asked about it—I told them briefly about my experiences. To make me feel good, they immediately arranged for a cake for me to cut. 'Victory Over Fears' was written on the cake. I was touched by their gesture.

✿

It had been over a week since I'd received the email about the TEDx talk. I knew it was time to begin drafting my speech, so I took a sheet of paper and decided to cast aside all doubts. I just started writing and the words just flowed. I underlined a few lines I thought would be especially important and finished the rough draft. Full of nervousness, I mailed it to Pooja and Ajit at TEDx. On 15 February, I received a reply that said the draft was fine, but I should make sure that I wrap up the talk within the prescribed time limit.

I decided to rehearse and time the talk today, as I had not done that so far. I was super excited to be going to Jaipur.

✿

20 FEBRUARY 2017

In the morning, I got a call from Ms Lobo from the Belgian Embassy. She told me the embassy had received a letter addressed to me from the Royal Palace and asked me to let her know when Consul General Mr Peter Huyghebaert could meet me to hand over the letter. I was speechless for a moment and said I would get back to her soon. I couldn't resist sharing the news right away with my family and friends. Then I called Ms Lobo and informed her I would come on 23 February to meet the consul general at around 1100 hrs.

By the evening, the news had spread among the media and I

started getting calls from reporters and journalists asking me how I was feeling on receiving such a great honour. They wanted to know what I was going to talk about, my dates of travel and so much more. The questions were endless and I was on calls all day.

On 21 February, *Mumbai Mirror* carried a headline about it, and so did many other newspapers. Many people started calling—I don't know how many phone calls I attended!

❧

23 FEBRUARY 2017

This was a big day in my life. I dressed in formals after almost a year and reached the consulate on time. They escorted Rupesh and me to Mr Huyghebaert's office. We had a good chat over a cup of tea and Belgian cookies. It was great to hear from him that my words had impacted many and that he was still following my story. In the end, he apologised for the occurrence of the blast. I told him, 'I can't complain because I believe a new life has been given back to me by you all. The amount of love I have received is infinite.'

He gave me his personal visiting card so I could get in touch with him directly in the future. It was indeed a lovely meeting.

I had to leave for Jaipur the next day and I needed to pack.

On the one hand, I was anxious about getting everything ready in time. On the other, I was happy about getting the opportunity to visit such a beautiful, historically rich city. I might as well buy something from there for the king and queen of Belgium, I thought. In fact, why not shop in Jaipur for gifts for all the hospital staff, including nurses, doctors, helpers, and policeman Alain, Sumita di, Madan bhai, Shabir bhai, the ambassador, Gurmail, Kurt, Joost and all the others who had helped me? And of course, for my family too. So I made a list.

Oh my God, by the time I was done jotting down names, I had more than eighty people on my list! We had only one day in hand at that, a Sunday, because we would reach on Friday evening, on Saturday was the event, and on Sunday evening we were to fly back.

Nidhi Chaphekar

I made many calls to find out where I could get antique mementos and noted down the location. I was taking the kids along for the first time for one of my events and I had asked Goldy di, who lives in Delhi (about five hours by road to Jaipur) to join us. Also, I had asked my mother to fly down to Delhi and accompany my sister.

❦

24 FEBRUARY 2017

I reached Mumbai airport in the afternoon. I had been asked to give the base a call before I arrived. The whole team was there to welcome me and to make my journey a memorable one.

When we landed, I saw a staff member standing at Arrivals, bearing a placard with my name. But before I could identify myself, someone came and offered a bouquet to me and said, 'I am a fan of yours,' taking me by surprise.

❦

We reached Hotel Clarks Amer. Soon, my sister and mom arrived. I was meeting them after four months. We enjoyed dinner together in the rooftop restaurant with live ghazals and slept really late. Ever since the incident, I need eight to ten hours of sleep, or else I would end up suffering a bad headache the whole day.

❦

25 FEBRUARY 2017

I woke up with a headache and wondered how I was going to speak. I meditated a while for relief. After breakfast, I went to see the stage. I saw many of the other invitees practising with the mic on stage, one by one. I was asked whether I wanted to practise, but I told them, 'It's okay, I want to be spontaneous.' But I did do a sound check. I needed to get ready and be back at the hall by 1400 hrs. I went upstairs, had a cup of tea with light snacks, and got dressed.

I was asked to sit in the first row and my family was seated in the second row. All the speakers were so inspiring. My turn was to come after the break.

When I went up on stage, I looked at the audience and smiled. I started narrating my story. I got emotional while talking about the incident because it all came back to me vividly, like a flashback scene in a movie. My hands started shivering, my voice trembled in between. But I didn't stop speaking. I kept going. People were applauding to boost my confidence. My heart started palpitating when I saw the timer had stopped. Yet, I didn't bother. When I finished, I received a standing ovation. I saw many, including my family, crying. Some had closed their eyes. Again, I felt I was doing the right thing by touching their hearts, by making everyone understand that yes, we are all human, we do have feelings.

Quite a few people came to me for autographs, and I gave my first autograph on a cap!

❦

26 FEBRUARY 2017

Today, I wanted to shop, but it being a Sunday, most of the shops were closed. I tried out different places and finally got what I wanted for the king and queen of Belgium. After that, I shopped as per my list for the rest. When my sister and I returned from our shopping expedition, it was time for her and my mom to leave for their bus back to Delhi.

At that very moment, Mom received a call—Dad was not well and had been hospitalised. He was in the ICU, so she needed to return immediately. We booked her on the first flight from Delhi to Amritsar. All of us prayed for Dad's health. Mom broke down and said, 'Bad days are coming back again.' I had to pacify her saying all would be well soon. Truth be told, my father had never been unwell, so it was a shock even to us. After a while, Mom calmed down and agreed that a lot depends on the way we think. We must think positive and nothing would go wrong.

Nidhi Chaphekar

We returned to Mumbai late in the night.

❧

27 FEBRUARY 2017

It was indeed a day full of worry as my father was still in the ICU. We were all praying for his health. The reason for his illness was still not known to us and neither to the doctors.

❧

28 FEBRUARY 2017

My parents' wedding anniversary. My father was in the ICU and my mother was feeling very low. In the afternoon, I got a call from my brother asking me to come to Amritsar, as our father's health was not improving. 'We need you here.' There was urgency in his voice. 'I always believe that it's your energy that can bring anything to you, and we need your positivity now.'

❧

1 MARCH 2017

I took the first available flight to Amritsar. I went to the hospital directly from the airport. As soon as I met my father in the ICU, I assured him, 'You are fine... nothing will go wrong.' He tried to talk and explain something to me, but I couldn't understand what he was trying to say. But after that, his condition started to improve as if he had got his energy back. He was out of the ICU by late evening.

However, the next day, the doctor was a bit worried about his test results. In the CT scan, they found an abscess in the liver and the surrounding area. The doctor called me outside the room. His hands were trembling when he said, 'I am sorry, but we need to do an endoscopy and will then send the sample for a biopsy.'

I steeled myself. I got a glass of water for the doctor and said, 'Don't worry, he is fine.'

The doctor though was not as hopeful. 'No, I am sure that your father is in the last stage of cancer,' he insisted.

I told him the tests would be negative but he felt that was very unlikely, and that I should keep my fingers crossed.

When the doctors were about to start the endoscopy, I was with my father, by his side. While the doctor inserted a big needle in my father's stomach, my father was fine, and I was holding his hand. Normally within two trials, the doctors are able to get the piece of tissue they need, but every time the doctor tried, he continued to find nothing. The third time my father started complaining of severe pain; I placed my cheek next to his and said softly, 'Just a few more minutes,' even though I too felt anxious. It reminded me of my situation right after the blast, when I too was assured of getting aid in a few more minutes. The doctor managed to take out the tissue on his fifth attempt—a tiny piece, maybe one-tenth the size of a mustard seed. My father was shivering as the pain was unbearable. I hugged him and continued to hold his hand.

Within a fraction of a second his condition worsened and his vitals started to drop. The head nurse called out for help to take him straight to the ICU. The nurse plugged in the oxygen and together we pushed the bed towards the ICU. It was a moment of sheer panic for all of us. Only my mother didn't know as she was in Dad's room, and I had told her in a very general tone that I was taking Dad for some tests, but I had briefed my brother about what the test entailed. My brother was called immediately. I had faith that everything would be fine. The situation was handled well and by night, his condition was under control and he was shifted back into the room. We were informed that the test results would be available in three to five days—I was confident the results would ensure there would be nothing to worry about.

✺

While I was in the hospital, I got a call from my office informing me about some people wanting to conduct a telephonic interview with me and asked whether I would be okay with doing it the next morning. It turned out to be a good forty-minute interview. I was feeling a little low as I had to return to Mumbai the next day; I was hoping my father would be discharged from the hospital and be back home that day. But the doctors hadn't said anything yet.

The next morning, the doctor examined my father and said he was doing very well. I asked him when we could expect the discharge.

'Well, it can be done even today. But he has to take some antibiotic injections at home.'

I asked him if the nurse could give the injections. He agreed and said, 'Okay, then you may take him home.'

I couldn't believe our luck! I thanked him and told him, 'I have to leave for the airport at 1300 hrs and I want to see him out of the hospital before that. Can we expedite things, please?'

We informed the rest of the family and my brother came to help. I was so glad when I sat in the car heading to the airport—at the same time, my father sat in another car that was heading home. I sent up a prayer of gratitude.

However, the moment my aircraft landed in Mumbai, I got to know that his health had again deteriorated, and he had been hospitalised. When my family asked the doctor why he had been discharged if he wasn't cured, the doctor said that it was because I had requested him to do so!

I felt really upset. I stayed quiet when I was told that the doctor was blaming me for this situation. Members of my family too felt I may have requested the doctor because my father kept telling me to get him discharged soon. I quietly prayed to God and told them, 'time will prove it... he will be fine.' I knew my father would be alright. If the doctor had discharged him on my request, he should have written so in the papers—'discharge given on request'. But for me, at that moment, my father's health was more important than proving myself right.

7 MARCH 2017

Today I had to complete my visa formalities for my Belgium trip. I got a call from Ms Pom—'Since you shared with us that while giving your TEDx speech you were shivering, we think it's time for you to undergo counselling for a few days.'

I agreed and connected with one of the counsellors. We had a few sessions together.

❧

8 MARCH 2017

When we reached the VFS office for our visa, we were told the rules had changed, and I would have to fill up the form online now. This change was effective from 1 February. (Our forms had been filled by Pradeep from my company and the appointment had been taken for the day.) We were dismayed when we were asked to fill the forms online and come back another time. Then I showed them my letter of invitation from the king and the official at VFS recognised me. He took the letter and went inside. After a few minutes, he came back and said, 'Please take a seat. We will fill your form right away. We have got instructions from the Belgium consulate not to charge any fees for the visa either.'

The concern shown by the embassy officials was heartening. We were there for just two hours and the work got done.

❧

Meanwhile, my father's condition was not stabilising and talks were on about what was to be done. My family finally decided to consult some other doctors.

❧

9 MARCH 2017

The day after the International Women's Day celebrations, I entered my company's premises for the first time after the blast. The last time I went there was to ask the planning team manager and the rostering team to put me on a US-bound flight in March 2016.

The moment I entered the office building—right from the office staff, trainers, instructors, crew—everyone started congratulating me. Some hugged me, some showered their love and had tears of joy. It took me nearly an hour to reach the room where the meeting was scheduled.

The rostering in-charge, Nandu, who had given me the flight that fateful day, had tears in his eyes. I smiled, 'If you had not given me the flight that day, how would I have become world-famous!' Everyone started laughing. It's true. It is because of the incident that I have been discovering wonderful things about myself. As the bestselling author and activist Christine Caine once said, 'Sometimes when you're in a dark place, you think you've been buried, but actually you've been planted.' Nothing was done on purpose; it was destined to happen with me.

❦

With only a week left for my Brussels trip, I started exchanging emails to connect with everybody I wanted to meet during my trip. On Saturday and Sunday, I shopped for all the gifts I wanted to take with me. There were so many that they did not fit even in the two, big, seventy-two-inch trolley bags. So I had to put some in a third bag as well.

I was very confused about what to wear while meeting the king. Finally, I decided to wear a traditional Indian sari. I was unsure about what kind of shoes I could wear. In Mumbai, I always stuck to a pair of very comfortable track shoes.

Even though I was looking forward to the trip, deep down I felt disturbed and anxious, wondering how I would feel and react when I see the same place where the incident from perhaps the darkest hour of my life happened. Would I be able to make peace with the past? Every day, for at least a week before my date of departure, I kept telling myself that it was all in the past, and rather than breaking down, I should try to set an example for others. I should meet and give confidence to those who had lost their loved ones. But the mind is sometimes restless and difficult to control.

❧

From the time the news of my invitation to meet the king went viral, many channels had got in touch with my company; so they asked me if I would give interviews with a few they had selected. I agreed to do one-on-one interviews.

Meanwhile, I received a mail from the protocol staff of the prime minister of Belgium saying they would be glad if I joined them at a ceremony on Wednesday, 22 March 2017, to attend the moment of silence at 0758 hrs at Brussels airport. I confirmed my presence. I also got a call from a counsellor cell informing me that while at the airport, one of their counsellors would be with me at all times. I decided, though, to not have any counsellor with me. But I was really touched to see how they were taking care of our sentiments.

❧

While my days were busy preparing for the Brussels trip, there was always a niggling concern at the back of my mind—my father was still quite ill. As he was not in a condition to be taken to another doctor for consultation, my brother was doing all the running around with Dad's medical records. Soon, a very senior doctor diagnosed that his gall bladder had burst and that was the reason behind his bouts of fits and acute illness. He said it was very rare for a person to survive after this sort of critical attack. He asked my brother to get him admitted in his hospital for treatment and further diagnosis. He was immediately shifted to the other hospital. And guess what, his biopsy report was thankfully negative.

❧

Nidhi Chaphekar

I got an email from a PR agency owned by Ms Beatrice Mondelaers saying they would be taking care of me in Brussels and asked me to pass their number to any media person who contacted me. Her email mentioned that the entire day, i.e., from the morning of the 21st of March to the evening, has been reserved for interviews with different media houses.

❧

16 MARCH 2017

After thirteen months, I decided to visit a beauty parlour. The lady who worked there recognised my voice and said, 'I have seen you somewhere.' After a pause, she asked, 'You are Nidhi, right? All of us were wondering if you are okay!'

After chatting with her for a bit, I told her how the hair on my arms and legs had grown thick and asked her whether waxing would work.

On seeing my scarred limbs, she seemed quite apprehensive and asked me if I was trying waxing for the first time after the incident. I assured her that I had the permission of my doctor. (I had sought his approval for waxing months ago.) The lady reluctantly agreed to do it.

When the first strip of wax was peeled off, a part of my leg looked like a cricket pitch... so clean and beautiful! What a feeling it is to see your legs nice and pretty after a parlour visit! But this time I was a little sad because without the hair on my arms and legs, the scars and deep wounds that seemed well-covered till a few minutes ago were now clearly and disturbingly visible. I felt 'unfeminine', if I can use that word. I wondered if I would ever again be able to wear dresses, the kinds where my legs would be visible. I wanted to, so I decided I would wear them with stockings. I resolved to myself – it doesn't matter if the uneven, deep patches on my legs get noticed; there is nothing as important and precious as one's health. As long as I am healthy, I should not pay attention to the insecurities in my head. Our skin never remains the same. It changes with time, so it shouldn't affect me, as nothing is permanent.

✿

18 MARCH 2017

What a coincidence. A year ago, on 19 March 2016, when I had asked for the flight from Mumbai to Newark via Brussels, they were not ready to give me the flight at first. Then I had called the rostering team while I was at my kids' school for their annual day programme, requesting them to put me on the flight, and Nandu had finally rostered me. This year again on 18 March, I was in the school attending the annual programme when, at around the same time, I received a call from my in-flight manager saying that my travel formalities have been completed. I felt my heart thundering away — it was the same region, the same time, and the same news I was receiving. The coincidence was so uncanny, it could disturb anyone. I couldn't help thinking — *why is the same pattern being repeated... what now?* This feeling of fear would be natural for anyone who has gone through so much, but I caught myself before I could let myself fall deeper — *don't forget, it is only your thinking; it is not the same situation.* And as a wonderful saying goes, 'A head full of fears has no space for dreams.' I don't want to let any fear come in the way of my dreams. I pulled myself out from thinking those miserable thoughts. I thanked my manager for her help and silently sent up a prayer asking God to keep His hand on our heads at all times.

I was not the only one to notice the coincidence. Many teachers and parents pointed it out to me too. 'Last year you had gone to Brussels right after attending the annual day function, and this year too you are travelling almost around the same date to the same place.'

I smiled and said, 'Incidents take place once, but our fear generates every single moment afterwards. So we have to conquer the self, otherwise it will conquer us.'

And then I got the good news that my father had been discharged from the other hospital. Two external pipes had been attached to draw out bile from the body. The surgery would be conducted only after bile formation completely stops. He was doing well and out of danger. Jai Mata Di.

❦

19 MARCH 2017

D-day finally arrived! I had an early morning flight to Amsterdam. We reported at the airport on 18 March at 2300 hrs itself. I was carrying the gift I had bought for the king in my hand as it was a fragile item. As usual, I was busy talking to many people I knew when Rupesh came up to me and said, 'there are no more seats available on the flight, so they have given us jump seats.' (One of the carriers had cancelled their flight and my airline was taking their guests on priority.)

'How will I travel on a jump seat!' I exclaimed.

Then the supervisor on duty asked us if they could put us on a Paris flight instead.

Rupesh and I boarded that flight in the nick of time.

All previously made arrangements had to be cancelled as now I was to land in Paris instead of Amsterdam. I had very limited time left to make the required calls. I called up Shabir bhai, but his number was unavailable, so I left a message to arrange for a taxi on our arrival. The duty manager in Paris was informed to call up Shabir bhai and inform him of the changes made. Photographer Ketevan, who had taken my picture on the day of the blast, had wanted to receive me at the airport. She was disappointed when I told her about the changes in my schedule. She had even booked herself for the night at a hotel near Amsterdam airport. I had to call people one by one and inform them about the inevitable delay in the schedule ahead.

Once again, the thought crossed my mind — *Why this change in plans? Why did this have to happen to us?* But I told myself, never mind, we are still following the schedule. Only it has been re-routed.

Exactly a year after the flight I had taken on 20 March 2016 to Brussels that had changed my life, I was taking a flight again today on 19 March 2017 to Paris. To my surprise, I found that five crew members out of the nine operating on the flight were a part of my crew set to Brussels on 20 March 2016.

On the flight I was to operate on 22 March 2016 from Brussels to Newark, all my crew members were still on the ground floor at Brussels airport except Shrungal who had reached Departure Level 2. She had been talking to a guest near the escalators when the blast took place. When I met Shrungal on the flight, she too expressed her shock at the coincidence, at how everything seemed to be exactly the same as that day. *Why*, she asked me. *Why*, I asked myself. But before I could give the thought more of my attention, I put my faith in God. I knew He must have planned the best for us. I told the others that maybe this was a happy reunion for all of us and hugged all of them. After the incident, I had not met anyone apart from Shrungal who had come home to meet me. I was tired and slept, and woke up just before landing.

On arrival, I met Jet Airways Duty Manager Shalaka and staff member Sami, who had bid me farewell on 5 May 2016 from Paris. They couldn't believe their eyes when they saw me. I was given a very warm welcome. I had told Shalaka to contact Shabir bhai to send a driver, but to my surprise he himself came to receive us. I had taken a lot of Indian sweets and gave two boxes to Shalaka and Ashutosh. Both of them had also come to see me while I was at Grand Hospital.

Shabir bhai had tears of joy when he hugged us. It was 0845 hrs when we all boarded the car. We reached the Crowne Plaza hotel in Brussels at noon. We talked nonstop throughout the drive. I told him in detail about my journey after the incident. He too shared his experience of that day. He told us how he had given interviews to a few channels over the phone because somehow they had got his contact number and they had heard that he had seen me in the hospital. They also asked him to share any latest picture he may have had of me, and he had forwarded the picture taken near the Atomium on the day prior to the attack. He told me he had never been so busy in his life, being on the phone continuously like that.

Some of those days had been maddening for him as he was the only one providing news to family members and friends especially in the first few days after the incident.

We talked so much that no one realised we had completed a journey of two hundred minutes.

The moment we reached the hotel, I saw Ketevan with her assistant photographer waiting for me at the entrance. It was the first time I was meeting her and her photographer clicked a lot of pictures.

I also met Justine from *RTBF* channel. I had only spoken to her on the phone so far, but this was my first personal interaction with her and her team. She had already taken permission and made arrangements to go to Brussels airport to do a photo shoot there. It was to start by 1300 hrs and go on for three hours. As we were late, she asked me if I could leave with them in twenty minutes. So I quickly checked into the hotel, put my bags in the room, and sat in the car along with Rupesh.

I was feeling a little low, but I knew I had to overcome the feeling. As we passed signboards giving directions to the airport, my heart began beating faster. When I saw the place where I had got down from the bus that day and then the signboard for Holiday Inn, I held on tight to Rupesh. Justine parked the car and we entered the airport from the opposite end. While walking towards the main entrance to the airport, I realised that my stretcher had been rolled somewhere there and then I noticed that yes, it was indeed a fire brigade parking hall where my stretcher had finally been placed. I saw the same shutter. I recalled everything in that moment. I could feel myself slowly losing control of my emotions. I was yet to face the exact spot where it had happened. We slowly walked towards the entrance. My legs were shaking, but I knew I had to conquer my fears. I kept walking. I saw Hotel Sheraton on the other side and my eyes filled up again. I pointed out to Rupesh and the others the place where my stretcher had been placed. While looking at the Sheraton logo, recalling how I had felt that day, thinking my captains would come soon, I just stood there for a moment in silence. I couldn't find my voice. I felt the same wave of pain choking me. I took a few deep breaths, knowing I had to now face the real ordeal when we enter the airport.

The place had changed a bit. There were cubicles outside now. A lot of military personnel were deployed in the area in view of the ceremony to be held on 22 March; there were just two days to go. Looking at the uniformed personnel, I was trying to identify the one who had helped me that day, but it was not easy. Justine showed the letter of approval to the security and they allowed us in. The cameramen entered ahead of me as they wanted to capture my reaction.

As soon as I walked in, from afar I saw that the bird sculpture that had been there earlier was no longer there. I was just next to Lane 10, where I believe the first bomb had exploded. As I slowly walked towards the spot where the second one had exploded, I saw the familiar Starbucks outlet to my left and my heart couldn't bear it anymore. The tears came fast. People around me were surprised to see me cry, but they noticed that the camera was on me. They probably thought it was a film shoot. Many gathered to have a look. I was trying hard to get my energy back to say something. Someone then asked me about the incident, and I narrated how I had been flung from where I was back then, and all that I had seen that day. We tried to locate the exact place where I had fallen and sure enough, to the left I saw the chair I had been sitting on when I had been thrown off my feet in the blast. Photographer Ketevan had been in the photo booth nearby, just ten to twelve feet away from me. I sat on the same chair in the same position to explain in a better way how I had sat there with my leg up, trying to stop the bleeding in my leg. I felt numb like I did on that day but I had to be strong. I could feel and hear the cries of people still ringing in my ears and the sounds of the rescue teams on their way. In front of that chair were the escalators that people had used as stairs to climb down to safety. None of the elevators and escalators had worked after the blast. Today I could see people using the same escalators as usual.

I sat on that chair for a few minutes, watching some kids playing nearby. *Life must go on*, I told myself. I must leave all the negatives behind and reach out only for positive energy. I prayed to God—*I can't ask so much in words but you have to listen to my silent heart.* I took the example of the building itself. It had been totally damaged, it had been reduced to rubble, but with everyone's efforts, it had been reconstructed and made much more beautiful. In the same way, I must rebuild myself with encouraging thoughts. Holding the hand rails, I prayed to God to give me strength to get up from the same chair today with no regrets and look forward to a fresh start, a new beginning.

❧

We had lunch and coffee and by the time I returned to the hotel, it was 1700 hrs. I saw Ketevan who had been waiting for me since the morning. She wanted to interview me to discuss my picture. I told her we could start in fifteen minutes. We walked to the botanical garden opposite the hotel. She first explained she had got many death threats over email, shaming her for taking the picture at that moment. So she felt that an interview with me would bring justice into the situation.

I told her, 'Well, in a hurry and a shocked state of mind, you posted the picture on social media without realising it could be misused, but it turned out to be a boon for my family for those ten hours until they could locate me. Because the picture showed that although my clothes were all burnt and I had visible injuries, I was okay. But it also showed I was in shock. Now the media should not have simply printed the picture like that... they should have cropped or blurred it a bit to maintain my dignity.'

She told me she had been offered a million dollars by a businessman from the Middle East who had asked her to sell my picture to him. But she never charged anyone anything. I found it surprising that a company would want to buy my picture. She had clicked twelve pictures in all—there were ten other people she photographed but I was the only one whom she photographed twice. 'that's the reason you appear in two different poses,' she explained.

The interview went on for an hour and a half. She also asked me to hold the copy of my picture in my hand. I had to repeat many things because of the sounds of police car sirens and the strong wind blowing in the background. I gifted her a box of Indian sweets and a handmade bag. She was delighted. We had snacks and coffee in the hotel. She also gifted me a Pandora bracelet. The next day, I saw some of my pictures online. During our conversation, Ketevan had mentioned that she had been offered money for my image to be sold to one particular media agency, but she had refused. So I told her that in case she receives money for the images, she should spend it on a good cause.

But she had declined the idea and said, 'No, no, not at all. For your picture I have not taken any money and I told everyone that it is free.'

By the time I returned to my hotel room, I was so tired, I had dinner and slept. I needed to wake up early to be ready to meet King Philippe.

❧

20 MARCH 2017

I woke up at 0630 hrs, had breakfast and started getting dressed. It was 0815 hrs when Justine arrived. She wanted to capture a few moments with me before I met the king and a few more afterwards as well. I thought I looked pretty but also funny, as I was wearing sports shoes under the sari. I didn't want to be uncomfortable while walking, well aware that I had to keep up with the tight schedule ahead of me. I couldn't afford to injure myself or even slow down. They shot a few photographs and interviewed me for fifteen minutes.

As she suggested, we left at 0915 hrs, to make it in time. We reached at 0945 hrs, parked the car a little away from the palace and at exactly 0957 hrs, we were at the gate of the royal palace. After verifying our identities, the security personnel requested me, 'Please wait for two minutes as Her Majesty the Queen of Belgium,

Mathilde, is arriving. Please wait in the car on the other side of the road. I will give you a signal to enter.'

Two bikes, one on either side of the road, with their blue and red lights blazing, their sirens sounding loud and clear, heralded the arrival of the queen. We were then given a signal to get the car in. Our car doors were opened by a royal house assistant and two people in uniform guided us into the room.

Alain Gerardy, chief of protocol of the royal household, told us, 'Many press people are waiting, so when you meet the king, please stand for a while to provide them with a good picture.' He then offered to take the gifts I had got for the king and the queen, so that the pictures would come out better.

I felt on top of the world when I shook hands with King Philippe and Queen Mathilde. Photographs were clicked by all the leading news agencies and then the king invited us in. The huge doors of the room were closed. We all sat down. The queen asked me many questions, about how I was doing and all I had gone through.

King Philippe asked me the question that was on everyone's mind — 'How did you reach that chair where you were photographed?'

I narrated my experiences to them. Queen Mathilde asked about my children's well-being. I told her that they wanted to be here but I was not sure if they would be allowed. She asked me to let their office know in case there was a plan to come to Belgium again and if their schedule permitted, they would surely meet our kids.

I could see that the king was feeling really bad for whatever had happened in his country. At the end of a good hour-long chat, King Philippe said to me, 'It was very unfortunate, what happened with you, but you were fortunate that if it had to happen to you, it happened in our country because we have the best doctors and the finest medical facilities.'

'that is true,' I replied, 'with the condition I was in, it is only because of the facilities and medical expertise you have here that I am alive today. I was told that you have plans to come to Mumbai this year. So hopefully we will see you then along with your children.'

We had a great time and a lovely cup of tea. They came out to see us off. This time there were no media people standing around. We were escorted by Alain and the staff of the royal household up to the door of the car. The same guard who had opened the car door when I had arrived again held it open for me. Meeting a royal family is a different feeling altogether.

❧

Justine was very eager to broadcast this the very next day; she wanted to be the first one to produce it on television. She wanted to take a few pictures and videos outside the palace for her documentary. So we spent a good ten to fifteen minutes before heading back to the hotel. She had also arranged my meeting with the doctors in Charleroi by 1300 hrs, so we had to rush back since I first wanted to change into more comfortable clothes. I changed, and by 1215 hrs, we left. It was an hour's drive; we were expected around 1315 hrs. On the way we chatted about my best memories.

I saw the first signboard for Grand Hospital, where I was treated. There was a small forest on one side. I noticed coal plates. On asking, I was told coal had been banned in the country for the past thirty years and that's why there was wire fencing around this place. They showed me the entrance of the hospital road just about two hundred metres away. I could feel my heart racing. When I caught the first glimpse of the hospital from the car, I shouted out like a kid — 'My hospital!'

When parking the car, I pointed out the spot where my ambulance had been parked when I was to leave for India. I explained with joy that this was the place where my wheelchair had been brought out and I had enjoyed fresh air for the first time. Then I showed them the place from where I was taken to the other side of the hospital for X-rays and CT scans. As I was about to enter the hospital visiting room, I was asked to wait for a few seconds while they took a few photographs of the room. The moment I entered, all the staff, including the doctors, nurses and head nurses, started clapping. Not having known that they had all gathered to welcome me like that,

I was dumbfounded for a moment. I couldn't control myself and hugged Dr Peeters and Dr Hans, tears of gratitude streaming down my face as I thanked both of them for all that they had done for me.

Then I hugged everyone else. I remembered some of their names. I told Carine, 'Look, I am still wearing the wrist band, to ward off the evil eye.'

I spent an hour talking to them. I could clearly see the happiness on their faces. Normally we never go back to places like hospitals, but I have a different opinion. We should always thank those who have helped us reach where we are today. Then I opened the big suitcases of gifts I had carried for them. For the men, I had handmade photo frames and for the women, handmade purses along with antique handmade earrings. I announced—'this is just a token of love for everyone, so please select the colour and design of your choice.'

Instantly, everyone gathered around my suitcases. Within minutes, everyone's hands were full. Some took gifts for the night shift nurses. Most of the administrative staff wore the earrings right away. The TV channel team interviewed Dr Hans and Dr Peeters. The doctors revealed my case study and stood beside me to have pictures taken. Dr Peeters said I was a miracle. He called it my rebirth. He said, 'Very rarely does anybody remember us later after the job is done, but she always keeps us in the loop.'

He added he was surprised to see me walking as they were expecting someone on crutches or using a walking aid, or at the very least, that I would be limping. 'We never thought she would walk without the bone graft but she proved everyone wrong,' he added. 'She is a tough lady and God has been kind to her. We never thought she would walk like this in the future.'

My speedy recovery was like a thunderbolt to them. He added that he was mesmerised with the results of the grafts on the marks and burns on my face.

Then Ms Lilane Lenaerts came up to me and introduced herself as the doctor who had accompanied me to this hospital from the Sint-Augustinus Hospital, Antwerp, in a helicopter. She had been with me throughout. She expressed how horrifying it had been. Dr Peeters said he had thought of inviting her to make this moment more beautiful, especially as she had called them up many times to check on my health.

She said she could never forget the state I had been in that day, and that I was truly blessed. After looking at the pictures she had clicked, I was wondering about the shock they must have been in. She said she had felt so worried for days together. She had prayed hard for me. I hugged her and asked her to share her email ID and phone number so that I could stay in touch with her. I requested her to accept a gift from me as a token of love.

I also gifted the handmade boxes to Head Nurse John, and all the three doctors. They loved it.

Although we wanted to stay a bit longer, we had to rush back so that Justine could finish her documentary. My suitcases full of gifts were finally empty. There were two more people I was to meet, but they couldn't make it. I told them I would see them when I come back on 23 and 24 March for my medical review. We left at 1600 hrs and reached our hotel at 1645 hrs.

I had even mailed the ambassador, Mr Puri, before my arrival and was informed that 20 March was his last day at the Indian embassy in Belgium. He had been transferred to Nepal. It was very important for me to meet him too and I had sent him a message. He told me to meet him at the office. I took with me the gift I had bought for him and some Indian sweets for the rest of the people.

Rupesh and I reached the Indian embassy with Shabir bhai. Mr Puri hugged us and gave a warm welcome. We started talking about the event that had occurred exactly a year ago. They told me how helpless they had all felt when they were unable to find me, as the area had been closed and no one was allowed in. Mr Puri spoke highly of me. He described how shocked he felt on seeing my photograph for the first time. 'I could never imagine the way you have handled it and have come out of it. You are so lively,' he beamed.

He said that later, when I regained consciousness and he came to visit me again, he couldn't believe his eyes. 'You are a true fellow of God, always being thankful to him in whatever situation He has put you in. It is because of your own will power, positivity and strength that you are alive and strong enough to handle any situation. I am glad I met you today and I have learnt a lot about life from you. Mrs Puri sends her regards. She would have joined us but is busy with all the packing, as we have to leave tomorrow night.'

I felt lucky to meet him. We had a cup of tea. The embassy usually closes by 1745 hrs, but everyone stayed back for my sake. I thanked everyone for their full support and help during our difficult times.

It was late by the time we reached the hotel. I was really tired but still feeling great thinking about how much love and affection we as human beings have for each other. We are the only species in the universe who can convey this love through words and gestures.

❧

21 MARCH 2017

Each day seems to be more beautiful that the previous one. The people I met and the experiences I've gone through continued to strengthen my belief that I could be a messenger of love and humanity, that I could inspire a few who find it difficult to face the challenges that life throws at them, to spread smiles and happiness and hope. I could feel a new confidence building in me.

Today, I had been scheduled to give interviews. After breakfast, we headed to the Hilton at Central. Beatrice from the PR agency was waiting at the entrance with two other people from the corporate communications department of my company, Monique Voorneman and Gilbert George. The session began and a variety of questions were asked but I answered all of them straight from the heart.

One question posed was: 'Would you like to shoot that terrorist?'

My answer was, 'No, then there would be no difference between me and them. The laws are made to punish them. Since this attack caused mass destruction, where so many people were killed or injured, I don't think I have the right to decide what is to be done with the terrorists. But given a choice, one thing I would want to do for sure is to send them for rehabilitation and counselling.'

The lady interviewing me laughed when I said that.

⁂

We took a lunch break at 1315 hrs for an hour. Beatrice knew that I was a vegetarian and had instructed the chef accordingly. After lunch, we started with the second round of interviews. One by one, we finished the remaining interviews on time.

The one common question raised by all of them was: What was your reaction after seeing your picture as it became the face of the terror attack?

Perhaps their words were different, I can't exactly recall now, but this was what they meant. I realise that of course I was upset with the fact that the photograph hadn't been blurred but I had decided to move ahead and focus instead on what the photograph did for me, my family and people from across the world whose prayers helped me recover.

'It is not the face of the attack,' I replied confidently, 'but the reflection in my face of hope, courage, resilience and strength of humanity around the globe.'

Monique then requested me to say something for the people at her workplace as well as she believed I was an inspiration for most. 'this is for the company's social media page,' she informed me.

I spoke for a good ten minutes. Afterwards, she watered an idea that had already been planted in my mind: 'Your thoughts can inspire more. Start a blog and let me know if you need any help.'

Even after speaking all day, I was not tired. When the work we do enriches us, we feel more energetic. I was to meet Amit in the hotel today as he had also come to attend the memorial ceremony arranged by the Belgian government and had arrived late in the afternoon. On returning to the hotel, we made plans to have dinner together, and have waffles afterwards.

'Let's do all the fun things I did with the rest of the crew on 21 March 2016, before we got injured,' I suggested. Amit was the only one who had not joined in when the rest of the crew and I had gone sightseeing. He had stayed back in the hotel. Amit agreed to my idea this time, and we asked Shabir bhai to join us too. We started with Sultan of Kebab, and from there we went to the Delirium. Then we did some sightseeing around the Grand Palace and Manneken Pis. We ate waffles from the same shop we had visited earlier. And how could I miss the Lady of Sorrow. I thanked her for being so kind to me. I touched her and prayed to her to be with me all the time. I cried a bit as I prayed, but I was really very happy to see her again.

As I walked on those familiar roads, I wanted time to stand still. At one point, I felt as if what we went through last year was just a dream. I asked Shabir bhai to take us by the Holiday Inn hotel as well. As we drove past it, I relived the feelings of that day.

When Shabir bhai dropped us at the rear entrance of Hotel Crowne Plaza, my heart felt heavy. I walked in behind Rupesh and Amit, feeling low. Revisiting all these places, though exhilarating at the time, had managed to take a toll on me, even though I tried my best to only look at the bright side. But thankfully, this feeling didn't stay with me for too long. As a saying goes: 'Every shadow, no matter how deep, is threatened by morning light.'

After a few steps, I heard Rupesh call my name. When I looked up, I saw policeman Alain Zachary with his wife Laurence and son Maxime along with his fiancée, Sarah van Der. I had not expected such a wonderful surprise; we had made plans to meet on the evening of 25 March.

He hugged me and said over and over — 'O Nidhi, O Nidhi! I am so glad to see you healthy, fit and fine!'

Words cannot express my feelings at that point. The hotel staff and people around us applauded.

Then he introduced me to his family. They had got a gift for me and he asked me to open it. When I did, I couldn't believe my eyes. It was a police jacket with his name 'Alain Zachary' written on it. He explained he had been wearing this jacket that day and had never worn it ever since.

'It's for you now, my token of remembrance.' And he made me wear it. I was really touched by his gesture. I invited them to have a drink with us at the restaurant. We talked a lot and Alain took more than a hundred pictures! We were all immensely happy. 'You have to visit our home too,' Alain insisted.

I didn't know if I would have time before we left, but I promised to surely try. He said he would check the calendar to see which day he and his son would be off duty and promised to call me to fix a date.

Even after they left, I didn't remove the jacket. The hotel staff spoke warmly about him, saying it was really nice of him to surprise me like this. They told me he had waited for us for quite a while. I went back to our room with beautiful memories that would last me a lifetime.

❦

22 MARCH 2017

It was a very special day for all of us. We had to be at the airport by 0700 hrs.

I slept soundly and woke up at 0540 hrs. It was the same date — 22 March. But the year had changed — 2017. Last year too, my alarm had been set for 0540 hrs as I had to report for my briefing with the crew at 0715 hrs.

We were to go to Hotel Sheraton. There were tables laid out based on the colour of the wristband worn by the attendee. Those attending only the ceremony at the airport wore a purple wristband; those attending it to see the inauguration of the bird sculpture, which was earlier at the airport but now relocated to the garden, were given a separate band. And there was a different coloured band for those attending the ceremonies being held in remembrance of the people who lost their lives at Maalbeek metro station.

We were given special guidelines to follow and were also instructed on security measures. We wanted to attend all the ceremonies, so we presented our invitation letter, which had a special barcode number. We were asked about which ceremonies we wished to attend. When we said 'All', they tied a red band around our wrists. We were asked to go upstairs where tea was being served.

There I saw Ketevan sitting with Sebastien, a famous basketball player who had been injured in the same blast. Ketevan had also taken his picture at the time of the blast. We were introduced to each other. I met many more who had been injured in that blast. One of them had lost his hearing.

As I was having coffee, a lady came running towards me and said, 'Hi, I am Inge. I work with the police and am based in Antwerp. I received a Louis Vuitton purse from the blast site. Are you missing one?'

I was shocked. I said yes. Inge told me she had tried to trace me but had not managed to get my contact details. When she found out I was attending the commemorative function, she decided to come see me and bring the purse. When she handed me the purse, I couldn't stop my tears. Seeing her love, affection and concern, I realised there is still an abundance of humanity, truthfulness and trust left in the world. Doing little things for others always brings love, respect and care. My money, bank cards, even the bills of my last purchase—for the shoes I needed to exchange for my son and husband—all were intact in the purse! It was as if nothing had even been touched.

I hugged her tight. 'thank you, Inge! What you did for me is really a surprise. I could never have dreamt of getting back my things, that too after a year.'

Let's be honest, who has time in this busy world today? And yet, we find human beings who care for us even if they don't know us. We shared email IDs and I made a new friend. I asked her, 'How did you know it belonged to me?'

'Well, from your card with the name written on it,' she explained, 'and your name was the one in the news and being published all over.'

Later, I sent her an email thanking her again for her kind gesture. She had had a feeling she would meet me sometime in life and had kept my purse safely. It felt so exhilarating to find something I had lost after a year's gap!

❦

We were asked to join the ceremony at 0715 hrs outside the airport. Security was very tight. The moment I stepped out in the open, I felt my heart sinking. I saw helicopters above. I had this horrible thought—for the terrorist too, today was the one-year anniversary. But I pacified my heart telling myself these were just the fearful thoughts of a negative mind. Those who were not wearing the red band were asked to stand near the media persons. We were asked to walk ahead and take seats next to the dais. I sat on one of the chairs to the right side. We were waiting for the prime minister, Mr Charles Michel, to arrive, and he was to be followed by the king and the queen.

After their arrival, the ceremony began. They offered condolences to the families of those who were not with us anymore. As a mark of respect, the national anthem was played and the heads of all the forces (the navy, army, air force) offered a salute. I couldn't control my tears. There was a lady in the seat behind me who had lost her mother in the tragic incident—she was sobbing in pain. I held her hand and offered her some water. The Flemish-Brabant military province commander, Colonel Koen Hillewaert, was sitting beside me. I noticed him observing me for a while. Later, he asked me how I was related to this event. When I explained, he said, 'Yes, I saw your interview in the morning and your photograph is in all the newspapers today as well.'

'thank you for recognising me,' I replied.

As the ceremony proceeded, I couldn't control my emotions when a person named Eddy Van Calster was called on stage to sing. His wife was just about to leave after her shift at the airport at 0800 hrs when she got caught in the blast and lost her life. She had worked for fifteen years at the airport check-in counter. He sang a song he had composed, and dedicated it to her. He sang it with so much love. He didn't cry, though his heart was in pain as we could all see. There was such depth in his words—she was alive in his heart, dreams, soul, so that no one could take her away from him.

Guman Lars Wactzmann was just about to leave for New York with his wife Jennefer when the attack occurred. He lost his wife. He spoke at the commemoration about what it would have been

Nidhi Chaphekar

like if they had left ten minutes later than they had. In a split second, the unthinkable happened and his world changed. But on that very day, he also started seeing the best of humankind, the unconditional love and help given by people around him. What a brilliant outlook on life. I was amazed.

We observed two minutes of silence in honour of all the victims, and then the king and queen, along with other dignitaries, went inside the airport departure hall to perform the rest of the ceremonies in the place where the bomb blast had occurred.

Meanwhile, Col. Hillewaert started talking to me. I told him I needed to find two people, including one military commando who had helped pick me up from the ground and made me sit on the chair, as well as the other person who had been with us in the fire brigade hall while I was waiting for medical aid to arrive. I told him I knew the airport staff very well, but I couldn't go inside the airport. I gave him a description.

I told him, 'the man who helped me in the fire brigade hall is fair, of medium height, lean, with blond hair, bluish-green eyes, probably in his forties. He used to be at the screening area most of the time. I don't know his name. They wear white shirts. But the military personnel I don't know at all.'

He told me he had a few friends in the military wing, so he would try to help me find the officer. We exchanged email IDs and numbers.

Next, buses had been arranged to take us from there to the memorial garden. While I was walking towards the bus, I saw the same man who sang the song in remembrance of his wife. I said to him, 'Can I hug you, please? Because I want to take some more energy and positivity from you. The amount of love you shared... God bless you for accepting the reality so gracefully and living life cheerfully to provide love to your family and the world. After all, this is what life is. It's really hard, but the show must go on. But the most difficult truth to express... you put it in words so simply, and so melodiously. Thank you for showing me another way.'

At the gardens, we waited for the CEO of the Brussels airport management to perform the inaugural ceremony. The bird sculpture was surrounded by sixteen trees that represented the victims who had succumbed to the explosions in the departure hall. We were also given ribbons to pin on our jackets, bearing the printed message — 'Always live in our heart 22/3.' I went up to the sculpture and hugged it tightly. My tears just didn't stop. My speech slurred. I offered my thanks to the sculpture — 'You were the one reason many were saved... otherwise, the full impact would have been on us.'

The sculpture had holes and marks — traces of the damage it bore during the blast — to symbolise the violence of the terrorist attack. The bird was wounded, scratched.

From there we had to go to the memorial placed at the venue of the ceremony while the king and queen and the rest of the dignitaries would go to Maalbeek metro station first and join us later. When we reached the venue, we had to stand on one side to watch the ceremony. Many people were looking from the windows of the surrounding buildings. People had gathered in full strength and there was a strong wind blowing. I was surrounded by the crowd and yet I was feeling very cold. I recollected the moments from that day last year and the vulnerable state I had been in. But this day I had clothes on and I could walk, and everyone I saw was fit and fine and talking to one another as they would on a normal day.

I met a couple who were present at the airport on the day of the blast, and they shared their story with me. They said, 'We don't like to move out much now, as we get scared.'

I told them, 'We shouldn't stop enjoying life. We shouldn't hold any hatred... we need to be good with everyone.'

I met someone who had lost his sister-in-law and was now taking care of her family. I told him, 'I am really sorry to hear about your loss. But God thinks you are capable of doing it and that's why he has given you this responsibility.'

I met the policeman who had lost his leg while running to help people from the site of the first blast towards the place where I had been standing, near the Starbucks outlet. Barely twenty-two, he was a young and handsome man. First I saluted him, then asked him if he would be comfortable if I took a picture with such a brave soul. He smiled. I told him that he was really a great human being.

Nidhi Chaphekar

After some time, the king arrived and the ceremony started. His words are engraved in my heart—'Let us dare to be tender. It is the responsibility of each and every one of us to make our society more humane. Let us just learn to listen to each other again, to respect each other's weakness.' The operations of the entire metro line were stopped for a minute to show that we had not forgotten, yet we remained standing together against hatred and terrorism.

The king inaugurated the memorial sculpture, on which were inscribed the following words—'Wounded but still standing in the face of the unthinkable'. It was approximately twenty metres long and two metres high, made of stainless steel slabs raised to the sky in a gesture of hope. The ceremony went on for more than an hour. Bands played, the national anthem was sung, the prime minister and the king and queen met many heroes. Later, an announcement was made that white roses would be distributed to us and if we wished to pay our tribute to those who had lost their lives and were harmed, we could offer the white rose at the sculpture. The barriers were opened and after the king, I had the honour of being the first person to pay a tribute. I bowed and stood there for some time, speaking to the lost souls in my heart.

At 1300 hrs, there was an announcement that we could proceed to the Residence Park hotel. I met Rakhee from the Indian embassy there who introduced us to the father of Raghavendran Ganeshan, the Infosys employee who lost his life in the suicide blast at Maalbeek metro station. I held his father's hand and for a moment, I couldn't speak. My eyes must have given away a lot, though.

'Are you fine now, beta?' asked Mr Ganeshan.

I replied, 'Yes. Uncle, I don't know what to say, but I am sorry for whatever you are facing.'

He simply said, 'It's destiny.'

We walked towards the hotel where a light meal had been arranged. I met many others who had either lost someone or had suffered in some way due to the blast.

A while later, I met King Philippe again. I was glad when Alain, the chief of protocol from the royal household, also shared his thoughts. He remembered the time he had met Rupesh at the hospital in Charleroi. I said, 'today, I have to close this chapter and welcome a new beginning of love, hope, peace and prosperity.' All of them agreed with me. I believe we should always close the bad chapters in our life and move forward with the good ones that provide us with encouraging thoughts and positive energy. This is the only way all of us can support one other. I try my best to practise the maxim — think good, do good, speak good and be good.

By this time, I began feeling pain in my legs, especially in my left foot; I had never been on my feet for such a long stretch of time in the past year. Right from the second day of our arrival in Brussels, it had started feeling heavy and painful. Either Rupesh or I would keep massaging my foot and even apply ice compresses at night. He would keep my leg in a raised position with the help of two pillows to make me more comfortable. He was such a great support as always. It was already 1430 hrs. I bid goodbye to everyone, including Prime Minister Charles Michel, and exchanged numbers and email ids with a few.

❧

23 MARCH 2017

Guess what? I received an email from Col. Hillewaert whom I had met at the commemorative event. He had good news for me — he had got in touch with the commando himself, and his name was Paul-Henry Beauvois. Mr Hillewaert invited me to his military barracks. We decided to meet on 27 March. It felt as if I was solving a puzzle.

❧

Just before leaving the hotel, I spent some time reading the e-newspapers that published my interviews when my eyes suddenly chanced upon an article about me by a critic who I choose not to name. I was shocked to read it! The critic very clinically pointed out that in my photograph — the one that became the face of the terror attack — it very clearly shows that only my feet are injured and nothing seems to have happened to my hands. He questioned how I could say that my hands were grievously injured. He alleged that my hands were absolutely fine and that I was just putting up a farcical show. He further went on to ask why the king of Belgium had chosen only to invite me and not the others who were also injured in the terror attack. If that was not enough, he also wrote that it can't be a coincidence that I met the king of Belgium just before the commemorative event. After this I couldn't manage to read. Tears pricked my eyes and my throat started aching. I couldn't believe the audacity of this person and failed to understand why anybody would think so. Just before I could fall prey to his negativity and cynicism, I checked myself and forced my mind to focus on all the good in the world and the blessings that have been showered on me. I wiped my tears, told my heart to stay strong and got ready.

We reached the hospital at 1000 hrs. Head Nurse John was anxiously waiting for us. He took me to Dr Hans. She said to me, 'Your result is an unbelievable one!' She wanted to take pictures of my skin grafts, wounds, face and back for their records. Then she took me to do the X-rays and CT scan to gauge inner healing and bone status. What a coincidence, on this day last year, I had been brought to this hospital in a state of induced coma and had undergone the same tests, but this time I was fully conscious. Last year, I had been on a stretcher on the same table and scanned by the same machine at the same hospital, but this year, by God's grace, I walked and sat down by myself for the scan on the same machine.

The e-report of my right foot's scan was made available immediately. Dr Hans took me to her cabin, matched the last scan report with the one done on 16 April 2016, and said to me, 'there is remarkable improvement.' She said she couldn't believe that the rarest bone ever to grow had already grown a bit but she added we need to be very careful.

'there are cracks in some areas, see?' she pointed out. 'On the heel as well. So you need to wear cushioned footwear all the time.' She also told me to rest well.

She explained there were many bits of shrapnel on the bed (base) of the foot, two of which troubled me while walking. She decided to do a CT scan of my left foot too, as she could see a bone growing downwards in the middle of my foot in the X-ray.

I had fractures with bone loss, which generated gaps in the centre of my left foot; it had opened up after the blast. She explained that when the bone joined, because of the gap, it did not match the natural line. Instead, it had started growing downwards, which was the reason I felt such pain all the time while walking. It felt as though a marble ball had been placed at the side of my left foot base. She saw pieces of shrapnel in the X-ray of my left foot as well. But the CT scan could be done only the next day, the doctor said, as in Belgium, they do not allow a patient to get two scans done on the same day.

She asked me in surprise, 'What do you do? How have you managed your skin and grafts so well?'

When a doctor tells you this, you feel you have achieved something. So I told her about how religiously I wore my gloves every day and had not removed them for more than an hour as instructed, applied the creams recommended by dermatologist Sophie, how I never missed wearing the silicone mask at night and was wearing it here too on my trip. Every day, I applied the pack of aloe vera and kiwi fruit at night and another one made of fresh cream with honey, lime and turmeric in the morning on my skin. That I drank turmeric milk every night before going to bed, did my physiotherapy regularly, got light body massages with pure coconut oil, restricted myself from going out in the sun and applied SPF 60 all the time, and most importantly, I did everything without seeing it as a burden. Instead, I enjoyed everything I did and daily, I would reaffirm to myself that today, I am going to be better than yesterday. I believe that's how the power of healing multiplies.

'You are the best result of our work,' beamed the doctor.

Then I asked how much longer I needed to wear the gloves. Dr Peeters advised wearing them for six to eight months more as he could see some areas were red, which meant they were still healing, and the sides were hard and protruding. Sophie said I could stop using the silicone mask but I still needed to apply the SPF 60 cream for a year before I could walk fearlessly. I also shared that till date I could only dab the cream on my face as instructed by them earlier; the moment I rub my skin to apply the cream, the skin would start stretching and I would feel a lot of pain. Sophie informed me that it would take a few more years for my skin to heal. I then showed them my fingernails, which had started growing in a twisted manner. The texture of the nail is rough too. Till date I face both these issues.

Later, when I met Dr Peeters, he asked me the same question. He had a look at my hands and face and was immensely happy. He was astonished by the results. They couldn't believe my recovery. I told him my secret too. He asked Dr Hans to take pictures of each part of my body that had healed. The hospital published their own magazine every six months and Dr Peeters informed me that they wanted my pictures to be printed in it.

For lunch, Rupesh and I headed to the visiting room where food had been arranged for us. Imagine our surprise when we entered the room and found it decorated! The staff gave us a very warm welcome. They had also invited Martine, the lady who had been injured in the bomb explosion that occurred at the metro station. She had become my family's friend during my hospital stay, when I had been in a coma. She had been treated in the same hospital but was discharged much before I could open my eyes. She had enjoyed bonding with our family. Tea with snacks had been her favourite time of the day. She had even visited us in Mumbai in the month of July.

As soon as she saw me, she became very emotional. We hugged each other. Then we enjoyed the small pizzas and sandwiches prepared by the chef in the canteen. Dr Hans handed both of us a gift pack—a scarf and a big box of handmade chocolates.

Martine said aloud—'I never knew hospitals gave gifts!' She too had brought gifts for us. When we unfolded the scarf, we saw the words 'Made in India', and everyone had a good laugh, especially the doctors.

We left at 1400 hrs and headed straight to Shabir bhai's house, where all his family members were waiting for us.

We reached at 1600 hrs and Fozia Baji (Shabir bhai's wife) hugged me close. I could see the satisfaction in her eyes when she saw me; when she had come to the ICU to speak to me last year, I had been in a very bad state. She had called her relatives home today—all those who had helped Shabir bhai in conducting the search for me on 22 March 2016—as well as those who had prayed for my recovery. Fozia Baji had also invited Baber bhai and his wife (Shabir bhai's younger brother and sister-in-law). His sister and her two young daughters were there too. Slowly, the house became full with no space to even stand! Every person in the room, in their own way, had either assisted Shabir bhai in locating me or helped him in many other ways during those traumatic days. Everyone thanked God for His mercy.

❧

Back at the hotel, Rupesh and I reflected on the day. We talked about how this unity across borders showed that we may be divided in religion, but in our hearts, we hold the same feeling of love and care. Humanity unites us more than anything else. None of these people we had met were related to me, nor was I from their country, but beyond all our differences lay a love that overpowered everything else. Putting his life at stake, Shabir bhai had come to see me in the hospital. We expect such care and concern from blood relations, but usually never from people you have befriended relatively recently. As former American president Jimmy Carter once said, 'the bond of our common humanity is stronger than the divisiveness of our fears and prejudices.'

❧

24 MARCH 2017

We had an appointment at Grand Hospital at 1600 hrs as Dr Hans had called two of her orthopaedic colleagues (experts in foot-related cases) to take their opinion as well. After breakfast, we wanted to relive something I used to cherish doing earlier whenever I was in town. There is a church near the city mall that I would go to every time I came to Brussels Central. But today, for the first time in nine years of visiting this place, I saw prayers being performed live. Maybe it was the first time I entered the church before 1100 hrs. The bells were ringing. I felt as if God was welcoming me. I had tears in my eyes looking at the statue of Mother Mary and felt as if I were talking to Lord Jesus. I stood there for a few minutes, lit a candle and came out. There was an amazingly different sense of satisfaction in my heart when I came out of the church; it felt as if I had personally spoken to the Lord and my prayers had been heard.

Later, I had to meet Mr Olivers (from the Belgian government authority personnel) for some official work. He was very glad to meet me in person because all this while we had been in touch via email. He spoke about my interviews that he had read in the newspapers and those he had seen on TV. He praised me on my outlook and the way I explain it to others. He expressed his sadness over all that had happened and told me they had never come across any such disaster; it was the first of its kind after the Second World War. All of Belgium was devastated by this tragedy. He shared with me that he had met many victims and felt quite sad for them. Some had been unable to come out of the trauma and were undergoing therapy. I asked him to let me know if I could be of any help to them. I would surely do whatever I could. He promised to reach out to me the next time I visited Belgium, since my schedule this time was already full. We parted on a very good note.

While waiting to hail a taxi, I saw a woman walking towards me. She conveyed more with her expressions and gestures than words. I gathered she was saying she had seen me on TV. I nodded in confirmation. A gentleman passing by understood we were facing a language problem and offered to translate. He told me the woman was praising my bravery and saying, 'God bless you'.

I smiled and said, 'Please tell her, "You are so sweet to acknowledge me, stay blessed."'

We took a taxi from there. The driver was from Afghanistan

and recognised me. He told me, 'How difficult it is to come out of an incident like this! I followed all your interviews and prayed to Allah for your good health, and for everyone else too.'

It still never fails to amaze me when people recognise me and say that they had prayed for me. 'People like you,' I said, 'can bring about a change in the world with your wonderful ideas and prayers. You have the strength to promote the spirit of humanity, keep up the good work you are doing. God will reward you for it.'

We reached the hotel and I thanked him for his love. As we entered the hotel, the receptionist came up to me and said, 'Excuse me, Ms Nidhi, my name is Milton. I have been trying to get in touch with you from the time you checked in but you have been busy all this while. There's always the media, camerapersons and so many people around you. But today since I saw you walking calmly with your husband, I thought of disturbing you.'

He said he was glad we were staying in their hotel, and happy to get the chance to speak to me in person. He had seen all my interviews, he said, and was very motivated by them. He was going through a very tough time, but listening to my interviews had changed his perception and outlook on life. He had become a very positive-minded person and he owed it to me, he said.

I shook hands with him, 'Now you have to share your positivity with others too. Keep smiling always, and thank you for being such a wonderful person.'

❧

It was 1300 hrs by the time we reached our room and in an hour, we had to leave for Charleroi. After having lunch at a restaurant owned by Uncle Kazi, a kind man who knew me by face and had tried to find out about me as soon as the news of the blast reached him, we left with Shabir bhai for Charleroi.

We reached the hospital at 1600 hrs, and I rushed to the waiting room where the head nurse, John, was waiting for me. He took me straight away to meet Dr Hans in the CT scan room. It was past duty hours for the staff but they waited for me. They took a scan of my left leg first. Then Dr Hans took us to her room, where she looked at the scans and showed Rupesh how badly and unevenly my bones had joined.

By this time, both the orthopaedic doctors arrived. They saw all my scans and X-rays, even the previous ones, and asked me to lie down. They examined my feet and asked me to perform different movements with my feet to check elasticity, pressing different parts to check the sensation. They asked me to walk straight and barefoot. It was tough as the pieces of shrapnel were pinching down on the sole like little pieces of glass. The bone growing downwards in the centre and side of the left foot caused disturbance and pain. The right foot heel always made me uneasy; it would feel as if the surface all around was uneven.

I was then made to walk on my toes, which was quite good. I asked whether I could walk on my heels, which was painful, but I did take just a few steps with help. I was asked to do some more stretches. But as my right foot was still swollen, I was asked not to do some of them. They asked me what I do in my physiotherapy and suggested what more I could add to that.

After an hour of discussion, the doctors said I was doing a commendable job; they appreciated my progress. Surgery would be required to remove all four pieces of shrapnel embedded in my feet, which caused pain while walking. 'First of all,' said one of them, 'calcaneum is the rarest surgery to conduct. And then if the injury is so bad, it is not advisable to do any surgery as most of the time it leads to infection. When an injury of such impact occurs, the bones become more brittle and when you open the area, it starts chipping. And in your case, the bones are very critical. Secondly, it becomes more dangerous to operate because we don't know from where the nerves are connecting as this foot was completely opened up, and because of the tender skin and grafting it becomes even more dangerous. With God's grace and your strength, you are walking and it's a miracle. We cannot expect such patients to walk and that too, so well!'

Dr Hans was appreciated for her work. They also said that delaying the surgery was a sound decision on the part of the doctors in India. In their report, they mentioned very clearly that if the left foot's middle bone posed further problems in walking in the future, they would operate on it. As of now, no surgery was recommended in the right foot. It all depends on further progress in the condition of the leg. 'Keep doing your physiotherapy,' they advised.

By the time they finished, it was 1830 hrs and all the other staff had left. Dr Hans had already called someone, from the same company that had provided me with the gloves and the special shoe earlier, to take measurements of my foot. He did so and asked me to come on 31 March to collect the special insoles. It would take them that much time to be readied as they had to be customised. They had decided to provide me with cushioned insoles to speed up recovery so that I would be able to walk more comfortably. Dr Hans was also worried about my fractured bone and the crack in it.

I went to say goodbye to the nurses and Dr Saidane in the burns hospital, in the adjacent building where I had been admitted. I asked them if I could visit my ICU room (Room No. 03). They told me to wear antibacterial clothing and to cover my head and mouth. They took me to the reception, which was right in the centre, surrounded by rooms on all sides. I was only allowed to see my room from the outside, as it was occupied by someone carrying a dangerous infection. He was on life support, they informed me. I looked at him from a distance and thought about how my family members must have felt when I had been in a similar place. I teared up.

Then I went to the operation theatre. I saw Dr Hans calling out to me. She gave me another wrist band that Carine had asked her to pass on to me as her shift got over at 1500 hrs. She had sent a message asking me to wear it. It would save me from evil, she had said. Dr Hans conveyed Carine's words—'Nidhi is very loveable and great.' I wore the band right there. It is red in colour with a cross on top. We then left for Sumita di's house, where we had been invited for dinner.

It was a beautiful drive. It took us about forty-five minutes to reach their house. They welcomed us in and we saw they had lit candles and decorated the house beautifully. We chatted over tea. Later, their sons joined us. We enjoyed our meal. Before we left, she

Nidhi Chaphekar

took me to the small altar in her home. She blessed me there and gave me a big gift along with a large pack of Leonidas chocolates. We both had tears in our eyes when we said goodbye.

We were back at the hotel at 0200 hrs. Before going to bed, I said a prayer of heartfelt thanks to God for keeping me alive, for bringing new, warm relations my way, and for letting me cherish their generous love.

❧

25 MARCH 2017

What a relaxed day. At 1600 hrs, just when we got back after lunch and a shopping spree, Alain called and requested me to visit the police headquarters on 28 March by 1030 hrs, or any other time suitable to me. He said it was very important as his boss wanted to meet me. To welcome us, he had also organised a grand dinner party on 29 March and requested us to be his guests. I could not say no.

At 1800 hrs, Martine took us out for dinner. She arrived ten minutes early. Everyone in Brussels is really particular about punctuality. She drove us to an Indian restaurant. We loved the beautiful décor and ambience, and the food was delicious.

Martine told me she got help for cooking, washing and household staff from the government. I was impressed. She still faced difficulty while writing, she told us, as she couldn't fold her fingers properly. She was now asked to do machine physiotherapy, which would help improve hand dexterity and help reduce pain. I assured her that she would clear this hurdle as well; she only needed to believe in herself. We parted on a good note.

I couldn't help thinking about how lucky I am, as now I have a good grip and can write well. In comparison, my hands had been in a worse condition. I thanked God from the bottom of my heart for helping me at each moment and prayed for Martine's quick recovery.

❧

26 MARCH 2017

We went to Belgaufra—one of my favourite places for waffles. The manager couldn't place me at first. When I reminded him, he said, 'You have come after such a long time! Earlier, you used to get ten to fifteen packets of waffles packed.'

When I told him about the incident, he was aghast! 'We didn't know that was you! We prayed for you and the rest of the victims in the church the very next day. There was a special mass organised for all the victims. I really didn't know it was you!'

I thanked him for his kindness. He didn't charge us a penny.

While we were walking around, I saw two young boys, pointing towards me. People nearby also looked at me. I felt self-conscious and checked to see if I had spilt something on my clothes, or whether my hair was a mess. One of them came up to me and spoke in English. 'Hello,' he said. 'My name is Zavier. I saw your interviews on TV. You are so optimistic. We need people like you, so we can progress in life. And I love your smile!'

Slowly, many people gathered near me. Some could only speak in gestures. Some asked me how I was doing now. One lady held my hand. I bowed my head in gratitude and said, 'thank you for your wishes and prayers. Merci.' When we left, many people waved goodbye with a smile.

I felt so moved.

Then I got a call from Alain. He told me he was waiting at the hotel to introduce his friends to me. I was just five minutes away and asked him to wait. I got to the opposite side of the road when I saw a huge fire-truck-like vehicle parked at the entrance to the Crowne Plaza. Alain must have seen me cross the road; he started announcing our names on the speaker—'Nidhi! Nidhi! Welcome, Nidhi, Rupesh, we love you!' I laughed and asked him to step out. I said hello to all his friends and we clicked pictures. I invited them in but they were on duty, so they promised a 'next time' before they left.

In the evening, I was to go to Gent to meet Kurt, the journalist from *Het Laatste Nieuws*. He had invited us for dinner. He had come to India six months ago to shoot a short documentary and interview with me, and asked me to inform him when I visited Brussels. We reached his house at 1800 hrs. It was an exceptionally beautiful house set in the woods. His wife had gone to pick up their son from school. By the time we sat down, made ourselves comfortable and had some water, she arrived. I had brought handmade earrings and a purse for her. She was so excited seeing the gift that she wore the earrings right away. She looked so pretty! We sat on the lawn and had drinks. Kurt's wife had cooked the yummiest food. Having known that I was a vegetarian, all the dishes, including the salad and soup, were vegetarian. She herself was a vegetarian by choice. Their son showed us a few magic tricks. They are really nice people, and we enjoyed the time spent with them and invited them to India. It was around 2300 hrs when we left.

❧

27 MARCH 2017

Another wonderful day I was looking forward to. After breakfast, we left for the military barracks at Col. Hillewaert's invitation.

When we reached, Col. Hillewaert welcomed us warmly and took us to his office upstairs. Paul-Henry, the commando who had helped me, was waiting there with their battalion cameraman. I got emotional when I saw him. We shook hands and sat down. He recalled he had been about to wind up duty on that day by 0800 hrs, when he heard the first bomb explode. Since he was one level below the site, he was unable to figure out what happened. When the second blast occurred, he was utterly blindsided, he said. He had never even dreamt of such a thing ever happening. Not wasting a minute, he ran upstairs. He recalled how he saw smoke everywhere and it took a few seconds before he saw me. He said, 'You were waving with your hand, saying, "Help me, please."'

He first pulled a wounded man aside, near the wall, and then came to help me. 'You asked me to hold you tight. You told me to lift you from the ground and place you on the chair.'

He was one of twenty-eight soldiers from 1 Star, the first sergeant of the Battalion of Horse Hunters posted there. After helping me onto the chair, he went to help others. He cannot forget that day, he told us.

I thanked him and said, 'If you had not been there to help me, I would not have been alive today.'

As an expression of my gratitude, I presented a handmade metal photo frame to him. I asked about his family. He told me he had two kids, and his wife was a caregiver for dogs. He said, 'She is very nervous after this incident. She is always worried about me.'

Then Col. Hillewaert showed us around the area. I saw a few tanks that were no longer in use but had been used in wars. The new tanks could accommodate four to five people, he explained, and told us how the tanks worked.

We visited the musical auditorium where everyone was practising for an upcoming event with the king. Later he showed us Paul-Henry's office too. We enjoyed the beautiful weather while we were there.

It was nearly 1230 hrs, and we had to hurry as we had to go to Antwerp as well. When we came back to Col. Hillewaert's office, he gifted me some beautiful books and a CD about the Belgium Air Force. The book I liked most is titled *Vampire 0204*. It's all about the three- to six-month posting they carry out in Afghanistan, how they feel when they are there, and what they do. The book is full of pictures of all the events and activities, showcasing their lifestyle during the time spent there.

What Col. Hillewaert did for me I can never forget. I thanked him from the bottom of my heart.

My wonderful time in Brussels strengthened my belief that I went through the difficulties I did because God had a different plan for me. He wanted to bless me with the most beautiful, unique, incomparable set of experiences and connections with lovely human beings. I have captured every moment in my eyes, my heart, and they will stay with me till my last breath.

We said goodbye to each other and with great gratitude, we left for Antwerp. Shabir bhai had accompanied us every day wherever we went and was speechless after witnessing all the events. Indeed, who has time in this world to get things elaborately arranged for others? But the experiences of the past few days taught us humanity and love exist in abundance, people around the world still take care of each other and no one can stop us from doing so.

❧

We had to reach Sint-Augustinus Hospital in Antwerp at 1400 hrs. Even before we could approach the reception in the hospital, a team of five, including the head doctor, Dr Nele Beeckman, came up to me and said, 'Hello, Nidhi, we have been waiting for you.'

I was astonished by their welcome. Their arrangements came as a complete surprise to us. After exchanging pleasantries, they took us straight to the meeting room where I was introduced to the doctors who treated me on 22 March 2016 and all the other hospital staff who had been involved in my treatment. A photographer was capturing these beautiful moments for the hospital newsletter. Except for the two nurses who couldn't make it and the two doctors who had joined other hospitals, everyone else was present in the room.

After asking about how I was doing, they shared their side of the story. They told me when I had arrived in the hospital, they had thought I was dark-skinned and only later did they learn my skin was actually burnt. They were seeing such burns for the first time, they said. They told me about how surprised they were when, despite so many injuries, I was still calm and composed.

'We first thought that it has affected you badly and you are in shock,' one of them recalled, 'but later we found that you are very alert. You gave answers to all our questions.' Another said, 'You were insisting that we inform your family. You gave us your husband's phone number and other details like passport number and such. You were consistently complaining about a lot of pain in your legs and also that you couldn't feel them. You even said, "I don't know who will come to see me from my company, but Shabir bhai will surely be here."'

Then Marc Hermans, the ICU head nurse, added, 'You asked two questions. First, "Are you going to amputate my leg?" I was not sure, so I kept quiet. Next, you wanted to know, "Is my face totally burnt?" and I said yes, and you replied, "Then I don't want to live. Please don't do any treatment on me. Let me die. How will I conduct my job? What will people think of me?"'

Believe me, I could not recollect any of their faces! I had a blank look as they spoke and they all had to introduce themselves to me one by one before they narrated their interaction with me.

Marc added that there was no prior information given to them that they would be receiving victims from the Zaventem airport blast, so they had not called for extra staff and that was the reason the nurses from the intensive care unit rushed to help when I arrived at the emergency.

He along with Anne Cannaerts and Kristen Roos were the first to speak to me in the hospital. I was with two other victims and I was conscious. Later, Anne and Kristen had gone with me to get the CT scan.

I was treated by the head doctor, Dr Beekman, along with Dr Leyman, an abdominal surgeon; Dr Jansegers, the orthopaedic; and two other doctors who worked on me at the time but no longer worked at that hospital. Marleen van Loock, who had worked in a burns injury ward earlier, had helped them do the bandages at night.

Later, after the surgeries were done, I was taken to the ICU on the first floor where Inge Vlegels took care of me in the late shift. It was Inge who received many calls on my behalf, calls from home, the embassy, my airline, and others.

Koen Cortebeeck and Dr Elkana Keersebilck helped them with my bandages after the surgeries. Elkana was an anaesthetist but also worked at the burns care unit of the military hospital, so he had helped with my bandages. For burns patients, the bandages are different from those used for other patients, and normally they didn't treat burns patients in this hospital, so I was lucky, they said.

It was Dr Luc Heytens who took the decision to shift me to a burns speciality hospital in the morning because of my deteriorating condition.

Nidhi Chaphekar

Out of the five doctors in their ward that day, four had operated on me in the operation theatre.

The doctors continued recounting the incidents of that day to me.

'You were so well behaved,' one of them said, 'and your heart was functioning in perfect condition, so we knew you were a tough lady. On our part, we did our best.'

'You were following all our instructions and even assisted us by providing a lot of information, and we were amazed as to how you were managing to keep that cool! You requested us to inform your family urgently, to tell them that you are fine. You kept repeating the words—"My legs are paining, they are very heavy... I can't feel them..."'

Dr Beekman said, 'We thought we may need to amputate your leg, given the worsening condition of your wounds.'

They had taken out as many metal pieces as they could at the time. In one surgery, they removed forty-nine metal pieces... they filled up two small boxes with all the pieces they removed! This was later handed over to the police.

'We wrapped you up completely from top to bottom,' a nurse recalled. After the surgeries were completed, this nurse had shifted me to the ICU room.

'Since you had not given any other name, we didn't allow anybody else to see you, as it was a terror attack.'

'People from the Belgium consulate also came late at night,' one of them added. 'Your company staff Melvin arrived the next morning, but since it was a high-alert case and we had to restrict entry, we could not allow anyone without prior information. Then Melvin said he just needs to have a glimpse of you to be sure you are the same lady they are looking for. A nurse took him inside while you were being bandaged. He could manage to see your face, which was swollen, but he confirmed that you were indeed the Nidhi he was looking for. In the morning, there was only one nurse in our hospital who knew how to bandage burns, and she removed many small fragments of metal stuck in your hands and feet while doing your bandages. Some of the pieces were tiny, like grains of sand! Today she is on leave, else you could have met her.

By then the doctor had taken the decision to shift you to a burns specialty hospital because your burns had worsened and your face, hands and legs were swollen. Your face had become double its normal size. So we sent pictures that were taken as soon as you had arrived in our hospital and of the treatment done here to the medical team at Grand Hospital, Charleroi.'

They showed us the pictures of each of my wounds before they operated on me—I was baffled. I was more concerned about the doctors handling someone in that condition! Hats off to them, I thought, as every situation they face in their line of work is different, and they put in so much hard work to fix the broken, shredded, uneven, open, deep and mismatched pieces of flesh and bones. One wrong decision of theirs could lead to complications. How mindful and skilful they have to be in such delicate cases. My belief grew stronger that doctors are indeed second to God.

'By the afternoon you were taken away from here to Loverval (the area where Grand Hospital is located),' they continued. 'Dr Liliane Leenaerts, who is an experienced emergency doctor, accompanied you in the helicopter. She was in charge of helicopter medical evacuations of severely injured patients from different intensive care units to burn centres. We also gave the bag containing your jewellery to her, to be handed over to the staff at Grand Hospital. You were flown from the military hospital in Antwerp to Charleroi.'

Dr Beeckman added, 'I couldn't even imagine someone with injuries like that would walk again, and even if you did, I did not think it would be possible without aid.'

She said she had been terrified seeing the scans, looking at the condition of my legs. It was one of the worst cases she had ever handled in her career.

'But you are a miracle,' the nurse beamed now. 'I am really happy to see you back!'

I requested them to show me the place where the ambulance had arrived and where I had been taken afterwards. Marc took me to the emergency gate from where I had been taken to Level 2, to the room where they spoke to me and took my details. I was curious to see the ICU room. And this time, an old lady was in that room. Marc introduced me to the lady and with her permission, we took a picture in that room. The elderly lady told me she felt good for me. I thanked her.

I re-visualized everything as they spoke. The nurse informed me they had three patients in all from the airport incident that day in the hospital, but my case was the most serious one. He recalled, 'We were writing down your details and at that time, we asked you whether you could remove your bangles or we should cut them, and you simply removed them even as your skin peeled off! We were so amazed at how you managed to stay so calm! From there we took you to the CT scan centre.'

Then the nurse who had done my CT scan the day after the blast spoke. She told me, 'I just can't forget that day. But you were very strong!'

I went to see the machine again. I sat on it for a few seconds, reliving the memory. That day I had just lain on it, numb. One of the nurses told me, 'Not even once did you say you were afraid. After the scan reports were made, we took you to the operation theatre. By then you were very low. We had called Dr Beekman as well. The doctors operated on you and the surgeries went on for the entire day. It was the first bomb blast case we handled.'

By then they had also called in more staff (nurses, doctors), including all those who were on leave or had a day off, to come and help, since they didn't know how many more such cases they would get. All of them had nearly done a double shift that day.

I was so moved listening to their account. I thanked all of them profusely; they had done such a wonderful job. Without their professionalism, knowledge, confidence and compassion, I would not have been here today. They made a quick and perfect diagnosis at the right time. It is thanks to their intelligence that I have my foot today. I expressed my feelings of gratitude and love for the entire team of doctors and nurses; they asked me to stay in touch. They took a few pictures and said they would post them in the newsletter they publish.

I had tears of respect, gratitude and joy running down my face as I left. I felt like taking them all along with me and cherishing their presence as much as I could. Words will never be enough to thank them for their invaluable efforts.

❧

We then went on to meet Mr and Mrs Jigar Joshi at their house. They narrated the entire story of that day. We had tea and snacks with them before we headed back. I thanked them for their immense generosity and kindness.

I had originally planned to leave Brussels on 28 March, but I decided to stay back for four more days as my work was not yet complete. The hotel room, though, was not available for those extra days. Due to a doctors' conference in progress in Brussels, most of the central city hotels were fully booked. We eventually found a room available at the Hilton, Central Station. We had to pack our bags and shift the next day.

We also had to go to meet Alain and his team at the police headquarters tomorrow at 1030 hrs.

❧

28 MARCH 2017

Gudi Padva, the first day of the New Year for Maharashtrians. We finished our breakfast by 0800 hrs and while I was about to leave, one of the serving staff named Lynn came to me and handed over a pack of goodies.

She said, 'Do relish these when you reach India and remember us.'

I was delighted by her thoughtfulness. I hugged and thanked her. It took a while before we could reach the reception with all our bags.

The checkout counters had a few people before me standing in line, and it took us more than fifteen minutes to complete all the formalities. It was already 1000 hrs, I noticed nervously when we started putting our bags in the car. We planned to check into the other hotel after our visit to the police headquarters. We left at about 1015 hrs and reached the address Alain had given me at 1041 hrs (ten minutes late). I was feeling embarrassed as I hate being late for any appointment. Alain had called me thrice to check where we were.

The moment we got out of our car, Alain and his team members came to escort us. Alain was the only one in civilian clothes. I saw more than thirty policemen standing on either side of the pathway and the moment I set foot on the path, they gave me a guard of honour salute, complete with a band playing on horseback. I was unable to believe my eyes! I didn't know how to respond! I had no idea that something like this had been planned! Then I met the DGA (General Directorate of the Administrative Police) and DAS (Directorate of Public Security) of Belgium Public Security at Federal Police, Mr Benoit Van Houtte. He welcomed us warmly, speaking into a mic so that he could be heard by the friends and family members of the police officers who had gathered there. I saw a cameraperson taking pictures. The DGA first said, 'Let's observe two minutes of silence as a tribute to the people who lost their lives in the disastrous event that took place on 22 March 2016.' Then he asked Alain to speak.

Alain's eyes were brimming with tears as he spoke. I couldn't understand everything he said because he spoke in French. The only thing I gathered was that he said that in all the chaos, he had heard a voice calling out—'Help, help! Please help!' And when he came closer to me and said, 'Hi, I am Alain. Are you okay?', I had replied, 'I can't feel my legs.' He couldn't make out what 'legs' meant, so he asked his friend Pascal to tell him the meaning of that word. Only then did he understand what I was complaining of and he started speaking to me, to assure me that medical help was on its way. He spoke about how they had reached the airport almost twenty-five minutes after the incident and had seen that people were badly injured. He said my voice had troubled him for many days afterwards, and even now, he could sometimes hear my voice calling for help and it disturbed him. In that dire situation, mine had been the only voice that he first paid attention to.

Alain then handed the mic back to Mr Van Houtte who said, 'We want people like her in this world. Even after suffering so much, she has the heart to think and speak positively. She is not only encouraging everyone in the world to love one another but also teaching others how to be a good human being.'

There was a special song sung for me after this, complete with a band on horseback—I was overwhelmed!

Not knowing what was coming up next, I heard Mr Van Houtte make an announcement, asking me whether I would accept their request to be 'Godmother' to all members of the Directorate of Public Security of the Belgium Federal Police. I was speechless! Such a big honour and privilege was being bestowed upon me.

I composed myself and said, 'Well, this life is a gift given back to me by them. If I have anything of value to offer to people today, it is because of them. It would be my honour to be their godmother.'

'You are the first and the last one to be honoured with this post,' he smiled.

I was asked to sign the certificate, which was counter signed by Mr Van Houtte, and I was honoured with a badge along with a few gifts. Alain's family and many other police officers with their families were present there. I thanked everyone.

We were taken to Mr Van Houtte's office, where we had a photo session. From there we were taken to see the special breed of horses the police have. There were hundreds of them, and I took pictures with many of them.

Then they showed us around the premises. I received such special treatment, it was flattering. I was asked to stand in front of vehicle number 29 and water was sprinkled on me as part of a welcome ceremony. They asked us to board the vehicle and took us to an empty area near the next building. Here they explained the features of this vehicle, which is used to disperse crowds in an emergency using water jets of very high force and also used in fire-fighting. They gave us a demonstration. They had put up big boards and metal barriers on the road, and they pointed these out and asked me and Rupesh to aim and release the water. My attempt was poor, but I managed to do it and the board flew off the ground like a sheet of paper! Rupesh, on the other hand, was very good on his very first attempt. What a wonderful experience it was!

Afterwards, we were escorted to the canteen where we had tea, coffee and snacks. I thanked everyone for making my visit so special. I expressed my respect and admiration for the kind of work they did – service that most of us lay people take for granted. We forget that the forces that protect and guard us – the army, the navy, the air force – they too have emotions just like the rest of us and they also need to be appreciated and cared for. They have families but they commit their entire lives to the people of their nation.

It was 1400 hrs when we left the place. Shabir bhai, who accompanied us, told me he had never seen such an honour being conferred upon anyone.

Rupesh was mesmerized and told me, 'I believe you will change many lives. It was something I could never have dreamt of.'

After checking in to our hotel, when I entered our hotel room, I realised that it was smaller than we had expected. When I opened the window, I saw it was covered with a white plastic sheet on the outside as maintenance work was in progress. I get very claustrophobic in such rooms and get an unbearable headache most of the time. So I immediately went down to the reception and told them about my problem. They told me they were fully sold out, though.

Disappointed, I was on my way back to the room when the staff who was tending to our luggage trolley recognised me and said, 'Hi, Ms Nidhi, how are you?'

We exchanged pleasantries. He expressed his admiration for the way I deal with things as he had seen my interviews. He said, 'My wife is a fan of yours. Can I take a picture with you?'

I readily agreed.

Then the bartender came out to greet me. He had seen me on 21 March, the day of my interview here, while I had been surrounded by the media. He offered me a cup of coffee now. He told me, 'I was so disturbed about the incident. So many innocent people were killed and injured. But listening to you that day opened my eyes. I realised that I am yet to perform the duties for which I have come into this world. Till then, the feeling of hatred had filled my head, but today I want to educate others to be human.' He thanked me.

Meanwhile, as I had not yet returned to the room, Rupesh came down thinking there may be a problem. But when he saw me talking to the hotel staff, he understood. Back in the room, we were sitting and talking when there was a knock at the door. When I opened it, the reception staff I had spoken with was standing there bearing a small cake and a plate of fruits. He first apologised to me and said they did have another room available, but that one too posed the same problem. We wouldn't be able to open the window because it was similarly covered with a sheet.

I thanked him for the thoughtful gesture. I told him, 'I tell the world to deal with tough situations. But sometimes I need to educate myself too to deal with such a small issue. I have to overcome this phobia. Anyway, I will hardly spend time in the room during the day.'

He thanked me.

Believe me, in the four days we stayed at the hotel, I didn't get a headache even once. It's all in the mind.

The rest of the day passed by meeting people I knew. It felt so good when people who saw me walking on the road recognised me, clapped and spoke words of praise—not because of what happened to me but because of the way I fought back. This is something we must all remember—the world will only remember us if we have changed and set a worthy example.

※

29 MARCH 2017

We had been invited to Alain's house at Waterloo for dinner. As the day was relatively free, I decided to shop a bit, and then just relax for a while. I went to buy gifts for my family and friends back in India. The kids had given me a long list as a year had passed since I last travelled abroad. One of the shop owners looked at me with curiosity, as if trying to place me. He asked me shyly, 'Excuse me, by any chance are you Nidhi?' I smiled.

He said he was very glad to meet me and immediately called his wife. She said she had been going through tough times, but after hearing my story, she changed her attitude and decided to only focus on the positives in life. I was so happy to hear that.

I purchased a lot of things but when it was time to bill us, the shop owner refused to take any money. I told him, 'Okay then, since you are insisting so much, I will accept one item as a gift from you, but for the rest I will pay.'

After a lot of arguing, he agreed. I was touched by his generosity.

While walking back to the hotel, I shared my feelings with Rupesh. The way everyone seemed impressed by my thoughts and talks gave me confidence and confirmed to me that words do matter, and how we use them does indeed make a difference wherever we go.

In the middle of all this, I received a call from Col. Hillewaert asking whether he could meet me today or tomorrow for a surprise. As today was already packed, I requested him to come tomorrow morning. We agreed to meet at 1130 hrs.

By 1600 hrs, we were ready to go to Alain's home with Shabir bhai. It was a little on the outskirts of Brussels, a historic place named Waterloo. The house was so beautiful and the surroundings so quiet. To welcome us in, Alain lit some firecrackers!

Alain had invited many of his friends. His wife, Margot Laurence, and his son and his fiancée were present. Since I was visiting them for the first time, I had gifts for everyone, including his three young daughters and his other friends. He introduced me to everyone. Then he told me he was so glad to see that I was still wearing the lucky charm he had given me while I had been in the hospital at Charleroi. He said he had seen it on my hand in every interview I gave, and even during my meeting with the king. I told him that I had never removed it, apart from the time when I was readmitted to a hospital for my surgeries. He asked me to close my eyes and stretch out my hand. When I opened my eyes, I saw he had placed another one in my palm, a strand of real pearls! I had tears in my eyes. He took permission from Rupesh, so he could himself tie it on my wrist.

Alain asked me to open a bottle of champagne for good luck. I think he must have popped open about ten or twelve bottles of champagne and the same amount of wine bottles, maybe even more. He didn't know I was a vegetarian. So when they asked us what I would prefer for dinner, I said, 'Anything is fine, but only vegetarian please.' That was a challenge for them. They ordered vegetarian sushi for me and non-vegetarian food for everyone else. We enjoyed the dinner and the company.

When it was time for us to leave, Alain said he had another surprise for me. He took out two canvas sheets and a marker and said, 'I want you to write something on it.' One by one, everybody wrote a special message. When I asked him why two, he said one sheet was for him and one was for me to frame and keep at my home as a fond remembrance. But he said he would give it to me later.

I thanked everyone for their love and time. It was midnight by the time we left. Rupesh, Shabir bhai and I had a great chat on our way back to the hotel, reflecting on how God has different plans for all of us.

I learnt today that wherever you go in the world, everyone's heart speaks the same language of love, care and affection. I believe what we do for others comes back to us. Love can truly do wonders, and every small gesture goes a long way.

❧

30 MARCH 2017

It had slipped my mind that Col. Hillewaert had said he would come to meet me today at 1130 hrs at the hotel. We reached the hotel lobby exactly at 1130 hrs and Col. Hillewaert was already there, on the dot. Over coffee, he talked about his experience of meeting me. He wished to hand over a special album his photographer had made for me. On the album cover were the words—*Best wishes and love to Nidhi from Koen*. I couldn't find the right words to thank him for this beautiful gesture. I couldn't help thinking how I didn't even know of him until a few days ago, and here I was, getting such a lot of importance and love from so many people.

He told me, 'I am doing this for you because you are a pure soul.'

I was moved listening to him speak. He was dressed in his uniform and I felt like saluting him. I thanked him for all his time and the great effort he had made for me, that too in such a short period of time. As a token of love, I presented him the last souvenir I was left with.

When he left, I just sat there for a few minutes thinking how beautiful the world is and how humble some people are. There are a few who are trying to destroy it, but they will never be able to accomplish their evil goal because the bond of humanity among people who love one another only grows stronger with every atrocity they suffer.

When I was about to pay the bill, the bartender said, 'It has been paid by the person sitting at the next table.' I turned to check but there was no one seated there anymore. Instead, the person who had occupied the table adjacent to ours had left behind a note thanking me and saying that I was doing a great job of spreading the message of love and peace, and that he wished to become like me. I felt overcome by emotion and hugged Rupesh in joy.

My children love waffles and in their wish list, this was the topmost request—to bring as many waffles as we could carry for them! I don't know when I would come back next, so I decided to order fifty packs of fresh waffles. I went to the familiar shop and the same tall guy was there behind the counter. I gave him the order and said I would collect it the next day at 1800 hrs. He didn't ask me anything and instead prepared two delicious waffles for Rupesh and me. He knew that I was leaving the day after, so he said, 'I will make it tomorrow evening so that it remains fresh.' I shook hands with him and we left.

The time had come to say goodbye to everyone I knew in Brussels. We went to Shabir bhai's house to say goodbye to Fozia Baji and their kids. It was a very emotional moment for all of us. We thanked the entire family for being so supportive. The bond

I share with them proves that geographical boundaries can never pull people apart. We left their home with our hearts full of love, compassion and affection, gratitude and peace.

While we were standing outside the hotel talking about how the days had passed, I saw Alain coming with his wife and two other people. First of all, I was amazed to see him at this hour. He wanted to surprise me, but to his luck, I was already standing outside at the time. He asked me to try and recognise the other woman accompanying him.

I couldn't recollect her face, so he said, 'She is Stefanie De Loof.'

She was the lady whose picture was captured along with mine on that fateful day. The lady who helped me at first and the lady who assisted Alain to trace my whereabouts. She was accompanied by her husband. We invited them in and had a long chat. She told me how I was breathing very heavily at one point and she calmed me by telling me to take deep breaths. She said she took help to place me down on the ground and also tied a band around my leg to reduce the bleeding.

I asked her, 'What made you sit there?'

She said she was dropped at the airport by her mother and just after the explosion, she decided to give her a call first, knowing she would get the news in a few minutes. And that was the only place she had found to sit. It was so great of her to travel all the way just to meet me as Alain had briefed her about my extended stay. I had spoken to her on the phone two or three times earlier, as Alain had shared her number with me. But the feeling of meeting her in person was incredible. I was feeling on top of the world and thanked God for being so loving to me. I had nothing to present her as all my gifts had been given away by now, but I gave her all my blessings and love. We had good fun chatting over drinks. It had indeed turned out to be a very fruitful trip for me.

Nidhi Chaphekar

Today was our last day in Brussels. I was a little sad. We went to the hospital in the morning. I felt good seeing the smiling staff, but there were some who couldn't hide their sadness too, those whom we knew we may not meet again. But I assured them that whenever I visited Brussels in the future, I would visit the hospital as well. And the staff appreciated my thoughts. The chants of Hare Rama Hare Krishna filled my ears. It felt great to know that they all remembered my favourite chant even after a year. My heart was thundering against my chest. I collected my customised foot insoles and asked the doctor how long it would take for me to adjust to them. Dr Peeters laughed aloud and said, 'Looking at you, just a day or two, but for others, it takes months at times.'

I laughed too. I thanked him for giving me such confidence. He said he felt proud that he was the one who treated me. I hugged Dr Peeters and Dr Hans and the rest of the staff present. I couldn't hold back my tears. I felt so much love and affection for all of them. I waved goodbye, sobbing as if I were parting from my own family members. While walking out, Rupesh noticed a bus parked at the bus stop; it was the same bus he used to take to travel from the hospital to the hotel and back. I also stood at the helipad and walked around the area from where my stretcher had been rolled in. I asked Rupesh to show me the hotel as well. On reaching, he pointed out the room he had stayed in. He also showed me the room my sister and brother-in-law had stayed in. He said with a smile, 'this was the balcony of the room where she would cook for you early in the morning.' I could not thank my dear sister enough for all that she did for me during my tough times. Tears of love and gratitude rolled down my face as I hugged Rupesh. No words can express the pain he had gone through. Usually, one hears the oft-quoted saying: 'Behind every successful man is a woman,' but in my case I can confidently say that behind each success of mine is a man who happens to be my husband. I was overwhelmed at the thought of all that they had had to bear for my sake.

Returning to Brussels in the evening, I collected the waffles

I had ordered. I could see that Shabir bhai was unusually quiet. When I asked him what happened, he said, 'With you around, I actually saw what life is all about. If it were in my hands, I would have asked you to live here.'

He was very sad that evening when it was time to say goodbye. After all, Shabir bhai had become a part of my family.

I got a call from Alain asking me what time we would be leaving Brussels for Amsterdam in the morning, as my flight back to India was from Amsterdam. I told him we would be leaving at 0645 hrs. He asked if he and Laurence could come say bye to us. I said, 'Please do.'

I packed my bags with a heavy heart.

❧

1 APRIL 2017

At 0545 hrs, I got a call from the reception informing me that Alain and his wife were there. We went downstairs to meet them. I could see tears in their eyes. They were both crying. Alain gave me the canvas sheet on which we had written messages at his house, along with a beautiful bottle of Japanese whisky for Rupesh. He promised me that he would definitely come to see us in India soon. His voice shook and he couldn't speak further. We hugged both of them and then they left. We were touched seeing them wave goodbye to us again from the other side of the hotel's glass wall. They still had tears streaming down their faces and as soon as they were out of sight, I too burst out crying. I was crying because my heart felt it would burst with the love we all have for each other.

It only proved once again to me something I truly believe in. That if you are good and pure at heart, you receive the best. Good karma always pays.

We checked out of the hotel and Shabir bhai came to see us off to the airport. The story that had been left incomplete earlier was completed in this journey. He accompanied us right up to the check-in counter. I got teary when it was time for him to leave. He told me, 'Nidhi, you are like our family member. So it hurts. As we don't know when God will give us the chance to be together again.'

I said, 'We will meet again soon.'

'Amen,' he replied.

I smiled and waved goodbye to Shabir bhai until he disappeared in the crowd. I was so overcome with emotions that I could not even speak for some time. The love people showered on me had crossed all barriers.

I was leaving Brussels with beautiful memories. I felt I was the luckiest person on earth to have survived all odds and received so much warmth and appreciation from the world. Today my job is to light up others' lives. To help people who are suffering to love life and tell them what it is truly all about. We serve, and in return, we receive what we serve.

My flight took off from Amsterdam, loaded with the best memories of my life.

And just when this book was about to go to print, life threw another pleasant surprise at me. Though I had pieced together most of what had happened and met nearly everyone who had played a key role in ensuring I am alive today, there was one person who I still hadn't been able to find despite my best efforts. Finally, with the help of Annet Ardesch, a Dutch forensic draftsman, and the support of VTM channel's show 'Make Belgium Great Again', I was able to meet Luc Lowel—the gentleman who helped me and a young boy when we were lying in the fire brigade parking hall, waiting for medical aid.

Luc and I connected through Skype; it was a very emotional moment for me. Luc had been working as a security agent at Brussels airport. He was on duty at the time of the blast, and like many others, did his best to help in whatever way he could. I remember him focusing on comforting the child who was lying beside me. I later got to know that this was more so because Luc had lost his nine-year-old daughter in 2003. He wanted to stay strong and ensure that the young boy—who was not severely injured but going in and out of consciousness because of the shock he was in and chaos he had witnessed – gets united with his family; he didn't want any parent to go through the pain that he had undergone.

Luc told me that he remembers a Belgian man on one side of the child and a dark-skinned lady on the other side, but despite my photograph going viral, he never associated the version of me he saw with the photo that was everywhere. I am so much in awe of people like Luc and the thousands of others in Belgium that day who went out of their way to help victims, overcoming their fears, transcending differences the world defines with words like 'race', 'culture', 'religion' and 'language'… not once thinking about their own safety. The spirit embodied by such people has inspired me so much.

I am on a new journey now. I live with a new purpose to my life. I have always thought and now firmly believe that what happens to you is your destiny, but how you deal with it is your future. I could see my future so bright and colourful. And I promised myself that one day I will fly again as a cabin manager. I will never give up hope.

Nidhi Chaphekar

ACKNOWLEDGEMENTS

From the bottom of my heart I wish to thank every person who has not only inspired me but touched my heart through their presence.

I would like to express my gratitude to Their Majesties King Philippe and Queen Mathilde of Belgium; the chairman of Jet Airways and his wife; Mr Manjeev Singh Puri, former Ambassador of India to Belgium, and his wife, Mrs Puri; DGA DAS Benoit Van Houtte of the Belgian Federal Police, who honoured me with the title of 'Godmother'; Pierre Cartuyvels, Deputy Head of the Cabinet and Diplomatic Advisor to His Majesty the King; Alain Gerardy, Chief of Protocol of the Royal Household; Peter Huyghebaert, Consul General, Mumbai, for their exceptional contribution in helping me in their own ways. Paul-Henry, a brave commando officer and the first person to help me after the explosion; Colonel Koen Hillewaert, the affectionate military province commander who helped me find commando Paul-Henry; Stefanie Chassagne De Loof, the kind lady who helped me at the site of the blast and also tied the first bandage on my leg; and Alain Zachary, the gracious senior police officer at Belgium Federal Police, for helping me stay awake in the first few critical hours.

I will always be thankful to Shabir Ahmad, my brother in Brussels and the first person to see me in the hospital after the blast, his wife, Fozia, and the rest of the family and friends for their unconditional support.

I am obliged to Sumita di from the Indian Consulate in Belgium, who was posted in the hospital at Charleroi before my family arrived, and her husband, Madan bhai; Ajay Aggarwal, and other members of the India Embassy in Belgium; the French Embassy in Mumbai for issuing emergency visas to my family members; Gurmail, who works for the Indian Embassy in Belgium and was responsible for all the pickups and drops from the airport to the hospital and back, for his prayers; Ketevan Kardava, for taking the photo that gave my family hope that I was alive; Inge Laurijssens, a police officer at Antwerp for returning my favourite Louis Vuitton bag after a year.

My heartfelt thanks goes out to the staff of Sint-Augustinus Hospital: Dr Nele Beeckman, the head doctor and a very dynamic personality; Dr Paul Leyman, abdominal surgeon; Dr Jan Van Leemput, intensive care surgeon; Dr Jansegers, orthopaedic; Dr Luc Heytens, who took the decision to shift me to the burns speciality hospital; Anne Cannaerts, Jean-maru Quartier and Kirsten Roos, ICU nurses; Nurse Koen Cortebeeck and Dr Elkana Keersebilck, who helped in doing my bandages after the surgery; Marc Hermans, head ICCU nurse—he was the first person to speak to me at the hospital, was always in touch with me through mails and also gave me all the information about my first day at the hospital; Marleen van Loock; Nurse Inge Vlegels for taking care of me after all the surgeries and attending the numerous calls from the embassy, my company, family and friends during the initial days after the blast; and Dr Liliane Leenaerts, who accompanied me in the helicopter from Sint-Augustinus Hospital to Grand Hospital at Charleroi.

I will be eternally grateful to my second family, that is, all the doctors, nurses, and staff at Grand Hospital, Charleroi: Dr Peeters, my general surgeon and one of the most intelligent doctors

I've met; Dr Nadine Hans, my orthopaedic surgeon, who is very loving; Dr Saidane, my always-smiling anesthesiologist; Dr Robert Van der Horst, anesthesist, a very patient and competent doctor; Dr Isacu Ciprian; John, head nurse, always smiling and at the patient's service; nursing staff Aurelie Iegrand; Gregory Fassiau; Amélie Ferrari; Aurélie Dumont; Arnaud Toussaint; Christine Helson; Sandrine Lefèvre; Aurélie Brancourt; Nourra Ghawi; Dr Masy Veronique; Laurence Depraetere; Carine Joué, (who was like a mother to me in the hospital); Étienne Marie-Catherine; Monique Hosselet; Fredric; and Agnes Pirotte. Thank you to both my physiotherapists, junior doctors and consultant specialists at the Charleroi hospital, whose names I unfortunately do not know. I also thank the canteen chef and the cleaning staff for being so supportive.

I would like to express my deepest appreciation to my family of Indian doctors: Dr Jamshed D. Sunavala, critical care specialist, consultant in internal medicine and physician; Dr Anil Tibrewala, my plastic surgeon and a lively gentleman who always boosted my confidence and believed in me; Dr Darius Soonawala, orthopaedic surgeon, for being supportive and patient with all my questions and also for respecting my decisions, which were sometimes dicey; Padma Shri Dr Milind V. Kirtane, otorhinolaryngologist, full of humility and energy; Dr Sudhir Warrier, a consultant and a gem of a person; and my physiotherapist Sabah for making the impossible possible and putting her heart and soul into my recovery.

The most enriching support system of my life — my ever-loving kids, Vardaan and Vriddhi, for having the courage and confidence that Mom will come back. My incredible husband Rupesh for holding my hand at every step and standing by me for all my decisions. My sister Jolly and her husband Amarjeet for being with us as strong pillars of support. My sister-in-law Madhuri and my mom-in-law for loving and taking care of my kids while Rupesh and I were away. Sakshi and Snigdha (Madhuri and Nilesh's children) for their sincere love and for being there with my kids. My brothers-in-law Nilesh and Ashish for taking turns to be with my husband at Grand Hospital.

My parents, for their day-and-night prayers, wishes and love.

My wonderful sisters Goldy and Meenu for nurturing me like a baby while I was totally dependent. My adorable nephew Abhimanyu for being with Rupesh at Charleroi and for teaching me how to use apps on my portable TV. My nephew Akshit for lending me his room for two months. My nephews Sameer, Rahul and Sahil for coming all the way to see me in India. My brother Rishi, his wife Inu and kids Ayaan and Inaaya for loving me from the bottom of their hearts. My niece Mansi for making me laugh all the time. Our friend Rohit and his son Karan for their love and respect.

Words can never express how grateful I am for the blessings showered by my late grandparents Srimati Swarn Devi and Sri Ram Lal ji, my guru Late Sri Premvir Singh ji and Guru Nirmal Swami ji.

Love to my editors Lakshmi Krishnan, Archana Ramachandran, Paloma Ganguly, Rashmi Menon and the team at Manjul Publishing House for believing in me.

A big thank you to all other members of my family, colleagues, officers, skin and blood donors, staff, management, passengers, friends, media members, award organisers, visitors, supporters and others from across the world who conducted prayers for my well-being.

It would not be possible for me to mention everyone by name, but you all stay in my heart. My blessings to all those across the world who took the help of social media with the hashtag #PrayForNidhi to send in all their prayers and good wishes.

Love and blessings to all.